BEYOND POWER TRANSITIONS

COLUMBIA STUDIES IN
INTERNATIONAL ORDER AND POLITICS

COLUMBIA STUDIES IN
INTERNATIONAL ORDER AND POLITICS

STACIE E. GODDARD, DANIEL H. NEXON, AND
JOSEPH M. PARENT, SERIES EDITORS

The Columbia Studies in International Order and Politics series builds on the press's long tradition in classic international relations publishing while highlighting important new work. The series is founded on three commitments: to serve as an outlet for innovative theoretical work, especially that work which stretches beyond "mainstream" international relations and cuts across disciplinary boundaries; to highlight original qualitative and historical work in international relations theory, international security, and international political economy; and to focus on creating a selective, prominent list dedicated to international relations.

Governing the Feminist Peace: The Vitality and Failure of the Women, Peace, and Security Agenda, Paul Kirby and Laura J. Shepherd

States and the Masters of Capital: Sovereign Lending, Old and New, Quentin Bruneau

Making War on the World: How Transnational Violence Reshapes Global Order, Mark Shirk

BEYOND POWER TRANSITIONS

THE LESSONS OF EAST ASIAN HISTORY AND THE FUTURE OF U.S.-CHINA RELATIONS

XINRU MA AND DAVID C. KANG

Columbia University Press   *New York*

Columbia University Press
Publishers Since 1893
New York   Chichester, West Sussex
cup.columbia.edu

Copyright © 2024 Columbia University Press
All rights reserved

Library of Congress Cataloging-in-Publication Data
Names: Ma, Xinru, author. | Kang, David C. (David Chan-oong), 1965– author.
Title: Beyond power transitions : the lessons of East Asian history and the
future of U.S.–China relations / Xinru Ma and David C. Kang.
Other titles: Lessons of East Asian history and the future
of United States–China relations
Description: New York : Columbia University Press, [2024] | Series:
Columbia Studies in International Order and Politics | Includes
bibliographical references and index.
Identifiers: LCCN 2023058641 (print) | LCCN 2023058642 (ebook) |
ISBN 9780231205368 (hardback) | ISBN 9780231205375 (trade paperback) |
ISBN 9780231555975 (ebook)
Subjects: LCSH: International relations. | Security, International—East Asia. |
East Asia—Foreign relations. | Regionalism—East Asia. | Legitimacy of
governments—East Asia. | National security—Case studies. | Political
stability—Case studies. | China—Foreign relations—Forecasting. |
United States—Foreign relations—Forecasting. | Common conjecture.
Classification: LCC LC3969 .M26 2024 (print) | LCC LC3969 (ebook) |
DDC 951—dc23/eng/20240316

Cover design: Chang Jae Lee
Cover image: Section of a handscroll titled "Four Events of the Jingde Reign:
Khitan Envoys Visit the Court," Song dynasty. Courtesy of the National Palace
Museum of Taiwan.

To Chen

—Xinru Ma

To Lao Lao and Lao Ye

—David C. Kang

CONTENTS

PART III. CONTEMPORARY U.S.-CHINA RELATIONS

PART IV. CONCLUSION

FIGURES AND TABLES

PREFACE

We began this project many years ago through many discussions about the vitality of East Asia itself, the paucity of Western scholarship that acknowledges that East Asian experience, and the disconnect between the East Asia we know and the theories and scholarship about the region that we regularly read in the mainstream English-language scholarly literature. Those discussions turned into a short article published in the *Washington Quarterly* in 2018, and they finally grew into this book. This book distills much of our thinking about how to bridge this chasm between the conventional Western scholarship on international relations and the East Asian experience.

Our book examines international relations in East Asia across an immense span of time and across an immense geographic region. Our purpose here is neither to contest nor to ignore the considerable subtlety and difference and individuality of each country in East Asia and their historical experiences. Every chapter we have written could be an entire book of its own. What we have done is attempt to be as sensitive to subtlety and context as possible, while still identifying long-enduring patterns, making systematic claims, and holding up social science theory to careful empirical examination. We realize we have made sometimes sweeping arguments that perhaps could be more nuanced. However, in assessing whether and how power transitions occurred in East Asia, we were forced to begin with a book that takes the broad swath of history first. This book is the beginning of what we hope will be far more research taking East Asian history as a starting point. It is not the end of research—it is our sincere hope that future research extends, refines, and perhaps even overturns the arguments and evidence that we have set forth here.

Many thanks to Jean-Francois Belanger, David Carter, Victor Cha, Alexandre Debs, Christopher Hanscom, Peter Katzenstein, Ji-Young Lee, Quan Li, Jonathan Markowitz, John Maurer, Nuno Monteiro, Lina Nie, Saeyoung Park, Brian Rathbun, Xie Tao, and Richard von Glahn for their detailed comments on various drafts of various chapters. We are particularly grateful to Stacie Goddard and Scott Wolford, and all the participants of a manuscript review we held at the USC Korean Studies Institute on November 5, 2021.

We also thank the careful reviewers at Columbia University Press and Caelyn Cobb for her superb editorial advice on this project. Thanks to Jill Lin, Ewon Baik, and Zoe Wallace for their extraordinary research assistance. David Cruikshank is a truly gifted copy and writing editor.

Earlier and more compressed versions of the arguments appeared in David Kang, "International Relations Theory and East Asian History: An Overview," *Journal of East Asian Studies* 13, no. 2 (2013): 181–205; Xinru Ma and David Kang, "Power Transitions: Thucydides Didn't Live in East Asia," *Washington Quarterly* 41, no. 1 (March 2018): 137–54; and David Kang, "Thought Games About China," *Journal of East Asian Studies* 20, no. 2 (2020): 135–50. We gratefully acknowledge permission from the *Washington Quarterly* and the *Journal of East Asian Studies* to elaborate on these ideas here. Partial and previous versions of this book were presented at the IR–ISS Joint Workshop, Yale University, on April 2, 2019; "The Political Economy of Security" conference at the USC Center for International Studies on January 26–27, 2018; and with the China working group, Marshall School of Business, on November 21, 2017. We gratefully acknowledge the support of the Laboratory Program for Korean Studies through the Ministry of Education of the Republic of Korea and Korean Studies Promotion Service of the Academy of Korean Studies (AKS-2015-LAB-2250002); and of the John D. and Catherine T. MacArthur Foundation, which supported part of this research. We have followed the Chicago Manual of Style conventions for transliteration and citation of Asian language sources.

BEYOND POWER
TRANSITIONS

I

INTRODUCTION

1

WHAT ARE THE LESSONS
OF HISTORY?

Are power transitions between a rising power and a declining hegemon particularly volatile? Is a war between China and the United States possible or even likely as a power transition draws near? Scholars and policymakers are increasingly worried about such a possibility. They often use events of the past to draw lessons for today. Susan Shirk argues, "History teaches us that rising powers are likely to provoke war. The ancient historian Thucydides identified the fear that a rising Athens inspired in other states as the cause of the Peloponnesian War."[1] As Richard Lebow and Benjamin Valentino point out, power transition theory "has become an accepted framework for many scholars and policymakers who focus on Asia."[2]

But are the "lessons of history" so obvious and universal? What historical record is Shirk referring to? By far the most commonly examined case studies of power transition in the scholarly literature are the Peloponnesian War in ancient Greece (431–404 BCE) and the rise of Germany under Bismarck and Anglo-German rivalry of the nineteenth and early twentieth centuries.[3] Analogies that liken China to the United States as Athens to Sparta or Germany to United Kingdom are obvious and have been made since at least Richard Betts's influential 1993 article "Wealth, Power, and Instability: East Asia and the United States After the Cold War."[4] In fact, the application of power transition theory to contemporary Asia relies heavily on the analogy of these few key historical cases.

Even when scholars argue that China might not follow the same path that Germany did, they are overwhelmingly debating interpretations of events and cases from historical Europe and which particular European analogy best describes China today.[5] Almost none of the scholarship on power transitions begins and ends with East Asia itself, which is a bit surprising. The strategy seems to be: get Europe right in order to get Asia right.

Had scholars of international relations (IR) and power transitions started with East Asian history rather than European history, they would have learned very different lessons. Most important, internal challenges were far more dangerous to the survival of regimes than were external threats throughout much of East Asian history. Specifically, with an examination of over 1,500 years of East Asian history, we find that majority of the dynastic transitions came from internal challenges. Wars of conquest were far less likely to result in the overturning of a dynasty than was rebellion or collapse. Fifteen of eighteen major dynastic transitions across premodern East Asia from China, Vietnam, Japan, and Korea resulted from internal challenges. Only three were a result of external threats. Furthermore, careful examination of these three instances of external conquest reveals that none of them followed anything like the contours predicted by power transition theory. That is, power transition theory does not apply across a huge swath of time and space.

If we are right, at stake is the common presumption that much western contemporary IR theory is universal. Rather, our research shows that at least in the case of power transition theory, it is far more circumscribed than generally thought by the field. If that is the case, then perhaps many other ostensibly "universal" theories need to be rethought. Just because an idea can be written down in abstract form does not mean that it is universally applicable across time and space. Rather, the historical experience of other regions of the world is different from the European historical experience and would likely yield both different "lessons of history" and different abstract theories to explain political phenomena.

Beginning with historical East Asia leads us to a second key insight: the central role in war and peace of a "common conjecture"—shared expectations about relative position and role in international relations—rather than the rise and decline of great powers relative to each other. A common conjecture about who is a legitimate participant in the system and whether there is a mutually accepted role is a shared understanding about the aims and identity of the participants. These are repertoires of legitimate practices, repertoires of power politics—patterns or practices of how countries legitimate themselves to each other. When these common conjectures existed, there was stability in East Asia. Often the most intense fighting occurred in the absence of these common conjectures. Furthermore, these shared understandings were durable: even after large disruptions, the East Asian international system would often snap back to a stable state. In other words, power transition theory can neither explain the wars of historical East Asia nor the periods of peace of East Asian history. Relative power and status quo satisfaction do not appear as key factors in war or peace in historical East Asia. The working of no international system is self-evident—they all need to be clarified, negotiated, and adjusted even if fundamental principles remain the same.

By focusing on East Asian history, we emphasize shared beliefs in explaining systematic patterns of war and peace over a remarkably long time period. The premodern East Asian international order is typically called "the tribute system" and involved a clear hierarchy based on culture and status, not necessarily material power.[6] Yet the precise manner and way in which relations between any two units were negotiated and resolved required framing, flexibility, adjustment, and diplomacy. Stabilizing practices and beliefs in historical East Asia were unique in content if not in mechanisms. All international systems legitimate certain actors and not others; all systems have legitimate practices and illegitimate practices. The particular culture of the East Asian system determined the manner and content of their legitimation—but all systems exhibit these same tendencies, and in all systems this is more important for war and peace than changes in the balance of power. Changes in the balance of power do not cause war—war is not a structural effect. Rather, the content of the common conjecture is critical.

Our frustration with the power transition literature begins with a fairly clear blind spot in empirical focus of power transition theory. From the time of A. F. K. Organski and Jacek Kugler onward, almost all cases are drawn from post-1820 European historical experience.[7] This approach is problematic at best. Scholars are increasingly recognizing that they have an intellectual blind spot that is Eurocentric and overemphasizes the importance and generalizability of the European and Western experience in the international relations literature. As David Kang and Alex Lin point out, "the median American scholar of [international relations] is deeply comfortable with European examples and analogies and has almost no exposure to Asian examples and history. Thus, when faced with Asian examples, they are considered within the context they are taught:

through the European lens."[8] J. C. Sharman explains how under-standing historical Asian polities might help change our long-held assumptions about power transitions in European history: "First, it disconfirms the idea of a single path to military effec-tiveness, of sequences of necessary and sufficient causes, either technological or tactical, by which war makes states. Second, it undermines stereotypes according to which relatively tran-sient successes by small European polities are too often por-trayed as epochal triumphs, whereas mighty, long lived Asian empires are characterized as merely failures waiting to happen."[9]

This blind spot is particularly vivid with power transition the-ory. Taking the conventional wisdom about power transitions at face value, it would appear that all power transitions in his-tory involved a Western power, and evidently nothing else hap-pened around the rest of the globe. From the Incas and Aztecs to the numerous polities on the Indian subcontinent, not to men-tion the rest of Asia and all of Africa and the Middle East, evidently none of them ever experienced a power transition. This may be the case, but there is scarce scholarship that actually asks whether all other regions of the world fall within or outside of the scope and boundary conditions for the theory to apply. In other words, scholars have rarely directly addressed whether power transition theory can be transposed outside the European experience and to what extent it is the appropriate lens to inter-pret the contemporary East Asian regional security dynamics.

Instead of using Europe's past to draw lessons about China today, why would we not use East Asia's past to draw lessons about China and East Asia today? What "lessons of history" might we find if we start with East Asia? Intuitively, why would we believe that the European historical experience is universal? Why would we look at a battle between two Greek towns from 2,500 years ago to draw insights about China today? To use only

European cases and assume that they constitute the entire pool of possible cases is to risk a blind spot by not exploring the wider set of possible cases on which to base the theory. In this sense, we are not refuting power transition theory; rather, we are pointing out that it is much less universal than is normally believed and that should raise questions about how applicable it is today in East Asia or even other regions of the world across time and space.

Viewed through the lens of East Asian history, there are two key questions, or insights, for contemporary East Asia. The first is the dangers of internal challenges rather than external threats. This insight leads us to examine the domestic situations in both China and the United States. There is an argument to be made that the domestic challenges in both countries are consequential and as likely to disrupt their rule as are the external challenge that each poses to the other. Both the United States and China face enormous problems in their domestic politics, society, and economy. While IR scholars may focus on the risks of a power transition war or conflict in the future because of these two great powers, it is also possible that these internal challenges will overcome or negate those external dynamics. U.S.–China relations clearly deteriorated in the early 2020s, perhaps to their lowest point since normalization of diplomatic ties in the 1970s. And at this writing, there is increasing talk in policy circles about the risks of conflict between the two sides. This may be true, but the lessons of this research call for directing focus on the internal dynamics of each country as much as on their external relations.

The second key argument running through this book leads us to ask whether a common conjecture remains among East Asian countries today and to what extent the United States understands and is a part of it. The nineteenth century disrupted shared understandings in East Asia, particularly beliefs about what is legitimate in international relations and what is expected. If this premodern conjecture is essentially entirely obliterated and if all East Asian countries are basically the same in their ideas, goals, structure, and norms as Western countries, then there is reason to believe that they will behave more according to power transition theory. To the extent that contemporary East Asian states know and understand what the others care about and how to accommodate each other and China, the region will be more stable than contentless structural theories such as power transition theory would imply.

Furthermore, it is also not clear the extent to which the United States—not a part of the East Asian historical conversation—will be able to apprehend the common conjecture among East Asian countries and craft its own shared understandings with East Asian countries. If an East Asian common conjecture remains, can the United States participate in it or understand it?

THE ARGUMENT: INTERNAL CHALLENGES AND THE EAST ASIAN COMMON CONJECTURE

In this book we address the issue of a blind spot in the choice of empirical cases to test in the power transition literature, and we counteract that blind spot by examining important cases from East Asian history. We argue that this oversight has led to an overexpectation that power transitions are a principal cause for war and that the theory is universally applicable across time and space. If we were to widen the empirical focus, particularly to examine important examples from East Asian history, we would find very different implications for the theory's applicability.

It is important to note that we are not claiming that power transition theory is wrong—far from it. Rather, we emphasize that it is less universal across time and space than scholars often recognize. The systematic contours of East Asian historical international relations do not reflect power transition theory or any structural theory of conflict that emphasizes relative power or status quo satisfaction. Scholars should be more careful about using power transition theory as a universal theory applicable across time and space. The theory is more bounded than scholars generally recognize.

To that point, East Asian history exhibits a different dynamic, focused on the content of beliefs. It was not relative power that caused war or peace, it was the presence or the absence of a common conjecture. Repertoires of power politics, patterns, or practices shared among the participants were essential to crafting stable relations; the strategic conception of practices was essential to legitimate themselves. As Sixiang Wang writes about Chinese Ming and Korean Chosŏn relations in the fourteenth century: "Addressing specific issues, whether concerning the goods, people, territory, or protocol, was certainly part of any Chosŏn envoy mission [to Ming China]. But diplomacy also depended on the cultivation and maintenance of shared frames of reference. Efficacy, in the latter sense, is measured less in whether imperial policies changed at the moment and more in how these frames of reference could be shaped in the long run."[10]

This conjecture is often called the East Asian "tribute system" of international relations. How this international system survived and evolved over the centuries, and how countries negotiated and renegotiated and improvised and modified principles and practices with each other and flexibly reinterpreted its basic principles and practices, generalize more broadly beyond East Asia. Legitimation is universal. But how East Asian countries legitimated themselves is particular to that cultural context. This could be called the "great East Asian conversation": about the appropriate role of power, the responsibility of those with power, and how different people within one society, and how different societies, should relate to each other. These are shared cultural beliefs about what is legitimate and expected based on foundational philosophical and intellectual notions. But we point out that these beliefs are not static or fixed; they are constantly evolving and changing. Yet the persistence of a core set of beliefs across time was remarkable, even as those ideas were debated, modified, and changed.

Furthermore, because of the durability and stability of the East Asian international system, wars of conquest were rare. These countries had a set of institutional and philosophical tools that allowed them to craft long-enduring relations with each other. As a result, internal challenges rather than external threats posed the most imminent challenges to the survival of political regimes. As noted previously, fifteen out of eighteen premodern regime transitions in East Asia came from internal challenges. Only three resulted from external invasion, and none of those follow the contours predicted by power transition theory.

We substantiate the argument in four steps. First, we show that historical East Asia experienced systematic patterns of war and other violence that were fundamentally different from the patterns of war in historical Europe. We find that the power transition itself among major powers almost never obtained in premodern East Asian history. Instead, China was so powerful that almost no other country ever came close to challenging it in material terms. East Asia was a hegemonic system rather than a balance of power system, as existed in historical Europe. China did rise and fall over the centuries, but even when China was divided or in disarray, in rare cases that other power was stronger than it. This in itself is an important finding. A massive section of the globe did not experience power transitions over more than a millennium, which begs for us to turn our attention to why we can extrapolate general claims from geographically bounded observations without further testing.

The fact that power transition occurred extremely rarely in much of East Asian history raises even more interesting questions that our current theories are ill equipped to address. Regimes in East Asia did rise and fall over time. If this did not result from power transitions, then what was the cause? To address this question, in the second step, we examine systematically the causes of the rise and fall of regimes in East Asian history. This points to the key observation that in East Asia the stable relations among the countries themselves meant that internal challenges were often more threatening than external threats. As Jean-Laurent Rosenthal and R. Bin Wong point out, East Asian leaders' primary focus has historically been the strategy of rule, not a strategy of conquest.[11]

In the third step, we illustrate this key observation with four critical case studies from historical East Asia. Each of these case studies illuminates a critical factor in the rise and fall of East Asian nations over time. Each of these case studies also shows both how remarkably enduring was the common conjecture, and how the order would snap back to equilibrium after a disruption. These cases also provide valuable insights into how difficult it is to apply power transition theory outside the European region from which it was inductively derived.

The first case is the Song–Yuan transition in the thirteenth century. The Mongol conquest of Song dynasty China (960–1279) that was completed in 1279 is one of the few cases of actual external invasion causing the collapse of a Chinese dynasty, and for that reason exploring the dynamics of the Mongol conquest is important. Debates about who was the legitimate heir to rule "China" was the central concern of the Song. Instead of viewing the rising Mongols as its threat, the Song were focused on recovering the lost "Sixteen Prefectures" from the northern Liao dynasty. That territory was considered innately "Chinese" and fundamental to Song's domestic legitimacy. This made the Song willing to fight wars at lower odds and higher costs against opponents who were not as dangerous as the Mongols.

Furthermore, what becomes clear from a close examination of this case is that while the Mongols were some of the most feared warriors the world has ever seen, their rise, success, and decline follows nothing like the predicted dynamics of power transition wars. We assessed relative power, at least, as much as is possible for that time. And it becomes clear that Song China at its height in the thirteenth century was the richest, wealthiest, most powerful, and most populous country the world had ever seen, with a population of over seventy million people. The Mongols had at best one million citizens in total, with a far smaller military than the Song. Yet, within fifty years, the Song ruling regime was completely destroyed and the Mongols had created the largest contiguous land empire the world has ever seen. Nevertheless, labeling the Song–Yuan transition as a power transition would be inaccurate. Rather, we find that some characteristics internal to the particular family and ruling regime of Chinggis Khan provide the most compelling explanation for why the Mongols started invading, and why they stopped after three generations.

The second case is the Imjin War of 1592 to 1598. This was East Asia's first "regional world war" and a war that was larger in scale than anything experienced in Europe up to that time.[12] Superficially, it could also potentially look like a war of power transition. In 1592, Ming China (1368–1644) was at the height of its power, yet Japan under Toyotomi Hideyoshi invaded Korea in an attempt to conquer China, failing miserably. Hideyoshi had grand designs for himself, and he clearly hoped to upset the contemporary order and create a new international order with himself and Japan at the top. The massive scale of the Imjin War makes it one of the most consequential events in East Asian history. As Kenneth Swope, a specialist in the military history of East Asia, puts it, this was "without question one of the most traumatic events [and] one of the most significant military conflicts in East Asian history."[13] Yet, as we show clearly, Japan at no time came close to matching Chinese power. The predicted power transition dynamics are almost entirely absent in this case.

This war affected the fate of what was unquestionably the most powerful and advanced country in the world at the time, thus constituting an important cautionary tale against taking at face value a theory of power transitions derived solely from the European experience. The fact that it did not follow any of the causal propositions laid out in mainstream power transition theory suggests that some nonstructural variables might be at play in governing interstate relations in Asia. The aims and concerns of all the participants reflected more their concerns about the common conjecture about status and appropriate behavior than simple structural or balance-of-power factors.

The third case we explore is the Ming–Qing transition of the early seventeenth century. The Manchu conquest of Ming China fifty years after the Imjin War, again, followed none of the contours of power transition theory. Having survived nearly three centuries, the Ming fell from within, beset by numerous rebellions. As central control broke down, the Manchus—a nascent state slowly growing in organization and power in Northeast Asia—were able to move in on a broken Ming dynasty and slowly reassert centralized control, a process that took decades. Naming themselves the Qing dynasty, they ruled China for three centuries (1644–1912). Here again we measure relative power and status quo satisfaction and find that none of the predicted power transition dynamics obtain at the time.

The fourth case we explore is really a series of cases: how Korea survived as an independent nation for over 1,500 years. Over the centuries, Chinese dynasties rose and fell, yet China has been the unquestioned hegemon for much of the previous two thousand years of East Asian history. As each massive new Chinese dynasty rose, their Korean counterparts needed to craft a relationship with that new, energetic Chinese dynasty. Korea managed to do so repeatedly over the centuries. However, none of the main China–Korea dynamics involved concerns about rapidly rising powers that were increasingly expansionist or revisionist or balance-of-power tactics. Instead, their relations with each other were fundamentally built upon the common conjecture and shared understanding. When the common conjecture was present, China–Korea relations were remarkably stable and enduring.

Again, our goal is not to replace Eurocentrism with another centrism, particularly Sinocentrism. What we advocate instead is to examine East Asian countries in the local political, economic, social, and ideational context. What kinds of lesson can we draw if we interpret East Asia on its own terms rather than as an antithesis of Europe? How would this help us interpret modern China's intentions and actions?

EAST ASIA TODAY AND CONTEMPORARY U.S.-CHINA RELATIONS

The fourth step in our argument applies the insights from historical East Asia to contemporary East Asian security and U.S.–China relations. There was an historical moment of globalizing regional systems: the arrival of the Western imperial powers in the nineteenth century challenged and, in fact, fractured the existing systems in East Asia. The globalization of the European state system transformed East Asia in numerous ways. For our purposes, the most consequential effect was that the East Asian common conjecture unraveled in the nineteenth century with the arrival of the Western imperial powers. What was taken for granted as legitimate and appropriate in international relations dissolved. All countries in the region had to adjust, adapt, and learn new ways of interacting with each other and the wider world. Perhaps most dramatically, Japan intentionally rose into the Western Westphalian international system, actively seeking out a wide range of practices and ideas from across Europe in its attempt to adjust to and survive in this new international system.

Japan was most successful in the twentieth century at adjusting to the new realities, and its dramatic rise and subsequent fall shaped much of twentieth-century East Asian regional relations. Indeed, as late as the mid-1990s, many analysts and IR theorists thought it was Japan that posed the most likely challenge to the United States for global hegemony. Yet within the space of a few decades, two events happened, both of which are consistent with our core arguments. First, for domestic reasons, the Japanese economic growth slowed dramatically, and it has remained low since the early 1990s. Japan's progress stalled not from any titanic struggle for power with another country but from internal reasons. The second event was that China moved out of its self-imposed isolation and began a dramatic and rapid economic, social, and diplomatic resurgence. Within the space of thirty years, China had far outpaced Japan in the region by almost any measure. Yet this transition occurred without any of the ramifications predicted by power transition theorists.

Today the focus is not on Japan as a potential challenger to anyone; rather, the focus is on a possible U.S.–China power transition, whether this might occur, and whether it might occur peacefully. We argue that whether a global power transition occurs is largely immaterial to actual U.S.–China relations. Those relations will play out most directly in an East Asian regional context. And, viewed in the region, the United States remains the more powerful actor. However, the speed and extent to which China has caught up to the United States economically, diplomatically, and in some cases even militarily cannot be ignored. No real transition has yet taken place, and the key question is whether U.S.–China relations will play out in the region as predicted by power transition theorists or whether domestic challenges and a common conjecture about key issues will be more important.

There are clearly major internal challenges to both China and the United States. Both countries face political, economic, and social issues that could be more consequential than their relations with each other, however they play out. While it is common to view China's domestic problems as great and rising, there is also a case to be made that the United States faces just as great domestic issues. If these domestic issues are not solved or managed in both countries, then it is unlikely that power transition dynamics will be the most important factors in their relations in the future.

Similarly, relations between the two countries have deteriorated rapidly in the past few years; although it is easy to portray this as a possible power transition and dissatisfaction or defending the status quo, the difficulties between the two countries appear to be deeper than that. Differences between authoritarian and democratic countries, between acceptance of international institutions or norms, and real contests over which country can have influence are not the only problems between the two countries. There are also genuine differences in viewpoints and attitudes toward the region, views of themselves, and views of each other. Differences in national identity and worldviews are also similar in some ways but different in others. Both countries view themselves as more than countries—both China and the United States view each other as the source of a glorious civilization. Yet the content of those worldviews is very different. If the two countries cannot find a common conjecture about how the world is and should be and what these two countries are and how they should interact, they will have difficulties interacting with each other no matter how democratic or authoritarian they are, or no matter how much each one buys into or forms an international economic order, for example.

ORGANIZATION OF THE BOOK

The book proceeds as follows. In chapter 2 we explore theories of power transition, noting that, while the logic for the theory is relatively straightforward, almost all of the empirical testing has been restricted to the European experience of the past few centuries. Rarely have scholars explored whether the theory has any cross-domain or out-of-region applicability, and we explore those issues in detail.

The remainder of the book is organized into three parts. The second part deals with East Asian history. We look for lessons in East Asian history and explore what the region looked like over the many centuries of its existence as a coherent international system. Chapter 3 explores the scope and boundary conditions for when power transition theory should apply, showing that the power transition itself rarely occurred among major powers in premodern East Asian history. To capture the historical patterns of this region, we systematically examine the causes of the rise and fall of dynasties in China, Japan, Korea, and Vietnam and show that only three of the eighteen transitions before 1920 came from invasion; the other fifteen transitions resulted from internal causes such as rebellion or a palace coup.[14]

Chapters 4–7 examine four key case studies: the Mongol conquest of Song China in the thirteenth century, the Imjin War of 1592–1598, the Qing conquest of China in the early seventeenth century, and Korea's relations with new and rising Chinese dynasties over the centuries. In each of these cases, long-enduring, mighty East Asian kingdoms faced enormous challenges: some fell, while others survived. These chapters discuss the ramifications for power transition theory for taking East Asian history seriously, pointing out in particular the dangers of internal challenges, not external threats. Furthermore, exploring these cases in detail reveals a number of nuances that bring into question the impact of power transitions on war, along with the importance of common conjecture on peace.

Part III takes these lessons of East Asian history and applies them to contemporary East Asian regional security and U.S.–China relations. Chapter 8 provides an overview of the East Asian region over the past thirty years, pointing out that a regional power transition has already occurred: within a remarkably short time span, China eclipsed Japan to return to its position as the unquestioned most powerful country in the region. This chapter reveals that East Asia continues to grow stronger, richer, more integrated, and also more stable and peaceful, not less, over time. Today, Western, and particularly American, policymakers and analysts overlook this fact about East Asia, instead emphasizing the dangers of China's rising power.

Finally, we focus on U.S.–China relations within the region, making two central arguments. First, internal challenges may be more consequential to both countries than external threats. Second, and perhaps more important for East Asian security, is that China has advanced quite quickly in integrating with and engaging the region. The United States, although it remains militarily powerful, appears to be far less interested in working with regional actors and institutions to craft economic and diplomatic relations. These two trends certainly appear to be leading to a regional transformation. Whether it will be peaceful or not will depend on a number of decisions made by all sides in the future. The concluding chapter thus explores the future of U.S.–China relations and avenues for future research, and it draws theoretical lessons for power transition theory and our understanding of international security more broadly.

2

THE COMMON CONJECTURE
IN WAR AND PEACE

Culture, Not Structure

Power transition theory often begins with reference to Thucydides, who wrote over two thousand years ago about the Peloponnesian War (431–404 BCE) that what made war inevitable was "the growth of the power of Athens, and the alarm which this inspired in Sparta" and "the strong do what they can and the weak suffer what they must."[1] These two quotations from one ancient historian's writings about Greek history animate a surprising swath of contemporary international relations theory, which is ostensibly deductive but is in fact influenced far too heavily by a few key stylized facts that are often presented as universal laws of nature.

In this chapter, we review the literature on power transitions, showing that it is based on an inductive reading of a small number of Western cases. We show that applications to East Asia proceed almost exclusively by analogizing to past European cases and by debating interpretations of European history rather than debating interpretations of historical and contemporary East Asia itself. We also discuss some important emerging mainstream international relations scholarship that questions assumptions inherent in power transition literature, and indeed much of the international relations literature itself.

More important than our critique of the power transition theory literature is our positive argument for explaining systematic patterns of war and peace. Rather than structural or material factors as the key to stability or instability in international relations, the key lies in the ideas that actors have and share about themselves and each other. That culture and not structure is central to explaining conflict in international relations is increasingly accepted. Both constructivist and rationalist approaches center on the role of ideas in their explanations for international conflict. Our argument can be generalized as well. Although this book will explain how particular ideas from a particular time and place explain large swaths of its international relations, these concepts are in fact fundamental to all international systems across time and space.

POWER TRANSITION THEORY

Power transition theory was first enumerated and later tested by A. F. K. Organski and Jack Kugler in *The War Ledger*. Three concepts are central to the theory: relative national power, status quo evaluation, and a hierarchical pyramid. In terms of the structural environment, power transition theory rejects the emphasis placed by balance of power theorists on anarchy, instead viewing the international system as a hierarchical pyramid, with the dominant power sitting at the apex above lesser great powers, other medium and smaller states, and dependencies. In terms of explanatory variables, power transition theory sees the probability of war being conditioned by two factors: relative national power and status quo evaluation (or degree of satisfaction).[2]

The logic of the theory is straightforward: a satisfied rising power, whose preferences for the ordering of the international system are closely aligned with the dominant power, has little motivation to challenge the status quo. Conversely, a dissatisfied challenger, whose preferences in international order differ substantially from the dominant one, seeks to alter the status quo.[3] Consequently, war is mostly likely between a dissatisfied rising great power and the dominant power. Organski and Kugler have a relatively mechanical view of power transitions, writing that "the fundamental problem that sets the whole system sliding almost irretrievably toward war is the differences in rates of growth among the great powers."[4] Among those states capable of contending for global leadership, "no wars take place without a transition."[5]

This basic framework has been followed by most power transition scholars since then. Steve Chan sums up the theory as "the danger of systemic war is greatest when a rising challenger catches up with or even overtakes a declining hegemon."[6] Jonathan DiCicco and Jack Levy find that "half of the observed transitions were followed by the outbreak of war."[7] Ronald Tammen and his coauthors concur that war is mostly likely when the states' relative powers are characterized by parity, while "the 'zone of contention and probable war' wherein the ratio of the dissatisfied great power's and the dominant state's capabilities lies between 4:5 and 6:5."[8] Robert Gilpin focuses more on the fears of the declining power rather than on the aims of the rising challenger, seeing preventive war as an attractive option for dealing with challengers.[9]

Over the decades, scholars have widened the scope of inquiry about power transition and its application, and the theory has been "a lively and expanding research program that has moved forward in several important substantive directions."[10] For instance, Douglas Lemke and Suzanne Werner enhanced the generalizability of the theory by extending the original focus on dynamics between major powers (the international system as a single hierarchy) to the role of minor powers in local and international hierarchies (hence, the international system as a series of hierarchies).[11] Scholars also relaxed the assumption of augmenting national power through internal growth, and there has been extensive discussion of how to measure national power and the implications of different measures. Recently, scholars have begun to pay more attention to the other variable—dissatisfaction—and have explored how to measure whether a country is satisfied or dissatisfied, how institutional features such as governance structures, regime type, or leadership affect the degree of satisfaction, how the leading state engineers satisfaction, and how alliances and alliance formation affect the probability of war, in addition to a wealth of hypotheses generated by formalization regarding risk propensity, the timing, speed, and trajectory of overtaking, and about integration as an opposite of war.[12] Four mainstream measures of dissatisfaction have so far emerged: Bruce Bueno de Mesquita's measure based on money market discount rates; Daniel Geller's detailed consideration of dyadic relations based on a state's specific demands for diplomatic or territorial changes; Werner and Kugler's measure of extraordinary military buildups by rising states; and Woosang Kim's measure of similarities with the alliance profile of the dominant state.[13]

THE DATASET AND EAST ASIA AS A DISTINCT REGION

While the logic of power transition theory is relatively straightforward, the overwhelming majority of the empirical testing of power transitions has been restricted to the European experience. The most influential scholars certainly did: Organski and

Kugler examined great power transitions from 1860 to 1975, focusing on five major hegemonic transitions: the Napoleonic Wars (1803–1815), the Franco-Prussian War (1870–1871), the Russo-Japanese War (1904–1905), and both world wars (1914–1918, 1939–1945).[14]

Gilpin examined the Peloponnesian War (431–404 BCE), the Second Punic War (218–201 BCE), the Thirty Years War (1618–1648), the Dutch War of Louis XIV (1672–1678), the War of the League of Augsburg (1688–1697), the War of the Spanish Succession (1701–1713), the French Revolutionary Wars (1792–1802), the Napoleonic Wars (1803–1815), and both world wars.[15] Richard Ned Lebow and Benjamin Valentino examine the past five centuries of European regional relations, mentioning Spain's sixteenth-century bid for hegemony, Frances's attempts in the seventeenth and nineteenth century, and Germany's two attempts in the first half of the twentieth century.[16] They briefly discuss Japan and China, but only in the context of twentieth-century geopolitics and their interactions with Western powers.

To offer a more specific breakdown of empirical cases examined by the power transition literature, we conducted a comprehensive search of articles published in peer-reviewed journals and coded the empirical cases discussed in each article (see the appendix). We found fifty-three articles about power transitions published between 1990 and 2016 in first-tier journals (figure 2.1).[17]

Among the fifty-three articles, by far the most examined case is the Anglo-German rivalry of the twentieth century: twenty-six of the twenty-eight quantitative studies certainly chose this case due to their heavy reliance on the standard datasets such as the Correlates of War (COW) project.[18] As William Wohlforth points out, "These studies are based entirely on post-sixteenth-century European history, and most are limited to the post-1815

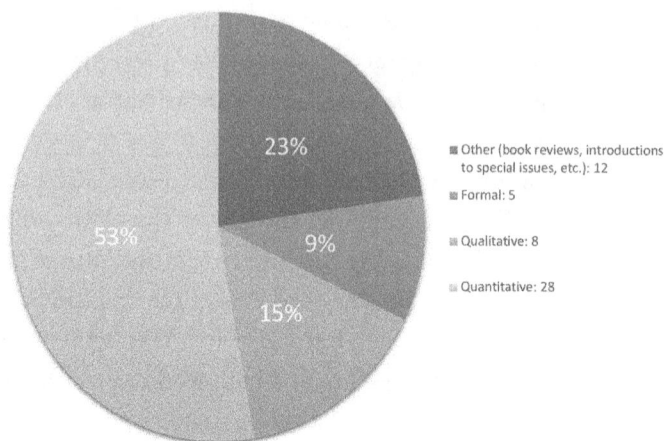

FIGURE 2.1 Breakdown of journal articles on power transition.

Source: Authors.

period covered by the standard datasets."[19] Although there is careful discussion of case selection, such discussion is mainly driven by the assessment of different data sources for measuring power.[20] The focus is on which power should be included in the system as a major power, whether the rise of certain power should be counted as power parity or transition, and, hence, which wars should be counted as major power wars. Cases are advocated for addition to the original list of wars defined by Organski and Kugler, but are still mostly limited to post-Napoleonic European history, such as the cases of Prussia and Austria in the Seven Weeks' War (1866), the Crimean War (1853–1856), the Wars of Italian Unification (1848–1850, 1859–1860), or the Russo-Turkish wars (1853–1878).[21] Only one study—Woosang Kim's 1992 *World Politics* article—examines great powers in the pre-1820 period, but again Kim's cases are restricted to European history.[22]

Non-European countries or cases appear only in passing. Only three articles among those that we examined focus on a non-European region. Kim tests power transition theory by examining thirteen East Asian wars from 1860 to 1993: the Sino-French War (1884–1885), the Sino-Japanese War (1894–1895), the Boxer Rebellion (1900), the Sino-Russian War (1900), the Russo-Japanese War (1904–1905), World War I (1914–1918), the Sino-Soviet War (1929), the Manchurian War (1931–1933), the Sino-Japanese War (1937–1941), the Chang-kufeng War (1938), the Nomonhan War (1939), World War II (1939–1945), and the Korean War (1950–1953).[23] Lemke and Werner examine the applicability of power transition theory to four persistent local hierarchies in South America between 1860 and 1980, including the Atlantic Coast (Argentina, Brazil, and Uruguay), the Pacific Coast (Chile and Peru), the land-locked states of the interior (Bolivia and Paraguay), and the Northern Rim (Colombia, Ecuador, and Venezuela). They find that power transition theory can account for war at both major and minor power levels. Specifically, they find that whether dealing with major world powers or the relatively weak states of South America, power parity provides the opportunity to act for those committed to changing the status quo.[24] In 2008, Lemke further extended the theory's applicability by testing it against the behavior of twenty state and nonstate actors in nineteenth-century South America and found that power transition theory may also predict wars among nonstate actors.[25]

As Lebow and Valentino point out, "minor powers like those in Latin America and Eastern Europe" are not the focus of power transition theory.[26] When Japan, China, or other non-Western cases are involved, it is almost exclusively in the context of the twentieth century or in relation to Western powers. Most strikingly, we were unable to identify a single article in our sample that examines an East Asian power transition earlier than the late nineteenth century as a reference to discuss the validity of using the theory as a framework to interpret contemporary East Asia.

It might be that it is straightforward to apply to Asia a theory inductively derived from the European experience. After all, a good theory should have clear causal mechanisms that can be transposed and translated beyond the domain in which they were first derived. Thus, the mere fact that the cases and original empirical examples of power transition theory are European should not necessarily disqualify it from application around the world. Rather, the real methodological question is whether the theory actually is universal over time and space. As Barbara Geddes pointed out long ago, one of the key "tasks crucial to testing any hypothesis [is] to identify the universe of cases to which the hypothesis should apply" and there are problems if "cases are selected on a variable—geographical region—that is correlated with the dependent variable."[27] To use only European cases to derive a theory of power transitions and then test that theory only on European cases and assume that Europe is the entire pool of possible cases is to risk making precisely the error that Geddes warned about.

POWER TRANSITION AS A "CANON" TO INTERPRET ASIA IN THE TWENTY-FIRST CENTURY

Despite the blind spot inherent throughout this literature, as Lebow and Valentino point out, power transition theory "has become an accepted framework for many scholars and policy-makers who focus on Asia."[28] At first glance, applying power transition theory might appear to be straightforward. Indeed, as China has become a major economic and political power, scholars have increasingly debated whether and in what ways the theory might apply to China, either in U.S.–China or China–Japan contexts.[29] Writing about China, Aaron Friedberg observes, "Realist pessimists note that, throughout history, rising powers have tended to be troublemakers, at least insofar as their more established counterparts in the international system are concerned."[30] John Mearsheimer believes that China is likely to imitate the United States in its pursuit of regional hegemony and predicts that China "is also likely to try to push the United States out of Asia, much the way the United States pushed the European great powers out of the Western Hemisphere."[31]

There are many who disagree that U.S.–China power transitions are dangerous. As Robert Art notes, the power transition perspective ignores China's "peaceful rise" strategy, although "we cannot predict the exact nature of Chinese intentions and goals a few decades from now."[32] Others have closely examined the rise of Germany under Bismarck and the eventual events of 1914, asking whether China's rise is anything similar to that of Germany in the nineteenth century.[33] Chan argues that the U.S.–China power transition will be more like the U.K.–U.S. power transition a century earlier, not the British–German power transition that caused World War I.[34] As Jingdong Yuan summarizes, "Comparing China to Wilhelmine Germany, against the backdrop of the centenary of the First World War, is a growing cottage industry and fills the pages of academic journals and think-tank reports."[35]

However, whether those scholars agree or disagree with the lessons of European history, they are still working within— and reacting to—the framework, ideas, and historical analogies derived from the European experience. Almost every dissenting voice about power transitions and China debates interpretations of historical Europe, not East Asia itself. For example, Chan is highly critical of Graham Allison's interpretation of Thucydides's *History of the Peloponnesian War*. Chan argues that Allison overlooks human agency and contingency, writing that "human emotions—such as envy, anger, resentment, arrogance, and even desperation in addition to fear—can possibly provide the missing link connecting power shifts to war outbreak because these feelings can incline leaders to undertake more belligerent actions." Chan also disagrees with Allison's interpretation of power transition theory that a rising power as likely to start a war—"a cocky, impatient upstart itching for a fight"—arguing that it is the declining hegemon that often may indeed be the revisionist power.[36]

And yet the debates about the same set of European historical cases hinges on who interprets the history the best. For instance, Yuan-kang Wang, in criticizing Chan for criticizing Allison, argues that "the Peloponnesian War, from which *Thucydides's Trap* is derived, was started not by the rising latecomer but by the existing dominant power (Sparta). The sixteen cases of power shifts in Allison's study, albeit problematic in case selection, include examples of wars initiated by *both* the rising latecomer and the dominant state."[37] Wang then corrects Chan on whether Allison treated the Crimean War (1853–1856) as a power transition war. All this debate about who started it—whether Greece or Sparta—whether led by Thucydides, Allison, Chan, or Wang—is ostensibly supposed to eventually provide insights into whether China in the twenty-first century will start a war.

The same pattern can be seen in debates about the lessons of World War I. Scholars probe the circumstances of why rising Germany started World War I, focusing on causal arguments such as rising nationalism or the importance of European geography as central to Germany's goals and fears. They then parallel a rising China in Asia with factors such as ostensibly rising nationalism and a geographic vulnerability. All this leads to the conclusion that if Germany started World War I, why would China not start World War III? Ian Chong and Todd Hall, for example, argue that "analogies can function to limit and distort the comprehension of problems. That said, we believe that the experience of World War I itself remains rife with lessons possibly more relevant now than ever. . . . Although not necessarily portents of another full-scale world war, the factors we identify do have the potential to exacerbate the risk of tensions or increase the likelihood of conflict in East Asia."[38]

As these two examples indicate, almost the entire debate about China's rise and East Asia revolves around "getting Europe right." If the analogy is correct, the reasoning goes, then one can understand China. Intuitively, this is odd: it is not clear that the better the historical examination of either ancient Greece or nineteen-century Germany, the better the insights into China today.

It may be that the experience of European power transitions is universal and that across time and space the most important factor for determining war is the change in relative capabilities between two great powers. But this needs to be shown, not assumed. The universe of cases is far larger than simply the European historical experience.

In short, power transition theory has used European cases for the majority of its empirical testing and for deriving its causal propositions. As Lebow and Valentino summarize, "Power transition theorists have been surprisingly reluctant to engage historical cases in an effort to show that wars between great powers have actually resulted from the motives described by their theories."[39]

RISING AND UNLIMITED AMBITIONS

Whether or not power transition theory is applicable to East Asia, it contains a number of commonly held assumptions that dominate the contemporary international relations literature. Most important, much international relations literature, and power transition theory in particular, takes the idea of "states" as unproblematic, assuming that all states behave, perceive, and want the same things across time and space. In particular, it is widely assumed that all states have rising and unlimited ambitions, which are bounded only by their material capabilities: the more powerful a state grows, the more its ambitions will grow as well. Consequently, states, especially those with limited knowledge about each other, believe in and act upon worst-case scenarios.[40]

The assumptions that states are uniform and have unlimited ambitions lead to a third assumption: larger states exploit smaller states to extract gains.[41] Invoking Thucydides's famous axiom, "the strong do what they can and the weak suffer what they must," theories grounded in power readily assume "the domination of the weak at the whim of the powerful."[42] Indeed, under anarchy, a larger power cannot credibly commit to not exploiting its bargaining leverage. Relatedly, if a state's expected decline in power is too significant compared to its costs of war, the inability to restrain another state in terms of future foreign policy demands makes preventive war rational.[43] These assumptions, therefore, complicate establishing credible commitments in bargaining theory, exacerbate the mutual insecurities central to the security dilemma, and serve as the key causal motivation for balancing.

Although some scholarship points out the problems with this set of assumptions, they remain easily the most influential in much of the power transition literature. In fact, if it were not at all clear that states have unlimited ambitions, then much of the power transition literature would lose its urgency, and indeed its relevance. As Kenneth Schultz and Henk Goemans point out, almost all international relations literature contains these assumptions about constant exploitation:

> a view of the world in which states have insatiable appetites for conquest, limited demands disguise unbounded ambitions, and any concession to an adversary only invites further aggression. This view is rooted in the belief, summarized by Holsti, that "whatever the window dressing, propaganda lines, and self-serving justifications for the use of force, the basic issue is always a power contest between two or more protagonists in which"— now quoting Aron—"the stakes are the 'existence, the creation, and the elimination of states.'" This view is echoed in Mearsheimer's argument that all states have a common aim: to maximize their power.[44]

Yet scholars have long noted little balancing behavior by smaller states,[45] and they have not found as much exploitation by larger powers as might be expected in a world ruled purely by coercion and domination.[46] Schultz and Goemans continue to point out that "historically . . . states bargain within far more limited confines defined by well-bounded claims . . . the size of claims is weakly related to the relative power of disputants and unaffected by dramatic changes in power, and smaller claims are associated with a higher probability that the challenger will receive any concession."[47] In other words, the assumptions underlying the power transition theory, which are often regarded as fundamental premises of how the world operates, warrant reassessment.

THE COMMON CONJECTURE IN
INTERNATIONAL RELATIONS

Rather than structural theories like power transition theory, a growing body of international relations scholarship from many diverse perspectives emphasizes the role of nonmaterial factors in both war and peace, and stability and instability. At the heart of this approach lies the fairly straightforward claim that beliefs about ourselves and each other are variable, not constant; those beliefs about us and them can create common expectations and stable understandings or can lead to fear, mistrust, and misperception.

Fundamentally, this comes down to the key concept in this book: a "common conjecture." Conjecture is a multifaceted concept, representing a higher-level framework that captures the strategic calculations and interactions grounded in beliefs and belief updating. Borrowing formal languages, stability can be thought of a specific equilibrium in a game that requires all share a common understanding of how they will play the game, including strategies on that equilibrium path. When participants share a common conjecture about appropriate and legitimate behavior, they share an understanding of each other's aims and identity.

In international relations, this means a set of beliefs about roles, rights, and responsibilities. These are repertoires of legitimate practices—patterns of how countries legitimate themselves to each other. What actions are legitimate? Who is legitimate? How do actors become legitimate? These are about social aims and identity: What do the actors care about, and how do they relate to each other? These common understandings about legitimate behavior, about relative role, are key to the parties being able to negotiate a stable relationship with each other.

In a 2013 special issue of the *Journal of Asian Studies*, David Kang, writing about hierarchy, legitimacy, and authority in East Asia, proposed two causal hypotheses regarding stability. First, if two states mutually agree on their relative statuses and capabilities, their relationship will be stable despite substantial differences in material capabilities. Second, conversely, conflict propensity increases regardless of the balance of power.[48] Moreover, common conjectures are inherently social. Sixiang Wang writes about Korea–China relations, "In the long view, no rhetorical or ritual gesture occurred in isolation as discrete statements. They were instead part of an ongoing conversation about the meaning and purpose of empire, one in which Korea's place in the imperial imagination played an important role."[49] From this perspective, our key claim is this:

> *The materialist or structural explanations based on power do not explain stability, nor do they explain conflict.*
>
> *Instead, the common conjecture shared between two countries accounts for both stability and lack of stability in their relations.*

Although an emphasis on the role of ideas is most commonly associated with constructivist theories, scholars working from diverse perspectives emphasize the importance of ideas. Where rationalists take preferences as given and constructivists endogenize them, James Fearon and Alexander Wendt note that "the rationalist recipe . . . embraces intentionality and the explanation of actions in terms of beliefs, desires, reasons and meanings," and "there is little difference between rationalism and constructivism on the issue of whether ideas 'matter.'"[50] Formal theorists have made this claim powerfully. Bargaining is not structural, despite Fearon's claim in 1995 that he was making a "neorealist" argument.[51] As Robert Powell writes, "Although some structural theories . . . seem to suggest that one can explain at least the outline of state behavior without reference to states' goals or preferences . . . In order to specify . . . a game theoretic model, the actor's preferences and benefits must be defined. Moreover, most conclusions derived from these models turn out to be at least somewhat sensitive to the actor's preferences and, especially, beliefs."[52] States bargain and negotiate all the time. As the surplus of peace grows, the link between the balance of power and war becomes less and less tight. Observing the conflicting empirical results on stability and balance of power, Powell argues that disparity of power itself does not disrupt the credibility of commitments. Instead, the probability of war is related to the distributions of both power and benefits. If the distribution of benefits is not controlled, the distribution of power and the probability of war cannot be assessed effectively.[53]

To that end, bargaining theory explicitly focuses on actor expectations and beliefs about what the other side wants and perceives. This disparity between the states' beliefs and the consequent different assessments of expected payoffs to fighting is the seed for conflict. The fighting can also be treated as a process for parties to update their beliefs, with beliefs converging over the course of the conflict.[54] Beliefs that the shared understandings will change can lead to a cascade effect of defecting from cooperation; conversely, enduring or recurring preponderance can build a stable set of beliefs as well. This is why practices that reinforce the value of peace can weaken the correlation between relative power and the probability of war.

Constructivists also treat ideas as being central to explaining stability. For example, Stacie Goddard observes that "whether an actor's claim is legitimate depends on whether it resonates with existing social and cultural networks."[55] This is a "focus on the intersubjectivity of meaning—both legitimate ends and appropriate means are considered social constructs [where] there is a broad consensus on a set of appropriate social actors, appropriate societal goals, and means for achieving those goals."[56] This emphasizes the "socially meaningful patterns of action which, in being performed more or less competently, simultaneously embody, act out, and possibly reify background knowledge and discourse in and on the material world."[57]

The presence of a common conjecture subsumes many more specific concepts in international relations, such as hierarchy, status, and legitimacy. All of these are elements of a common conjecture. A system exists when units regularly interact; an order structures how those units interact. Although the contemporary Westphalian international order's fundamental organizing principle is sovereign equality among states, many international orders have had different organizing principles and have recognized a wide variety of units as legitimate members. A common conjecture is about social relations: Do units have different expectations for their rankings in the system? Do different units have different expectations for behavior? Do the units understand each other's roles and responsibilities? The system's principle might be hierarchical or equal; however, whichever it is, the conjecture needs to be commonly constructed and believed to be legitimate by all parties.

A common conjecture is about social rank order, role, and responsibilities: Who should do what? Figuring out exactly what those shared expectations are will vary depending on the given historical, geographic, or cultural context. For example, in the contemporary era, which actors can be a "nation-state" in the contemporary Westphalian order is about ideas, not about the material composition of various actors. Bridget Coggins argues that which political actors become recognized "nation-states" in the international system depends on far more than simple governance and authority over a geographic area. She writes that "the strongest members of the international community have a decisive influence over whether today's secessionists become countries tomorrow and . . . most often, their support is conditioned on parochial political considerations."[58]

In East Asian history, the organizing principle of international relations was hierarchy, and the system and order were quite different from that of historical or contemporary Europe.[59] Different international orders will have different principles and norms, different cultures, and hence different common conjectures. Furthermore, different systems may have more, or less, shared understanding; and different systems and orders may have more durable and robust common conjectures, or they may be more fragile. What happens when there is destabilization? What happens when there is disruption? How do the units repair and rebuild their shared understandings?

Another concept that fits under our definition of a common conjecture is that of hegemony, which arises when units accept the leadership and influence of another unit. The simple fact of material preponderance connotes only primacy or unipolarity, and hegemony implies more than mere size. Ji-Young Lee points out that, "a country does not automatically become a hegemon by virtue of preponderant power but instead needs legitimation of its identity as such. . . . An important aspect of hegemonic power is about using cultural resources for strategic purposes, 'rendering some activities permissible while ruling others out of order.' "[60] In this way, leadership or hegemony is social: both leader and follower understand their different roles and responsibilities.

Power transition theory was mainly derived from—and subsequently tested on—a small set of geographically and temporally confined cases. To our knowledge, there have been only rare attempts to actually test whether power transitions obtained as the theory predicts outside of either the contemporary era or historical Europe. When applying power transition theory to East Asia today, the debate proceeds almost exclusively by analogy to past European cases as providing clues or lessons for how China might behave today. This approach has deep theoretical problems, as we have shown in this chapter. But even more important, empirically, power transition theory tells us very little about East Asian history, nor does it provide actual insights into China today.

In contrast to structural theories like power transition theory, we emphasize the shared beliefs and understandings that can exist between actors. In both the contemporary and historical eras, states negotiate all the time. This observation lies at the heart of both formal theories, such as the bargaining theory of war, and also many constructivist approaches to international relations. Both conclude that if two states are able to craft a common conjecture, then their relations will be far more stable than if they cannot do so. This insight lies at the heart of our analysis of both historical and contemporary East Asia, to which we will now turn.

II

HISTORY

3

THE LESSONS OF EAST ASIAN HISTORY, 500–1900

Internal Challenges, Not External Threat

G iven the oversight of East Asian history ingrained in the power transition literature, it is natural to ask whether different regions of the world actually experienced different patterns of power transition and the rise and fall of great powers. In this chapter, we will provide an overview of East Asia's historical experience with the rise and fall of great powers. We find that there is one key difference between historical East Asia and historical Europe, and one key pattern within East Asia.

The key difference between Europe and East Asia is that East Asia was a hegemonic system, while Europe was a multipolar balance-of-power system. China in the twenty-first century is not a rising eighteenth-century European state competing desperately for survival in a multipolar system. China is a massive and ancient country with an enduring civilizational influence that is rebounding from a temporary century of turmoil. Intuitively, it would seem obvious not to expect China to act like a mid-sized European state from centuries ago.

The key pattern in East Asia was that internal challenges were far more likely to cause the fall of dynastic regimes than were external threats. East Asia experienced long survival of the main actors in the system and remarkably stable relations between them, especially as compared to those in Europe. The common conjecture among the countries was also remarkably enduring, and there were extensive cultural and institutional resources that the participants shared and could draw upon in their relations with each other. As a result, relations among the participants in the order were often stable for long stretches of time. Thus, war was not the typical main threat to the existence and survival of the various countries.

CHINESE HEGEMONY

From the time of the Han dynasty (206 BCE–220), although Chinese power waxed and waned over the centuries, East Asia was mostly a hegemonic system, not, as we have said, a multi-polar balance-of-power system as existed in Europe. As Joseph MacKay observes,

> For more than two millennia . . . a relatively consistent idea persisted of what Imperial China was or should be. When China was ascendant, as during the Han and Ming dynasties, this identity justified Chinese regional dominance. When China was in decline, it provided a source of aspiration. When foreigners occupied the country, as did the Mongols under the Yuan dynasty and the Manchus under the Qing dynasty, they justified their rule by claiming the Mandate of Heaven (*tian-ming*) for themselves.[1]

Every other political actor that emerged in the past two thousand years emerged within the reality or idea of Chinese power. Korea, Japan, Vietnam, the peoples of the Central Asian steppe, the societies of Southeast Asia—all had to deal with China in some fashion and decide how best to organize their own societies and to manage their relations with the hegemon. The reality of Chinese power, Chinese ideas, and debates about the proper role of government and state–society relations and different ways to conduct foreign relations—these were all a fact of life in East Asia. Surrounding peoples could choose to embrace or reject the idea and fact of China, but they had to engage it no matter what they chose.

More than that, when China did fail and fall apart, it was almost always for internal reasons. As Yuri Pines writes, choosing particular start and end points,

> The Chinese empire was established in 221 BCE, when the state of Qin unified the Chinese world. . . . The Chinese empire ended with the proclamation of the Republic in 1912. . . . For 2,132 years, we may discern striking continuities in institutional, sociopolitical, and cultural spheres throughout the imperial millennia. . . . The Chinese empire was an extraordinarily powerful ideological construct. . . . The peculiar historical trajectory of the Chinese empire was not its indestructability . . . but rather its repeated resurrection in more or less the same territory and with a functional structure similar to that of the preturmoil period.[2]

Walter Scheidel, writing about the Han dynasty, delimits the centuries between its fall and the eventual reunification under the Tang, and concludes that sixth-century China restored a bureaucratic state that succeeded, "albeit with substantial interruptions, in maintaining a core-wide empire under Chinese or foreign leadership until 1911 and, in effect, up to the present day."[3]

In contrast to Pines's and Scheidel's point about the decline and rise of China, much of the scholarly literature on Chinese foreign policy and military strategy over its history suffers from two limitations: temporal and geographic. Temporally, some of this literature treats two thousand years of Chinese history as stagnant, repetitive, and unchanging.

In fact, as we show in this book, East Asian history exhibits two trends: some astonishing continuity and some remarkable change as well. East Asia grew, changed, evolved, and innovated as much or more than any other region on the planet, and scholarship on war and violence should reflect that historical reality. China spent much of its history in disunity and divided, as well as being powerful and hegemonic at other times. Furthermore, the challenges it faced and the wars that occurred across time were not simply a cycle. The East Asian region evolved over time, and the challenges facing the various countries evolved as well.

The Qin dynasty from two millennia ago had no other recognizable counterparts. By the fourth to sixth centuries, however, recognizable countries—institutionalized, territorially delimited, centrally administered—had begun to emerge in Korea and Japan.[4] By the tenth century, Vietnam, Tibet, and other actors had also emerged, creating a truly "international" system. Not only were there new and different actors across time, but the sophistication, complexity, and interconnectedness of the region also changed and deepened substantially over the centuries. Thus, while there were enduring cultural and institutional threads that run across two thousand years, there was also substantial change.

Another potential blind spot with the scholarship on historical East Asia is that it overwhelmingly focuses only on ancient China. Geographically, the extant literature is Sinocentric to the point of ignoring—much less addressing in any serious manner—the experience of other countries in the region. It is precisely this lack of taking the totality of all East Asia seriously that keeps scholarship so narrowly confined to either Eurocentric or Sino-centric preoccupations. "It takes two to fight": only by considering both China and its regional neighbors can we assess patterns of peace and conflicts and test competing causal claims.[5] Only by taking the region as a whole, in all its diversity, can we truly begin to craft accounts of state interaction that reflect the reality on the ground.

Scholars frequently approach East Asia with a disproportionate, almost exclusive, focus on China, drawing comparisons between Europe and China rather than between Europe and the broader East Asian region.[6] Earlier scholarship on the tributary system often uses the term interchangeably with "a Sino-centric order," which overemphasizes China's pervasiveness in the historical system rather than the norms and practices that persisted even when China was not involved.[7] It may seem odd to call for *not* focusing only on the hegemon. Our point, however, is that we need to place more emphasis on the agency that existed across the entire East Asian region. The region under consideration can be defined as emerging with the founding of the Qin dynasty in 221 BCE and lasting until the full arrival of the Western imperial powers, marked by the first Opium War between the United Kingdom and the Qing dynasty in 1839–1842. There were, in fact, numerous countries that existed alongside China—Korea, Japan, and Vietnam are the longest enduring, but also the peoples of the Central Asian steppe, and even the many *mandala* kingdoms of Southeast Asia, such as Siam. This shift in emphasis is necessary if the international relations discipline is going to widen its inquiry beyond China and address regional patterns of international relations across the breadth of historical East Asia throughout the two thousand years that it encompasses.

Given this revised view of the historical East Asian region, it becomes clear that East Asian history would reveal that the conditions for power transition almost never obtained in East Asian history. China was a hegemon and predominant through much of East Asian history. Even when China was weak and divided, peer competitors were rare. It was rare that any other country could compare to the various dynasties, as determined by conventional "power" measures.

ENDURING PATTERNS IN EAST ASIA: STABLE EXTERNAL RELATIONS, DANGER FROM WITHIN

The fact that the historical East Asian system was hegemonic did not rule out the rise and fall of particular regimes. Nor did China remain unified and predominant over the entire two millennia. If the rise and fall of dynasties did not result from power transitions, then what was the cause? Perhaps the biggest lesson to draw from East Asian history is the dangers of internal challenges rather than external threat.

Table 3.1 provides an overview of the causes of the rise and fall of these dynasties. Most strikingly, only three of the eighteen dynastic transitions before 1920 came as a result of external war. The three exceptions were the Tang–Shilla alliance that crushed Koguryŏ in 668, the collapse of the Song dynasty, and the Ming intervention in Vietnam in 1407 on behalf of one Vietnamese dynasty against a usurper.

Every single Japanese ruling coalition fell from internal causes, whether the transition from the Heian to the Kamakura shogunate, the triumph of the Tokugawa clan in 1600, or the

Meiji Restoration of 1868. Indeed, the only external invasions that Japan faced in its entire premodern experience were the unsuccessful Mongol invasions of 1274 and 1281. For its part, Japan involved itself in the mainland only twice before the late nineteenth century: in 663 in support of Paekche—one of the three Korean kingdoms—during the Korean War of Unification; and its failed invasion of Korea and China in 1592, which we will discuss in detail in chapter 5.

China itself was conquered only once in its history, by the Mongol hordes in 1279. The only other "foreigners" to gain power in China were the Manchus in 1644 as they moved in on the remains of the collapsed Ming state. We will discuss both foreign arrivals in detail in chapters 4 and 6, because neither of them fits the expectations of power transition theory. All the other dynastic transitions were internal—due to decay and collapse, whether the Qing in 1912 or the Tang in 907.

For its part, Korea was one of the most stable countries the world has ever experienced, with unified rule from 668 to 1910. Indeed, Korea experienced only three dynasties during that entire thirteen-century span of time. Both the Shilla (57 BCE to 935) and Koryŏ (918–1392) dynasties fell to internal revolt; it was only in the twentieth century that Japan colonized Korea, in 1910, ending the 518-year reign of the Chosŏn dynasty.

Vietnam emerged from the disintegration of China's Tang dynasty in the tenth century. Although contemporary Vietnamese nationalist historiography emphasizes continual Chinese threats, the reality was far different—China challenged the border with Vietnam only once in eight hundred years, but the Vietnamese state doubled its size through conquest to its south. Moreover, of the successive Vietnamese dynasties, only one—the short-lived Hồ (1400–1407)—fell from external interference. Every other dynasty collapsed from within.

Even the Ming intervention in 1407 was initiated by the Vietnamese. This one break in the China–Vietnam relationship is important to explore in more detail, because it presents insights into how the two countries managed their relations. Although China had invested the Trần dynasty (1225–1400) as rulers of Vietnam, that dynasty began to lose control in the 1390s. In 1400, a rebel, Hồ Quý Ly, deposed the Trần ruler and declared himself the founder of a new dynasty. The Trần royal family sent emissaries to appeal to the Chinese court for help in overthrowing the usurper, and China initially sent troops and an envoy merely to restore a Trần as king. Having easily dispensed with Hồ, the Ming do not appear to have had any idea what to do with Vietnam once he was overthrown. The Trần family was in disarray, so a return to the preceding dynasty seemed unlikely to succeed. Eventually the Ming decided to reclaim the territory, although clearly that had not been the intention behind the original intervention. A few years later, successive Ming emperors decided that holding Vietnam was an unnecessary distraction, preferring to return the relationship to a tributary one under a Vietnamese ruler.[8]

Also notable is the startling longevity of these countries. In stark contrast to the European experience, there were literally centuries when most of these countries did not face existential threats from external powers. These four countries, recognizably the same countries today, spent centuries living and interacting but only rarely fighting with each other.

In sum, even a cursory glance at East Asian history would lead to very difficult conclusions about how international systems and international relations operate. The lessons of East Asian history would emphasize the dangers of internal

TABLE 3.1 DYNASTIC CHANGES AND THEIR CAUSES IN EAST ASIA, 600–1920

Country	Dynasty	Dynasty dates	Cause of fall	Internal or external
China	Tang	618–907	Zhu Wen rebellion	Internal
	Song	960–1279	Mongol invasions	External
	Yuan	1271–1368	Zhu Yuanzhang rebellion	Internal
	Ming	1368–1644	Li Zicheng rebellion	Internal
	Qing	1644–1912	1911 revolution	Internal
Japan	Nara	710–794	Growing power of Fujiwara clan	Internal
	Heian	794–1185	Minamoto no Yoritomo seized power	Internal
	Kamakura Shogunate	1185–1333	Conquered by Nitta Yoshisada	Internal
	Ashikaga Shogunate	1336–1573	*Sengoku jidai* (Warring States Era), Hideyoshi (second great unifier), Tokugawa (third great unifier)	Internal
	Tokugawa Shogunate	1600–1868	Meiji Restoration	Internal
Korea	Koguryŏ	37 BCE–668	Tang–Silla alliance and decade-long war	External
	Silla	57 BCE–935	Aristocratic families, civil war, king was only a figurehead for last century; Koryŏ eventually conquered	Internal

(*continued*)

TABLE 3.1 DYNASTIC CHANGES AND THEIR CAUSES
IN EAST ASIA, 600–1920 (*CONTINUED*)

Country	Dynasty	Dynasty dates	Cause of fall	Internal or external
	Koryŏ	918–1392	Yi Sŏnggye rebelled	Internal
	Chosŏn	1392–1910	Japanese imperialism	Imperialism
Vietnam	Lý	1009–1225	Trần Thư Độ forced Lý Chiêu Hoàng to give the throne to Trần Cảnh	Internal
	Trần	1225–1400	Hồ Quý Ly rebellion	Internal
	Hồ	1400–1407	Ming China intervened on behalf of Trần dynasty	External
	Later Lê	1428–1788	Mạc rebellion	Internal
	Mạc, Lê, etc.	1527–1788	Many rival civil wars	Internal
	Nguyễn	1802–1885	French imperialism	Imperialism

Note: Identifying a singular event that causes the collapse of a dynasty can be challenging and subject to interpretation. In this context, we identify the pivotal event in the final years of a dynasty to illustrate the underlying cause, with an emphasis on distinguishing between internal and external factors.

challenges. East Asian history also teaches us that political units of vastly different size and power can craft remarkably long-enduring, indeed centuries-long relations with each other. China and other countries rarely sought to exploit or renege on their relations with their neighbors.

PATTERNS OF WARFARE IN
EAST ASIAN HISTORY

East Asian patterns of war were clearly different from European patterns of war. The European experience was of constant warfare and continuously rising and declining great powers, whereas East Asia shows a clearly different pattern dominated by Chinese hegemony, which lasted much longer than any European hegemon. This suggests that we should look at the long-enduring Chinese hegemony for clues about how China might behave while ascendant. Over the centuries, China expanded in some directions but also crafted enduringly stable relations with many countries. As Mark Dincecco and Yuhua Wang observe about China, "The most significant recurrent foreign attack threat came from Steppe nomads. . . . External attack threats were unidirectional, reducing the emperor's vulnerability."[9] Chiu Yu Ko and colleagues point out that "it is well established that interstate warfare, or military conflicts between sedentary societies, was more common in Europe, whereas military conflicts with nomads from the Eurasian steppe featured more prominently in China."[10] David Wright observes that "for two thousand years, the primary military and diplomatic preoccupation of the Chinese empire was the northern frontier."[11]

Rarely do scholars ask, however, why these threats were unidirectional and arose mainly from nomads rather than from powerful states such as Japan, Korea, and Vietnam. Explaining how and why these historical patterns developed over time will likely provide better insight into China's priorities and how East Asia as a region dealt with China than looking at European history. Perhaps more important, it is striking that the hegemon is the country that is fearing and facing threats rather than the other way around. As noted in chapter 2, this is the opposite of what extant theories predict: that the most powerful country is the aggressor.

It is here that the common conjecture becomes central to any explanation for systematic patterns of war and peace in East Asian history. Further chapters will explicitly show how the common conjecture operated across time and space with regard to selected specific cases. Here we simply describe the overall pattern of war and peace. Warfare in historical East Asia has been studied extensively elsewhere, and here we will only summarize those findings. Kang makes one key empirical claim about early modern East Asian international relations: "China's relations with the Central Asian peoples on its northern and western frontiers were characterized by war and instability, whereas relations with the Sinicized states on its eastern and southern borders were characterized by peace and stability. Unipolarity—Chinese military and economic predominance—cannot account for both of these simultaneous outcomes."[12]

In *East Asia Before the West*, Kang created a dataset of more than eight hundred entries that code interstate and intrastate violence from 1368 to 1841 in East Asia.[13] The initial dataset was based largely on an important Chinese-language source, 中国历代战争年表 (Chronology of Wars in China Through Successive Dynasties).[14] In subsequent scholarship, Kang, Fu, and Shaw introduced a valuable Korean-language source, 한민족 전쟁통사 (Chronology of Wars of the Korean People), and subsequently Kang, Nguyen, Shaw, and Fu added a key nineteenth-century Vietnamese-language primary source, 欽定越史通鑒綱目 (The Imperially Ordered Annotated Text Completely Reflecting the History of Viet), originally commissioned in 1859 and last published in 1884.[15]

This dataset, with its centuries-long record of internal and external violence across these three countries, reveals many interesting findings. In the case of Vietnam, for example, the authentic imperial record that was examined suggests that the monarchs of the Đại Việt period (968–1804) were usually much more concerned with internal stability than with aggrandizement or invasion from China. The Vietnamese court explicitly recognized its unequal status in its relations with China through a number of explicit and formal institutional mechanisms and norms. Vietnamese rulers also displayed very little military attention to their relations with China, which were conducted extensively through the institutions and principles of the tributary system. Rather, Vietnamese leaders were clearly more concerned with quelling chronic domestic instability and managing relations with the Champa and other kingdoms to their south and west.

Of 279 total incidents of violence in Vietnam between 1365 and 1789, 31 percent were external, while 69 percent dealt with internal violence of some kind (table 3.2). In other words, the Vietnamese court was much more concerned with internal than external threats to its survival. Of the internal violence, there were roughly the same number of internal revolts (36 percent) as regime contestations (32 percent).

Vietnam experienced interstate war in only 27 of the 424 years covered by the data, or 6 percent of the time. Moreover, the bulk of security preparations mentioned in the source material bore no relation to the northern border but predominantly involved troop movements to preempt intra-elite conflict.

As for Korea and China, an examination of the dataset from 918 to 1841 indicates that internal violence was far more prevalent in early modern China than in early modern Korea. The

TABLE 3.2 TYPE OF VIETNAMESE CONFLICT, 1365–1789:
SUMMARY OF "THE IMPERIALLY ORDERED
ANNOTATED TEXT COMPLETELY REFLECTING
THE HISTORY OF VIET" DATASET

	Number of incidents	Share of external incidents (%)	Share of total incidents (%)
External incidents	87	100	31.2
Border skirmish	18	20.7	6.5
Interstate war	69	79.3	24.7
Conflict not involving Vietnamese dynasties	3	—	1.1
Internal revolt or conflict	100	—	35.8
Regime contestation	89	—	31.9
Total incidents	*279*	—	*100*

Source: David C. Kang et al., "War, Rebellion, and Intervention Under Hierarchy: Vietnam-China Relations, 1365–1841," *Journal of Conflict Resolution* 63, no. 4 (2019): 896–922.

authors did not investigate the causes, but it also may be a result of the extraordinary stability of the Chosŏn dynasty (1392–1910). Put differently, the dataset reveals that Chinese and Korean sources contain similar incidents, and both essentially confirm that Chosŏn Korea had almost no wars with the Ming or Qing on its borders once both dynasties had consolidated their control. Indeed, the real problems for Chosŏn, which are well documented, arose from attempting to avoid the fighting between the Ming and the Qing.

Indeed, in China, it appears that intrastate violence was more worrisome and prevalent than interstate or extrastate violence. During a time when the Ming rose and fell, the Qing rose and fell, and the Qing doubled the size of China's territory through conquest, the Korean Chosŏn dynasty remained the same, both politically and geographically. Finally, piracy was a major concern, and Chosŏn suffered 110 pirate raids during this time period.

By the eighth century, Japan's foreign borders had been largely fixed in relation to the continent and remained unquestioned for centuries into the future, even while it gradually expanded and consolidated control among the islands themselves. Bruce Batten notes that "the most important section of the border was the Korea Strait, located between the island of Tsushima and the Korean peninsula. . . . Aside from the late sixteenth century, during Hideyoshi's invasions . . . the strait has always defined the western limit of Japanese territory." In fact, after the defeat in 663, Japan had no military interaction with the peninsula, and "with the exception of Hideyoshi's invasions in the 1590s, Japan never crossed the East China Sea to encroach upon Korean ground (or vice versa)."[16]

The historical Japanese state was involved in war so rarely that most scholarship on Japan treats historical foreign relations as a subset of cultural history. There is, in fact, an historiographical consensus that Japanese leaders engaged in foreign relations with Asian states mainly for economic or cultural exchange, not war and conquest. As Batten writes, "in order to gain access to luxury goods, ideas, and other aspects of 'advanced' culture . . . this culminated in the Nara period with Japan's full integration into . . . the 'East Asian world.'"[17]

Indeed, the entire Japanese historical experience in its foreign relations is a puzzle when viewed through a Eurocentric lens.

Unlike England, Japan never played the role of an "offshore balancer" intervening on the continent to restore a balance. Mearsheimer argues that "the United Kingdom has consistently acted as an offshore balancer in Europe, as offensive realism would predict. Specifically, it has committed military forces to the continent when a rival great power threatened to dominate Europe and buck-passing was not an option."[18] Japan experienced centuries of stable relations with China, Korea, and the rest of the continent, interrupted only by the Mongol invasions of 1274 and 1281, six centuries after the Korean War of Unification, and the Japanese invasion of Korea three centuries after that (1592–1598). Put differently, over the twelve centuries from its emergence in the seventh century as a recognizable state up until the late nineteenth century, Japan suffered only one set of invasions and initiated only one invasion. Abbey Steele and colleagues note that Tokugawa Japan (1600–1858) "was remarkably stable; Japan saw no foreign or domestic wars . . . and even the threat of such conflicts, until the mid-nineteenth century."[19]

For its part, Korea had only three dynasties throughout its existence from the time of the unified Shilla dynasty in 668. Both Shilla and Koryŏ, having survived centuries as a coherent government, fell from within. Indeed, as will be discussed in chapter 7, Koryŏ managed to survive in a particularly tumultuous time, when Northeast Asia was experiencing weak, divided Chinese dynasties. Koryŏ fell only from internal decay, not invasion from any one of these giant northern neighbors. The Chosŏn dynasty (1392–1910) was ultimately colonized by Japan in the early twentieth century, a victim of the dramatically changing world.

Although Vietnamese like to talk about centuries of war with China, the historical reality was quite different. Vietnam came into existence not to fight China but rather to coexist within the shadow of hegemony. There is an anachronistic twentieth-century nationalist myth of Vietnamese history that tends to be taken at face value by Western scholars and most Vietnamese themselves: that historically Vietnam feared China and saw China as its main external threat. So deeply has this modern Vietnamese meme of chronic war with China taken root that it is often repeated without reflection by observers and scholars of East Asian security and used uncritically to argue that Vietnam fears China in the twenty-first century. It is widely accepted today that Vietnam's history has been one of constant struggle for autonomy against China. Yet this narrative is a recent, twentieth-century nationalist narrative that was originated during a time of Vietnamese colonization by France and that was aimed at uniting Vietnamese in struggles against larger imperial powers, including the United States.

Viewing the thousand-year-old China–Vietnam border as simply the result of a military balance between the two sides is imposing a European lens on East Asian history, and it obscures how tribute relations moderated risk and stabilized the China–Vietnam relationship over the centuries even as the military balance shifted over time. Particularly important was the negotiated status within the tribute system that established Vietnamese regional independence while maintaining a check on Chinese incursions. Liam Kelley is worth quoting at length:

> Dinh Bo Linh . . . established a dynastic enterprise in the Red River delta in the 960s. He did this not by fighting off the Chinese . . . but by allying himself with a Cantonese warlord and defeating other warlords in the region. In the 970s Dinh Bo Linh then dispatched envoys to the Song court to establish relations. The court first granted him the position of military

commissioner and then commandery prince, continuing a common Chinese practice of granting titles to individuals who had fought their way to power in the region and over whom China had no effective control. What would be different this time, however, is that the Song eventually elevated the title of Dai Viet's ruler to "king of the state," thereby establishing Dai Viet's position not as Chinese territory but as a tributary state. Viet "independence" thus came in the form of an unequal relationship with China.[20]

From that time on, the Vietnamese court explicitly recognized its unequal status in its relations with China through a number of formal institutional mechanisms and norms. Explicit recognition of the hierarchy began with Đinh Bộ Lĩnh in 968 and continued essentially unquestioned until the arrival of the French in the nineteenth century. The historical record suggests that the rulers of the Đại Việt period (968–1804) were usually much more concerned with internal stability than they were with invasion from China. James Anderson observes about Vietnam that "by 1086 a clear border had been mapped out between the two states—the first such court-negotiated border in China's history. . . . The existence of a formal border between the two polities was successfully challenged only once in the next eight hundred years."[21]

In sum, the Historical East Asian War dataset—and a qualitative examination of patterns of war and other violence—emphasizes that stability was easier among like units than between different types of units that had different types of preference. Furthermore, the stability among like units does not fit easily into any category of balancing or bandwagoning, nor does the violence conform to our existing theories. While this is not to argue that they are "anti-theoretical," the point is that significant scholarship to theorize carefully about cases in early modern international relations that contains a diversity of political units has not yet happened.

The analysis so far reveals that power transition theory suffers from a presentist and European focus in its choice of empirical cases to test. With rare exceptions, cases examined in this literature are almost all European, and mostly from the post-Napoleonic era. This has led to an overexpectation that power transitions are a primary cause for war, along with misplaced concerns resulting from comparing China to various rising powers in European history. By examining premodern East Asian history, we show that it is exceedingly difficult to find instances of power transition among major powers, and the scope and boundary conditions for power transitions almost never obtained. Rather, a more prevalent transition is dynastic transition, with fifteen out of eighteen resulting from internal rebellion. What these findings reveal is that the European experience is in fact not universal, and that power transition theory is less common or applicable than one would think from simply reading the scholarly literature.

The key point that arises from an examination of a grand sweep of over 1,500 years of East Asian history is the recurrent centrality of a massive China despite disruptions. Also notable is the extraordinary longevity of East Asian states, which was in large part a function of their ability to craft stable relations with each other. Given that external stability, the greatest challenges to these regimes were not from war or invasion but were internal. If modern social science scholars had started with East Asian history instead of European history, they would have drawn the lessons of how central to war and peace are a common conjecture and shared understandings, not changes in the balance of power. To further explicate our argument in detail, in the following chapters we explore four key case studies taken from East Asian history.

4

THE MONGOL CONQUEST OF THE THIRTEENTH CENTURY AND THE SONG-YUAN TRANSITION

천고마비 天高馬肥 てんこうひば 秋深塞馬肥

The sky is high and the horses are fat in autumn

The Mongol conquests of the thirteenth century are often considered to be one of the most impressive military achievements the world has ever seen. Arising out of the Central Asian steppe, in less than a century the Mongols conquered China, much of Asia, and as far west as Moscow, Krakow, Budapest, and Egypt. Superlatives do not adequately convey the Mongol accomplishments. The Mongol Empire was the largest contiguous land empire in history. The Mongols achieved this in two generations, whereas Rome took four centuries to conquer a smaller area.

The Mongol impact was economic as much as political. Deep commercial ties under Mongol rule were forged between Asia, the Middle East, Europe, and India. The Silk Road—for centuries a loose network of trade routes roughly connecting China to Turkey—became a highway under the Mongols. Thomas Allsen emphasizes "the centrality of the nomads to East–West exchange."[1] As Marie Favereau points out, the Mongol conquests were undoubtedly the impetus for Columbus's search for a new path to India. She writes, "in truth, the Columbian exchange should be seen in part as a legacy of the Mongol exchange."[2]

In East Asia itself, Kublai Khan—grandson of Chinggis Khan, the founder and first Great Khan of the Mongol Empire—renamed his empire the Yuan dynasty in 1271, after the division of the Mongol Empire. Marveled by the Mongol's sweeping success across the globe, the conquest of the Chinese Song dynasty in 1279 by Kublai's Yuan dynasty is often conveniently interpreted as a typical example of power transition.

Such a claim may have a point on the surface. Ever since the Tang dynasty came to an end in 907, China had been in a chaotic era of political division and disturbance known as the Five Dynasties and Ten Kingdoms (907–979). When Emperor Taizu centralized power in the Central Plain and established the Song dynasty in 960, there still existed quite a few concurrent polities, in particular to the north and west. In this sense, the unification under Kublai and the replacement of the Song dynasty by the Yuan dynasty marked an end to centuries of division of China. Moreover, the unification under the Yuan dynasty had a profound impact on the conceptualization and the construction of "China" in later generations. Emperor Hongwu, the founding emperor of the Ming dynasty (1368–1644), wrote to Emperor Yuanshun of the Yuan dynasty and said, "In ancient times, the emperors, when seeking unification, often stopped in the Central Plain and the four barbarians (*siyi*) were not ruled. Only the ancestors of His Highness treated different people and territories both within and outside the Four Seas as the same, which is unparalleled in history."[3] Emperor Yongzheng of the Qing dynasty also said, "The unification of Central Kingdom began in the Qin dynasty, but the unification beyond the Central Plain started with the Yuan dynasty."[4]

However, was the Mongol conquest of the Song dynasty a power transition? More precisely and more relevantly, did the process of conquest follow the contours hypothesized by the power transition theory, that is, a rising power surpasses and ultimately displaces a declining hegemon? A closer look into the demise of both the Northern and Southern periods of the Song dynasty and its relationships with its rivals in each period indicates otherwise.

We use the Song–Yuan transition to illustrate two key points. First, the demise of both the Northern and Southern Song dynasty was caused by internal, rather than external, factors. In particular, we argue that the Song dynasty's systematic focus on territory that it considered Chinese led it to sideline the threats from the Jurchen Jin and the Mongols for decades. The Song had decades of evidence that both these steppe regimes were unusual and not just another ephemeral steppe federation. Yet the Song decided nevertheless to ally with the rising powers. Second, the Song's legitimacy crisis was rooted in the lack of common conjecture on who the legitimate Son of Heaven is and how to reconcile the relationship between *hua* (华, civilized) and *yi* (夷, barbarian). After conquering the Southern Song dynasty, Kublai redefined "China" and maintained ethnic diversity within the territory under the premise of national unity. In other words, when the common conjecture was reestablished, peace was obtained.

In the rest of this chapter, we illustrate our arguments in the following steps. We first explain the centrality to the Song's identity and legitimacy of recovering the lost "Chinese" territories—the Sixteen Prefectures. We will then examine how this led the Song to sideline threats from the rising powers and to even form alliances with them twice, and how the cost of such alliances, in both cases, was the collapse of the Northern and

Southern Song dynasties. The fact that the Song was aware of the rising threats but was far more preoccupied with recovering what it considered to be lost "Chinese" territories shows the central themes of this book—how the absence of a common conjecture leads to the most violence, and subsequently how internal factors tend to be more important than structural factors.

We then turn to the other side of the story and briefly survey the rise and fall of the Mongols in the thirteenth century. We argue that the power transition theory has little to say about the Mongol conquest of China, or about the abrupt collapse of Mongol power in China in the fourteenth century. In the case of the Mongols, the decision to adopt elements of the East Asian common conjecture and found the Yuan dynasty was deliberate. Consciously adopting many of the norms, conventions, and institutions already extant in China made Mongol rule far easier. The Mongols also kept many of their own institutions and norms, combining the two approaches in synthetic ways. In addition, the strongest explanation for their behavior—their rise, coherence, and ultimate decline—is internal to the particular leadership qualities and family dynamics of the Chinggis Khan clan. The Mongols themselves were not conquered from without; there was no new power transition where a rising ambitious power attacked and conquered the Mongol Yuan dynasty. Rather, the end of Mongol rule in China came from internal implosion.

THE SIXTEEN PREFECTURES
AND THE SONG'S DEMISE

The Mongol conquest of the Song needs to be put in proper context. The Mongols were not the first northern power to conquer the Song. A century earlier, in 1127, the Jurchen Jin had captured half of the Song territory, leading to the Southern Song reestablishing itself south of the Yangtze River, with its capital at Hangzhou. As Peter St. Onge puts it, "What should unsettle the historian is that despite this unprecedented [Song] economic strength and the technological advances that accompanied this strength—gunpowder (including exploding iron shells), movable type, textile machinery, new seed varieties, paddle-wheel ships, modern windmills—the dynasty was ultimately conquered twice by bands of nomads with a fifty-to-one disadvantage in numbers."[5]

Some argue that the monetary policies of the Song dynasty led to their downfall. The Song evidently were inflationary. St. Onge writes, "a series of inflationist emperors returned to the policies of the doomed unified Song . . . increased burdens on the private sector, launched war against the Jurchen Jin, and built up the economic situation to one of hyperinflation."[6] However, the worst episode of paper money depreciation occurred during the Song–Jin wars of 1204–1217, and afterward the monetary system stabilized. Another steep depreciation occurred after 1265, in the midst of the Mongol wars, when the Song introduced a new paper money system, but the Song was suffering military defeat and fiscal distress before that happened. After all that, Kublai imitated the Song paper money system in designing his own pure fiat currency monetary system.[7]

Harold Tanner argues that property seizures antagonized powerful landowners, who defected to the Jurchens and later to the Mongols in increasing numbers.[8] But this also cannot explain the Song collapse; the infamous seizures of the 1260s occurred in the Yangtze Delta, where there were no Mongols to defect to at that time. Others point to the Song's military weakness.

The Song identity: The Mandate of Heaven and the Sixteen Prefectures

From its inception, the Song struggled with a sense of legitimacy crisis. The Song arose out of the chaos of the Five Dynasties and Ten Kingdoms era, following the collapse of the Tang dynasty (618–907). In the wake of the final collapse of the Tang arose multiple different claims to be the legitimate successor to the Tang. Zhao Kuangyin, the commander of the Imperial Guards serving the Later Zhou dynasty (the last of the Five Dynasties), founded the Song dynasty by a coup d'état in 960.

Thus, the Song's focus on claiming the Mandate of Heaven as the legitimate ruler of all China was more than simply an affectation. A central piece of that claim was the Sixteen Prefectures of Yanyun. Originally at the core of the Central Plain, the Sixteen Prefectures contained the "Great Wall" (notional at this time), the main barrier of the Han dynasties against the northern nomads. This strategic area was ceded to the Khitan Liao by Shi Jingtang, a general of the Later Tang dynasty, in exchange for the Khitan Liao's military assistance during his revolt against the Later Tang. The Sixteen Prefectures then became a central site of contention. Nomadic control of the Sixteen Prefectures circumvented the "Great Wall" frontier and left the entire North China Plain completely exposed to the northern nomads. The nomads could easily roll across the North China Plain, leaving Han Chinese in the north ruled by outsiders.

This bitter legacy inherited from the Five Dynasties became the source of endemic fighting for the subsequent three centuries, and a central sore point of the Song rulers. Emperor Taizu, the founder of the Song dynasty, set up a Reserve Treasury (封桩库, *fengzhuang ku*) as a deposit treasury deliberately to accumulate funds to recover the Sixteen Prefectures either by direct purchasing or military conquest. Taizu lamented,

> Shi [Jingtang]'s Later Jin bribed the Khitans by ceding the Youyan area to benefit himself, leaving [Han] people in that area to be ruled from outside the borders of China, people to whom I feel very sympathetic. Once three to five million [of wealth] is stockpiled, I will send an envoy to make a pact with the Khitans to redeem the territories and people with gold and silk. If a pact is not made, I will disperse the wealth and recruit warriors to recover the land militarily.[9]

When Emperor Taizu conquered the Later Tang and unified the southern parts of the Central Plain, officials of the Song dynasty wanted to congratulate Taizu by crowning him with the title flattering Taizu's achievement in unifying *tianxia* (一统太平, *yi tong tai ping*). This title intended to reinforce him as the legitimate Mandate of Heaven. Taizu rejected the title and rebuked that the Sixteen Prefectures "have not yet recovered, how can I claim a unified and peaceful *tianxia*?"[10]

The Alliance Conducted at Sea and the Humiliation of Jingkang

Taizu launched another expedition to recover the lost territories before he died in 976. After his death, his successor, Emperor Taizong, launched two grand expeditions to recover the Sixteen Prefectures, leading to 25 years of sporadic wars between the Song dynasty and the Khitan Liao. The expeditions initiated by the Northern Song dynasty and the expeditions initiated by the Khitan Liao made the two parties realize that neither of them was powerful to conquer the other by force. The Khitan Liao thus chose to settle for the next best thing: firmly occupying the strategic Sixteen Prefectures and taking advantage of this to extort material compensations from the Song dynasty. In 1005, the successive battles between the two dynasties were concluded by the Covenant of Shan-yuan (澶渊之盟, *chan yuan zhi meng*).

The 1005 treaty introduced a new diplomatic language of equality: the two states often addressed each other as "the northern dynasty" and "the southern dynasty," and different rules of etiquette applied to visiting Khitan envoys compared to other "barbarians."[11] Additionally, the Song immediately abolished all place names containing characters such as "barbarians" (戎, rong), renaming prefectures such as Jing-rong (静戎, "Calming the barbarians") to An-su (安肃, "Peaceful and silent") and Ping-rong (平戎, "Pacifying the barbarians") to Bao-ding (保定, "Protect and stabilize").[12]

The Covenant of Shan-yuan is often viewed positively as it ended large-scale military conflicts between the two dynasties, allowing the Song and the Liao to live in peace for decades. However, it also marked the official admission by the Song of the permanent loss of the Sixteen Prefectures. As a result, the symbolic value of the Sixteen Prefectures as a sign of military weakness transcended their original, strictly military, significance.[13]

Moreover, the negotiations over the Sixteen Prefectures did not end with the signing of the Covenant of Shan-yuan. For instance, in 1041, Liao demanded the Song to cede a large area of Guannan (关南), an area included as a part of the Sixteen Prefectures in Shi Jingtang's initial cession but later controlled by the Song dynasty. Fu Bi, an envoy of the Song dynasty, forcefully conveyed the Song's determination to defend the territories even at the cost of ruining the Covenant of Shan-yuan. Specifically, Fu Bi said to Emperor Xingzong of Liao,

The emperor of the South [Song] dispatched me to tell His Majesty that he heard the Northern dynasty [Liao] wanted to seize the ancestral homeland. How is it possible that the Southern dynasty [Song] be willing to lose the ancestral homeland? The honor of seizing land on Liao's side means the humiliation of losing it on the Song's side. As countries of brothers, how can we honor one and humiliate another?[14]

Fu Bi successfully negotiated a peace with Liao by increasing the annual payment (岁币, *suibi*) from the Song dynasty without ceding the land. After his return, Emperor Renzong of the Song dynasty wanted to give him a promotion. However, viewing the increased payment as a humiliation, Fu Bi refused the promotion and advised Emperor Renzong to never forget the national humiliation and to continue to cultivate military strength. This contention over Guannan is not a single incident. As Gao Hongqing points out, multiple fierce negotiations took place between the two sides over disputed areas of the Sixteen Prefectures. The Northern Song dynasty often compromised and made concessions in the form of increasing the annual payment to the Khitan Liao.[15] The humiliation that came with it accumulated to the Northern Song's unique complex about the Sixteen Prefectures.

Perhaps most obvious—and often overlooked—is that the Song identity played a key role in its decision making and in the dynasty's ultimate demise. Nicolas Tackett has argued most forcefully that the Song China was a "nation" in the modern sense of the word, a transdynastic entity that viewed itself as a homogenous cultural and ecological zone, and that "these beliefs fueled the sentiment that the Song had the moral right to seize 'former' territory that lay beyond the limits of its political control."[16]

As a Chinese dynasty, the Song identity was inextricably bound up in a worldview involving the great East Asian conversation about civilization, and the common conjecture about what China's role and position are in that civilization. Thus, one specific element is central to explaining the Song identity: the idea of what China should be and the legitimacy of the Mandate of Heaven built on that concept of China. As far back as 800 BCE, Chinese rulers claimed the Mandate of Heaven to justify their rule. Timothy Brook writes, "Centuries of custom regarded the [Chinese] emperor as Heaven's son . . . he was the only person entitled to approach Heaven in sacrifice and to communicate with it."[17] For the Song, claiming the Mandate of Heaven was a key legitimizing goal. In the Song's eyes, the emperor must be the supreme *tianxia*, reflecting "all under Heaven." At the time, during the eleventh century, scholar-officials such as Ouyang Xiu (1007–1072) used their writings to help "construct a legitimate transmission of the Mandate of Heaven from the Tang dynasty to the Song dynasty."[18]

A hierarchical investiture–tribute relationship is so central to the legitimacy of the Mandate of Heaven that Shi Jie, a scholar-official of the Northern Song dynasty, tried to free the dynasty from the moral shackles and obligation of obtaining and maintaining this hierarchical relationship by redirecting the debate on the Sinic-barbarian relationship from a relational one to a geographical and cultural debate. In his essay "On China" (中国 论, *zhongguo lun*), Shi Jie argues:

> Heaven presides above and the earth presides below. That which is situated in the center of the two is known as the "middle kingdom" (*zhongguo*). Those who dwell on the edges of heaven and earth are known as "the four outlanders." . . . The "central kingdom" is on the inside. The boundary between

inner and outer was created to strike a balance between heaven and earth. . . .

Those who do not reside beneath the twenty-eight constellations, nor within the nine domains, nor in the positions of ruler and minister, father and son, husband and wife, older and younger brother, guest and host, and friends: they are beyond the frontiers . . .

The four outlanders among the four outlanders. The central kingdom in the central kingdom. For each to not disturb the other. And that is all![19]

As Gao Hongqing writes, by emphasizing mutual independence and irrelevance, Shi Jie defined the geographical boundary of China as those within the nine domains (九州, *jiuzhou*) beneath the twenty-eight constellations and abandoned the debates on superiority and inferiority. The concepts of "center" versus "edge" were still mentioned, but the focal point was on the geographical scope of the nine domains. Unfortunately, the Sixteen Prefectures of Yanyun fall within the boundary of the nine domains by any measure.[20] Shi Jie's argument helped the Northern Song justify its "equal" relationship with Liao, but at the same time, it inevitably bound the Song's legitimacy with the recovery of the Sixteen Prefectures.

One challenge faced by scholars when studying China of the twelfth and thirteenth centuries is the severe "biases of survival" that are endemic in the accountings of the Song's legitimacy. Since the Song dynasty, in retrospect, was regarded as the orthodox dynasty from a Sinocentric perspective, any data that have survived—Chinese official documents, elite Chinese chronicles—are written from a strong pro-Song perspective, downplaying the recognition gained by the Khitan Liao and the Jurchen Jin. The problem of Sinicization is so acute that as a result it is almost taken for granted that the Song's legitimacy, as an orthodox dynasty established by Han Chinese, was never questioned. However, Ge Zhaoguang argues that Shi Jie's "On China," as the first-ever political essay that features discussion on what China is, reflects unprecedented anxiety about Han China's legitimacy among Han scholars.[21] The dilemma faced by the Song dynasty was not an accidental loss of territory to nomadic minorities but chaos resulting from the lack of a basic common conjecture amidst competing discourses on who has the legitimate Mandate of Heaven. Questions discussed in essays by Shi Jie and other Song scholars—including whether the Song dynasty had political legitimacy, how the regime gets support, and how the Song frames the history of others in relation to its own—would not be mentioned at all if the Song ruler had not experienced severe doubts about its legitimacy.[21] To some extent, the later establishment of the Yuan dynasty by the Mongols and the Qing dynasty by the Manchus was erected on a foundation built by the recognition of the Khitan Liao and the Jurchen Jin dynasties, not only politically but also psychologically, by actors in that regional system.

The legitimacy crisis faced by the Song dynasty was so acute that the Khitan Liao and the Jurchen Jin also started to label themselves as "China" in pursuit of strategic legitimacy. Liao's changing attitude toward an alleged imperial seal reflects this challenge well. After the collapse of the Qin Empire in 207 BCE, generations of Han emperors struggled to possess the imperial seal, which was deemed to be the official representation of the emperor and an indispensable component of imperial legitimacy.[22] The Khitan Liao acquired one in its expedition to Later Jin in 947, but the Liao emperor did not pay much attention to it. However, after the Covenant of Shan-yuan, the

Liao emperor, knowing that the seal was forged, regarded it as something of supreme ritual significance and "manipulated the seal to produce a discourse of genealogy of empire that explicitly claimed the heavenly mandate transferred from the Tang to the Later Jin, and eventually to the Liao, and implicitly denied the Song of legitimacy." Moreover, the Liao built five capitals, devoid of actual administrative functions, to link the Liao dynasty to the Tang, furthering its contest of legitimacy with the Song.[23]

The idea of what China should be and the legitimacy built on top of it was profound, and giving up the Sixteen Prefectures was unthinkable to the Song rulers. The Sixteen Prefectures were a lodestone in the Song thinking. For example, in 1190, Song official Huang Shang (1146–1194) wrote, "It has long been the case that the territory of the Central Plains included Yan in the north, with the Great Wall marking the boundary. It was only during the Five Dynasties that Shi Jingtang abandoned the Sixteen Prefectures and offered them to the Khitans. It has been over three hundred years and [this territory] has yet to be returned to our possession. . . . This surely fills one with indignation!"[24]

Tackett elaborates on this point to argue that the recovery of the Sixteen Prefectures was the touchstone for the creation of a Chinese national identity. This is not imaginary revanchism: the Song elites genuinely felt that this was their heartland. As Tackett points out, the Sixteen Prefectures "was lost to the Khitans before the founding of the Song. Asking to have it 'returned to our possession' made sense only insofar as the pronoun 'our' referred not merely to the Song state, but rather to a political entity that transcended dynasties."[25] As Gari Ledyard points out, "the issue was simple: the aliens [Khitans, Jurchen, or Mongols] did not deserve to govern China; the Song did."[26]

After a century of peace with the Khitan Liao, the Song violated the long-established Covenant of Shan-yuan and formed an alliance with a rising Jurchen Jin against the Liao. Under the Alliance Conducted at Sea (海上之盟, *hai shang zhi meng*),[27] the Song and the Jurchen Jin agreed to jointly invade the Khitan Liao. If they were to succeed, the Song would transfer its annual payment to the Khitan Liao to the Jurchen Jin; in return, the Jurchen Jin would hand over the Sixteen Prefectures to the Song.

As the Song's ally, the Khitan Liao had always endeavored to preserve the Covenant of Shan-yuan. Before his death, Emperor Daozong of Liao repeatedly advised his grandson, Emperor Tianzuo, saying: "We've been at peace with the [Song] dynasty for a long time. You have a strong personality, but you must not make trouble." He further instructed the Liao officials to stop Emperor Tianzuo if he were to make any irrational moves to disturb the peace.[28] Peter Lorge notes that the Alliance Conducted at Sea among two very suspicious partners occurred because the Song was "so fixated on the Sixteen Prefectures that their ambitions could be limited to gaining that piece of territory. . . . From the perspective of a steppe leader it made no real sense."[29] The Song was so focused on regaining the Sixteen Prefectures that it chose to sideline the potential threat of the Jurchens. In 1125, the Khitan Liao fell as the Jurchen Jin captured the fleeing Liao emperor. However, the joint expedition also exposed the Song's military weakness, and the Jurchen Jin only transferred part of the Sixteen Prefectures. In 1127, two years after the fall of the Khitan Liao, the Jurchen Jin captured the Song ruler, Emperor Qinzong, along with his father Emperor Huizong, and sacked the Song capital city of Kaifeng. This incident, in which the Son of Heaven was taken prisoner, is remembered as the Humiliation of Jingkang (靖康之耻, *jing kang zhi chi*), marking the end of the Northern Song dynasty. The Song imperial family fled to southern China, establishing the Southern Song dynasty.

Song alliances with the Mongols

As a result of the manner of its inception, the Southern Song dynasty was characterized by revanchism. Lorge notes that even when the Song was pushed to the south, "the court could never explicitly abandon the idea of recapturing the north."[30] Morris Rossabi writes, "like any other Chinese dynasty, the Sung aspired to reunify China. Revanchism played an important part in policy debates at the Sung court."[31] After more than a half-century of stable relations with the Jin, in 1206, the Song invaded the Jin with 160,000 men.[32]

The Song was so focused on recapturing lost territory that it appears to have consciously chosen to view the Mongols, then a rising power, as an opportunity instead of a threat. After paying the Jurchen Jin for over a hundred years, the Southern Song allied with the Mongols in an attempt to crush the Jurchen Jin. Lorge observes,

> The Song court's attempt to establish a more productive relationship with the Mongols fell foul of its own irredentist ambitions and serious underestimation of Mongol military power. . . . A less emotionally driven court might have been able to accept that the . . . Mongol army was the superior force, and wiser course would have been to subordinate itself to the new dominant power. This was obviously beyond the emotional and intellectual capabilities of the Song court.[33]

Charles Peterson also observes,

> It has in hindsight struck observers since the thirteenth century
> that, with the Mongols rising in the rear of [Jin], it was not a good
> idea to assist in the destruction of that regime. But was there ever
> a genuine choice? The Sung were prisoners of a powerful revan-
> chist heritage which in turn rested on fundamental conceptions
> of their place in the world and in the cosmos. The former
> demanded unremitting efforts to recover the ancient Chinese
> heartland, the latter, uncontested Chinese supremacy over the
> nations of the world, morally and politically.[34]

It is important to note that the Southern Song may have been
just fine without recovering the Sixteen Prefectures. After all,
the Song continued to rule for another 150 years as the Southern Song dynasty; and under the Southern Song's rule, southern China continued to flourish, characterized by growing
urbanization of the society and expanded maritime trade.[35] It
had been defending its version of the Maginot Line, a network
of canals and irrigation ditches between the Huai and Yangtze
rivers, against the Jurchen Jin for over a century. After the loss
of the north in 1127, the Southern Song dynasty established China's first permanent standing navy, which underwent a massive
expansion from 1243 to 1247 in view of the Mongol invasion of
Korea in 1231 and conquest of Jin in 1234. In contrast, despite the
Mongols' spectacular expansion on land, where their mounted
archers had been irresistible and invincible, the Mongols made
little headway on water. For thirty years the Mongols were
unable to cross the Imjin River to take the island of Kangwha,
to which the Korean king had retired, and for forty years they
were unable to penetrate the Southern Song's defensive system
of canals and ditches.[36] John Man comments on the battle of

Xiangyang, a city with impenetrable walls dominating the Han River: "The siege went on for five years. The Chinese could not break out, the Mongols could not break in. There were countless attempts to sneak in, to break in, to break out—all foiled."[37]

Sugiyama Masaaki highlights two acute difficulties faced by Kublai Khan when conquering the Southern Song dynasty: the Mongols' expeditionary style being restricted by seasonal patterns; and their weakness on water. The Mongols lived a pastoral-nomadic life with a fixed seasonal pattern of scattered grazing in summer and living in sheltered camps in winter. Expeditions planned by the Mongols needed to accommodate this seasonal pattern. This is why famous expeditions by the Mongols—the expeditions of Chinggis Khan, of Batu, and of Hulagu—all moved from east to west in areas of similar geographical and meteorological features, especially areas with a colder, drier climate favoring animal husbandry. This strategy was compatible with the nomadic life. However, conquering the Southern Song dynasty required an expedition from north to south, passing vast areas with extremely rare grasslands. The long-lasting war between the Jurchen Jin and the Southern Song dynasty had also devastated this area. Consequently, the pastures and other supplies could not meet the need for a large-scale nomadic expedition. At the same time, the long distance between the Mongols' base and the Song territory made it hard for them to finish the expedition before the winter. In Sugiyama's words, "Jiangnan [the Song's heartland] is outside the 'effective shooting range' of the Mongols."[38]

In its late years, the Jurchen Jin dynasty faced both domestic and external crises. Since the 1120s, the Yellow River had continuously flooded for more than thirty years, wiping out crops over a large area. Tax revenue of the Jin government plummeted, and there was a shortage of bronze coins and copper deposits.[39]

At the same time, the Southern Song dynasty discontinued its annual tribute payments to the Jurchen Jin. The Mongols started attacking the Jurchen Jin in 1206 and took its capital of Beijing in 1215. Pressed by both internal and external problems, in 1217, the Jurchen Jin attacked the Southern Song dynasty, "devoting considerable resources to an inconclusive war with the Song."[40] Allsen describes the Jin attacks on the Song in 1217 as "foolish."[41] Herbert Franke writes that "although the strategic situation seemed hopeless, the [Jin] court in K'ai-feng decided to attempt to compensate for its losses in the north by means of a southern campaign against the Sung."[42]

In the summer of 1231, the Mongols sent envoys to the Southern Song to discuss forming an alliance, leading to a small-scale joint expedition in attacking the Jin capital of Kaifeng. In 1233, the Mongols again sent an envoy to the Southern Song, proposing a joint attack on Cai Zhou, promising to return Kaifeng to the Song along with the surrounding area of Henan, part of the lost Chinese territories of the Central Plain controlled by Jin. In 1234, faced with a joint attack of the Southern Song dynasty and the Mongols, Emperor Aizong of Jin committed suicide, while Wanyan Chenglin, who had just succeeded Emperor Aizong, was killed in the chaos, marking the end of the Jurchen Jin dynasty.[43]

However, as the Jin fell, the Mongols returned only part of the promised territory to the Song. After the Mongols withdrew to their northern base, the Southern Song initiated a hasty military expedition to recover Henan. This move to reclaim Henan can be explained only by nonmaterial reasons. The Henan area was the main battlefield for the Jin dynasty and the Mongols, and it was severely damaged. Regaining the area could not increase the Song's power but would only become a burden on the Song court. After all, even if the Song were to successfully reclaim the area, a large army would have to be stationed there, while supplies would need to be transported from the Southern Song's heartland Jiangnan via the Yangtze River for thousands of miles. This is exactly what happened. After the first battle in Luoyang, the Song army was almost wiped out due to the shortage of food. The huge failure to regain Henan marked the beginning of the Song–Mongol hostility, in which the Mongols claimed moral ground by blaming the Song for breaching the alliance.

In short, the Song focused on reclaiming land that it considered to be "Chinese heartland" to the point that it made a series of strategic decisions that led to its own demise. Allsen writes about the Song,

> Hoping to regain territories long lost to the hated Jurchens, rejected the Chin overtures and instead negotiated an alliance with the Mongols. . . . The Sung, eager to benefit from the Jurchen collapse, made an ill-advised attempt to occupy the whole of Honan. The Song forces, woefully inadequate to the task, were soon put to flight by the Mongols, who had no intention of sharing the spoils of victory with their recent ally.[44]

In hindsight, the Jurchen Jin could have formed an alliance with the Southern Song against the rising threat of the Mongols. The image of Song–Jin fighting that comes to mind is two men grappling as they both roll over a cliff. The Song had decades of evidence that the Mongols were unusual and not just another ephemeral steppe federation. The Song could see country after country falling to the Mongols and had watched their longtime rivals—including longtime nemesis Xi Xia—be conquered one by one. It is unrealistic to argue that the Song overestimated their chances in war. Rather, the Song allied with the Mongols

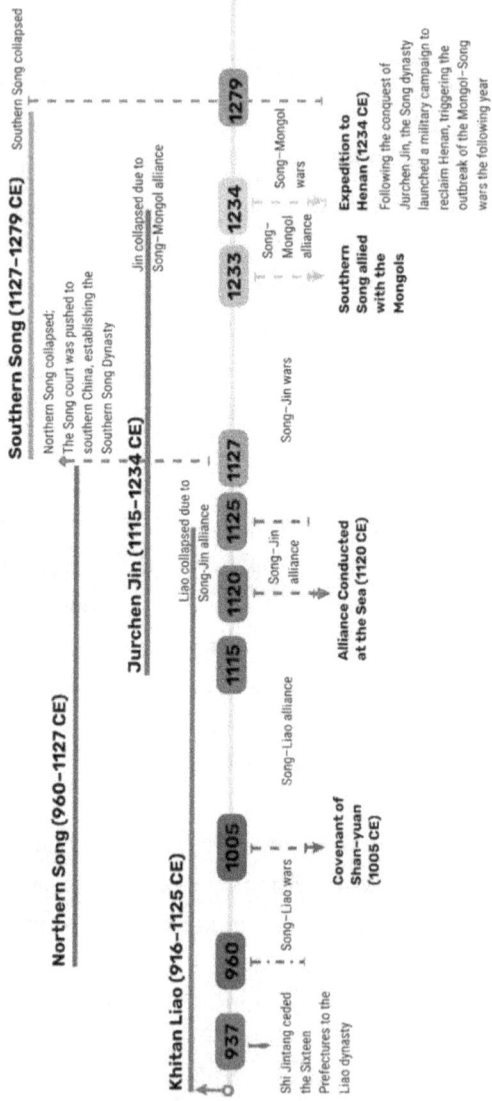

FIGURE 4.1 Alliances in the Song-Liao-Jin period.
Source: Authors.

in order to recapture territory from the Jin. Then, after the collapse of the Jin, the Song decided to provoke its ally, which had already withdrawn to the north, and initiated an attack to reclaim lost territories.

THE WEAKNESS OF POWER TRANSITION THEORY EXPLANATIONS

So far, we have briefly explained the centrality of the Sixteen Prefectures in the Song's identity and legitimacy and how the Song twice formed an alliance with a rising power to reclaim lost "Chinese" territories, both of which led to its downfall. We are principally concerned with assessing whether power transition theory can explain the dynamics of the Mongol conquest of the Song. Fairly clearly, the answer is no. Most basically, the conquests were not about a fearful, declining power and an ambitious, resentful rising power. Chan's extensive review of the literature concludes that "power transition theorists are explicit in arguing that great-power wars are started by rising upstarts."[45] In 1958, Organski originally argued that the challenger's motivations are to use its power to restructure the international order and benefit from its increased power and the new system.[46] However, there is no agreement about when the rising power will initiate war: some argue that power parity must be achieved with the declining power, while others argue that the challenger initiates war once it reaches 80 percent of the dominant state's power.[47] Yet, no matter what the mainstream international relations literature concludes, it is obvious that these conditions did not apply in the Song–Mongol relationship.

The Song–Yuan transition should not be treated as a simple power transition for at least two reasons. In terms of relative power, it is far from clear to what extent the two nomadic empires that crushed the Song—first the Jurchen Jin and later the Mongols—were actually superior to the Song dynasty. Philip D. Curtin notes,

> Between the foundation of the Song dynasty in 960 and the conquest of northern China by the Jurchen nomads in 1127, China passed through a phase of economic growth that was unprecedented in earlier Chinese history, perhaps in world history up to this time. It depended on a combination of commercialization, urbanization, and industrialization that has led some authorities to compare this period in Chinese history with the development of early modern Europe six centuries later.[48]

A standard narrative of the Song dynasty was that, in contrast to its vibrant social, economic, and cultural development, the Song was always militarily inferior to its neighboring steppe dynasties such as the Khitan Liao, the Jurchen Jin, or the Mongols. However, as Lorge points out, such an interpretation is ultimately historiographical rather than real and ignores the simple fact that the Song ruled a far more populous and wealthy empire for far longer than either the Liao or Jin dynasties. Moreover, the Song dynasty maintained an immense standing army throughout its entire history. A significant number of important civil literati spent most of their time on military tasks and military policy, while the Bureau of Military Affairs (枢密院, *shu mi yuan*) was so prominent that it had to be separated from the civil bureaucracy to prevent any single official from gaining undue power at court.[49] Even when the Song lost control of the traditional birthplace of Chinese civilization along the Yellow River to the Jurchen Jin, the Song economy was not in ruins, since the Southern Song dynasty still controlled 60 percent of China's population and a majority of the most productive agricultural land.[50]

By any conventional measure, the Mongols were not as powerful as one would assume. The Song China at its height had a population of more than seventy million people, and eleventh-century per capita income in China, at $1,458 (in 1990 international dollars), was almost twice that of England at just $754.[51] Chinese war technology was unsurpassed, and the Song had vibrant commercial, cultural, and artistic sectors. The Song capital, Hangzhou, was considered one of the wealthiest cities in the world, with widespread domestic trade and commerce. The Song certainly was not the declining power attacking the rising power out of fear: Even by the thirteenth century, "the Song was, on the surface, prosperous."[52]

The Mongols at their height had an army of perhaps 120,000 men, with perhaps two or three times that many troops who had switched allegiances from defeated lands.[53] In contrast, the Song standing army contained over one million men, and the Song navy had more than two thousand ships.[54] The entire population of the Central Asian steppe was about one million; Allsen writes "in Chinggis Qan's day the population of the eastern steppe . . . was somewhere between 700,000 and 1,000,000," a small fraction of China's population.[55]

Apart from their relative powers, the history that unfolded prior to the collapse of the two periods of the Song dynasty also does not fit the power transition theory. If the power transition theory holds, we should anticipate that the Song dynasty, the *supposedly* declining hegemon, would engage in either preventive or defensive wars with the Jurchen Jin dynasty and Kublai's Yuan dynasty, the respective rising power in the two periods of the Song dynasty. However, examining the diplomatic negotiations and alliance formation among dynasties before the demise of the Northern and Southern Song reveals that rather than fight against the rising power, both the Northern and Southern Song chose to sideline the threat from the rising powers; instead, the Song chose to form alliances with the rising powers and engaged in a series of wars not to expand its influence or maintain its hegemony but to recover lost territories—territories that were not even ceded during the Song's rule but by previous dynasties—with the aim of restoring the Song dynasty's legitimacy as the authentic ruler of all under Heaven. The Song's determination to recover the lost territories was so strong that it ditched the 115 years of peace with the Liao constructed via the Covenant of Shan-yuan and allied with a rising Jin to crush its old Liao ally, which in the end led to its own demise. When the Song court was pushed to the south, history repeated itself when the Southern Song formed an alliance with the rising Mongols, which led to the collapse of the Southern Song. As Yuri Pines writes:

> At times, lofty pronouncements appear so divorced from the realities on the ground that a student may be tempted to dismiss them as nothing but a meaningless brouhaha. Yet discourse of inclusiveness and universality in China . . . was also a powerful political force in its own right. Firmly entrenched values, perceptions, and ideals could at times direct the ruling elite toward a certain course of action that was hazardous from military, economic, or sociopolitical points of view.[56]

THE RISE AND FALL OF THE MONGOLS

While half the puzzle of the Song–Yuan transition is why the Song fell, the other half is why the Mongols succeeded. This chapter is not a comprehensive analysis of the Mongol conquests, the Mongol Empire, or the Mongol exchange that intensified global trade long before the Columbian exchange. Rather, we are concerned with a narrower but equally important conceptual issue: How do we explain the Mongol conquest of the Song China?

As noted in chapter 3, it is widely acknowledged that for two thousand years China's primary external threats came from the steppe and were unidirectional. Brantly Womack writes, "The primary curse was that the nomadic neighbors to the north and west were more attracted by China's wealth than by its virtue, and their combination of mobility and a vast, inhospitable hinterland made them a border problem for which there could not be a final solution."[57]

Regarding the Mongols specifically, Peter Frankopan writes, "Although the Mongols seemed to be chaotic, bloodthirsty and unreliable, their rise was not the result of a lack of order, but precisely the opposite: ruthless planning, streamlined organization and a clear set of strategic objectives were the key to establishing the largest land empire in history."[58] Before the twelfth century, the Mongol tribes were virtually unknown. Yet within a few decades a young leader named Temüjin began to build up a personal following. Defeating local smaller tribes, eventually Temüjin was named *khan* (or *khaghan*), or leader, of the Mongols. He took the name Chinggis ("boundless"). Chinggis Khan conquered much of the Central Asian steppe and united the various peoples under one Mongol banner. In 1206, he declared the formation of the Great Mongolian State (Yeke Mongghol Ulus). Unifying the Mongols under one leader had never happened before, at least not on this scale and this durably. As impressive as Chinggis's accomplishments were, Pamela Crossley notes that Chinggis himself "intentionally conquered nowhere outside of Mongolia and only a few locations by accident. . . . It was his successors . . . who made fundamental contributions to transformation of the medieval world."[59] For the next two generations, Mongol armies expanded the conquests and empire that Chinggis had begun. These three generations—from Chinggis to his sons and grandsons—created the largest land empire in world history.[60]

The Mongols initially attacked states in Northeast Asia around China in the early thirteenth century, conquering the Xi Xia and then the Jurchen Jin dynasties in northern China. Beginning in 1207–1209, the Mongols initially attacked the Xi Xia. The Xi Xia tried to ally with the Jurchen against the Mongols, but when the Jurchen failed to help them, the Xi Xia attacked the Jurchen, even as the Mongols continued to invade their lands. The Mongols regularly won battles with far smaller forces. For example, in the assault on the Xi Xia capital, Kharakhoto, Chinggis had 75,000 men and the Xi Xia had between 150,000 and 300,000 troops.[61] Yet by 1227 the Mongols had conquered Xi Xia. The Mongols then turned their attention to the Jurchen Jin, conquering the Jin by 1234.

For the next twenty years, the Mongols made little attempt to conquer the Song China itself. Then, beginning in 1259, Kublai Khan (1215–1294), Chinggis's grandson, turned his attention to the Song. Kublai began his conquest of the Song in the southwest, initially invading and conquering Yunnan. Over the next few years, the Mongols captured Song cities one by one, with the Song ruling family fleeing farther and farther south. In 1271 Kublai declared the Yuan dynasty in China (table 4.1). Eventually the Song ruling family was killed off when Lu Xiufu, the Left Imperial Chancellor (左丞相) of the Southern Song dynasty, carrying the last Song emperor, an eight-year-old boy, committed suicide by jumping into the sea in 1279.

TABLE 4.1. TIMELINE OF MONGOL CONQUESTS IN EAST ASIA

1207–1227	Conquest of Xi Xia
1211–1234	Conquest of the Jurchen Jin dynasty
1219–1259	Pacification of Korea
1259–1279	Conquest of Song
1271	Yuan dynasty declared
1274, 1281	Attempted invasions of Japan
1283	Burma expeditions
1286–1287	Champa and Vietnam expeditions
1289–1292	Java expeditions
1298	Temür reverses expansionist policies of his ancestors, readmits Đại Việt as a tributary state, cancels planned invasion of Japan
1368	Mongols ousted from China, Ming dynasty proclaimed

As Kublai was completing his conquest of the Song, he also sent expeditions against Java, Japan, and Burma in the 1280s. However, within a few years of Kublai's death, the Mongol regime had switched its focus from conquest to administration. Endless conquest was neither inevitable nor necessary. By the 1290s, the Mongols had stopped expanding and started administering. Planned invasions were canceled as too expensive. As Hsiao Ch'i-Ch'ing writes, the reign of Temür (Kublai's grandson and successor) "was significant as the transition between a period of continuing conquests and one of general peace. All the foreign conquests that [Kublai] had launched late in his reign

had ended in failure. Apparently admitting that further conquests would be fruitless and costly, Temür . . . reversed the
expansionist policy of his predecessors."[62]

The Mongols may not have been political innovators, but they
were able administrators. They adapted Mongol institutions to
rule sedentary society (for example, the appanage system used
to govern North China after the conquest of the Jin in 1235) and
adapted existing systems (for example, the Liao–Jin dyarchy) to
their own purposes. The Mongol system of communication,
control, and coordination was unparalleled in the premodern
world. It was this ability to communicate that allowed them to
conduct multiple simultaneous military operations and then
subsequently to keep the empire together. This administrative
capacity included a remarkable postal system set up across the
empire. In its most robust form, stations existed every twenty-
five miles, by far the fastest postal service up until the modern
era. Brook concludes that "mounted couriers were expected to
cover up to 250 miles in a day."[63] Regardless of whether this was
achieved, the reality certainly far exceeded anything known to
the world up to that time, and this administrative capacity
allowed for a massive increase in global trade, which became
known as the "Mongol exchange."

Adopting the appearances and conventions and norms of the
East Asian common conjecture was not simply superficial but
central to the Mongols' attempt to legitimize themselves and to
govern China. Although the Mongols retained many of their
own customs and values, they also readily adapted to the reality
of the Chinese situation. As we will see in chapter 7, Koryŏ
Korea and the Mongols were finally able to craft a stable relationship once the Yuan granted Koryŏ tribute status, ending
decades of skirmishing between the two sides.

Nevertheless, the Mongols by 1300 had stopped expanding, and the Mongol Yuan dynasty (1279–1368) lasted less than a hundred years. Evidence of the importance of family and leadership factors is that the Mongols began to disintegrate almost as soon as they reached the apogee of their power. By the time of Chinggis's grandsons, the great Mongol Empire had fractured into four smaller empires, and those empires began to fracture almost immediately. In China as well. Kublai Khan died in 1294, and succession battles within the family began to tear the dynasty apart. During the mid-Yuan, "the country was free from foreign wars, campaigns of conquest, and popular revolts." Yet at the same time, over thirty-nine years, nine *khaghans* ruled China for an average of 4.3 years each; six of them became *khaghans* only after armed struggles, while three were killed. "Bloody purges always followed in the wake of a succession struggle."[64]

The second strand of our argument explains much about the Mongols: internal dynamics were much more important to the rise and fall of the Mongols than were external threats. By 1368, the Ming dynasty had been proclaimed as succeeding the Yuan. As Weiwen Yin notes, "After the Mongolian Yuan Dynasty was defeated by the Ming Dynasty in 1368, the Mongols retreated to the north and resumed the nomadic lifestyle. Although the Mongols continued to be a threat to the Ming, they never conquered the agricultural zone again. One reason is that, unlike their predecessors, the Mongol tribes since year 1368 were largely divided."[65]

For our purposes, there are two lessons of the Mongol conquests. First, the Mongol conquest of the Song China, which initially seems like a power transition, does not align with the patterns anticipated by the power transition theory. Second, the most compelling explanation for both the arc of the Mongol conquests and the fate of the Song dynasty is the same: internal dynamics, which were more important than structural or external causes in explaining the decisions and actions of both the Mongols and the Song.

The Song identity and the concern for an imagined "Chinese" homeland explains more of their behavior than any material interests. The Song, like all Chinese dynasties since the Qin and Han of 200 BCE, existed within an unquestioned worldview that took for granted the idea or vision of the "traditional" Chinese homeland. Conventionally, scholars view the formation of national identity as a Western, nineteenth-century creation. But countries in East Asia have had well over a millennium of a corporate identity. Nowhere is this clearer than in the attitudes and behavior of the Song.

In many ways, there was an identifiable Chinese national identity by the middle of the first millennium. This Chinese identity will be contrasted to Korean identity in chapter 7, where it becomes clear that the Korean worldview did not include primacy in the international order or even dreams of primacy. Part of the East Asian common conjecture involved relative role: the Koreans were content when they were able to find a negotiated status and had no notion of primacy as a Korean ambition. A key element of East Asian political and social organization has been the enduring idea of a universal form of kingship arising from the Mandate of Heaven. The Song elites could not conceive of submitting to the Mongols simply to survive. This would have been literally unthinkable at the time.

On the other hand, the Mongols do not fit in most conventional theory that begins with assumptions about the character of the type of units that make up a system. Unlike many conventional fifteenth- or eighteenth-century European empires, there was no metropole, no core. The steppe was not the source of material wealth or political organization, although it was a religious and spiritual center. The ostensible capital of the entire empire was a planned city, Karakorum, that never had a population of more than twelve thousand and did not exist before 1200.[66] It was not really even a capital: Chinggis kept moving, and wherever he was, that was the capital. Favereau writes that "scholars have begun to sweep away old stereotypes of marauding plunderers showing instead that the Mongol Empire was a complex political, social, and economic entity resembling a federation or a commonwealth."[67] As Michal Biran argues, "Mongol expansion began due to both practical and ideological reasons, and ideology played a major role in shaping the Mongols' spatial concepts. . . . Chinggis Khan had no grand design of world conquest. However, the steppe ideology of supra-tribal unity, which he had employed while unifying the Mongolian tribes, included a strong universal component."[68]

Moreover, the Mongols did not transform the international order—in East Asia, at least—in the way that revisionist states in power transition theory are hypothesized to behave. The Mongols certainly were not motivated by the goals typically hypothesized about a revisionist power: resentment of the dominant hegemon and a desire to change the rules of the system to benefit them. To be sure, the Mongols upset centuries of political arrangements and had a lasting impact across much of the world, but in East Asia they did not create a new international order in their image that outlasted them, at least in East Asia itself.[69] There were no new ideas of sovereignty or of how relations should work among the units in the system. Rather than force local populations to adapt to foreign ideas, the Mongols were often content to leave religions, politics, and leaders in place and simply rule administratively above them. In East Asia, when the Mongols adopted the elements of the common conjecture about how "China" should behave, its relations with other countries such as Koryŏ Korea became relatively stable. This was most notable in the Mongol adaptation of the institutions, trappings, and rituals of the traditional Chinese dynasties, and their establishment of the Yuan dynasty in 1271. Despite retaining many of the practices and principles of Mongol rule for the Mongols themselves, the Yuan dynasty in many ways continued and adapted existing Chinese institutions, such as the examination system for selection of civil servants.

5

THE SMALL ATTACK THE LARGE

The Imjin War, 1592–1598

不屑國家之遠、山河之隔, 欲一超直入大明國, 欲易吾朝風俗於
四百餘州, 施帝都政化於億萬斯年者, 在方寸中。

Regardless of the distance between nations, the barriers of
mountains and rivers, my heart desires to go straight to the
Ming, change the customs throughout China's territories into
ours, and implement the imperial governance eternally.

—Toyotomi Hideyoshi

I n 1600, Ming China was the most powerful and sophisticated country on the planet. Frederick Mote writes that in
the early seventeenth century, China was "the largest, richest, and most populous society in the world at that time. . . . it
ensured local social order, collected revenues, and reinforced the
normative system. . . . How could any enemy challenge a structure of such weight and stability?"[1] This was a hegemon, a source
of "civilization" for the entire region. Chinese ideas, legal codes,
political institutions, and religious and philosophical views were
borrowed throughout the known world. Access to China for

purposes of trade was critical throughout the region for both commodities and luxury goods.[2]

Yet, in 1592, Japan invaded Korea with more than 160,000 troops on approximately 700 ships, intending to conquer China after first subduing Korea.[3] More than 80,000 Korean soldiers, eventually supported by almost 100,000 Ming Chinese forces, defended the Korean Peninsula.[4] After six years of war, the Japanese retreated, having failed spectacularly in their quest to conquer China and Korea.

Explaining why Japan initiated a war against the Ming when Japan's power was nowhere close to that of the Ming is a key to understanding the complex dynamics of possible power transitions in East Asian history—but more. We chose the Imjin War for four reasons.

First is the importance of the war in East Asian history. The long-enduring East Asian countries had the logistical, organizational, and political-economic capacity to wage war on a scale unimaginable in Europe at the time. These countries could also project power over water—there was no "stopping power of water," to use one of John Mearsheimer's arguments that was adapted to explain the European experience. Mearsheimer writes, "The United Kingdom too, has never tried to dominate Europe. . . . The reason it did not do so, however, is basically the same as for the United States: the stopping power of water."[5] By way of comparison, the English Channel is twenty-one miles wide at its narrowest; the Korea Strait, between Pusan, Korea, and Fukuoka, Japan, is 120 miles at its narrowest. The staggering scale of the Imjin War on both land and sea and the conduct of war across a far larger body of water than the English Channel in themselves should be sufficient cause for international relations scholars to explore its causes and consequences.

Second, Hideyoshi's invasion of Korea marked the *only* military conflict between China, Japan, and Korea for over six centuries. Between 1281 (the second Mongol invasion of Japan) and 1894 (the Sino-Japanese war over Taiwan and Korea), the Imjin War was the only military conflict between any of these three countries. This is a remarkably long period of stability. Three major powers in East Asia—and indeed much of the rest of the system—could peacefully coexist for an extended time span, despite having the military and technological capability to wage war on a massive scale. The centuries of peace between these three countries were clearly a political choice, not a by-product of material constraints. The common conjecture and shared expectations are central to the explanation of six centuries of peace between China, Japan, and Korea.

Third, as we will show in detail in this chapter, the Imjin War clearly represents an enduring general pattern of East Asia. Power transition was not the principal factor for war; debates over the common conjecture, especially that over a shared understanding of relative role and status, explain the outbreak of this massive war far more fully than the balance of power. Furthermore, given the remarkable stability of the countries' relations with each other and the many normative and institutional tools that they had to manage their relations, internal factors and domestic issues were often more important than external threats in explaining state behavior. Put another way, if one of the most important wars in East Asian history—or even world history— did not follow any of the causal propositions laid out in mainstream power transition theory, then it shows vividly that power transition theory is more temporally or geographically restricted than often believed.

The fourth reason we focus on the Imjin War as an unusually instructive case study is the lack of attention paid to this case in the international relations literature. As Kenneth Swope notes, "it is nonetheless surprising that such an important and well-documented event has . . . received so little scholarly attention in the West."[6] James Lewis argues that "the Imjin War was very significant to Northeast Asia and offers comparisons with the great international wars of Europe and continental Asia. . . . If we in the West wish to understand East Asian international relations, the Imjin War is an excellent starting point."[7]

THE IMJIN WAR, 1592–1598

Before the Imjin War, the most recent major military action that had involved Korean forces were the Ming–Chosŏn negotiations over their border in 1392, and those negotiations did not devolve into actual fighting. War had been avoided in that instance by Chosŏn's accepting tribute status with the emergent Ming dynasty, while the Ming gave up the land it had potentially claimed from Korea, accepting as Korean the lands below the Yalu (Amrok) River. As will be discussed in chapter 7, relations between China and Korea were close and stable for 250 years.

With the stabilization of its border with Ming China in the fourteenth century, regularization of relations with the Jurchen tribes to its north, and the waning of piracy along its coasts, Chosŏn Korea had been so peaceful for two centuries that on the eve of the Imjin War of 1592, it had fewer than a thousand soldiers in its entire army.[8] Kenneth Lee writes, "After two hundred years of peace, Korean forces were untrained in warfare and were scattered all over the country in small local garrison troops. Koreans were totally unprepared on land."[9] Ki-baek Lee describes the quality of the Korean military in 1592 as "meager and untrained."[10]

In contrast, Japanese troops were deeply experienced, honed by over a century of fighting within Japan itself. Known as the *Sengoku jidai* (戦国時代, "Age of Warring States," 1467–1603), the fighting within Japan for domination had created hundreds of thousands of experienced Japanese fighters over the years. They came equipped with arquebus guns and had better training and more experience than the Koreans.

In 1592, the Japanese, under the leadership of Toyotomi Hideyoshi, launched an invasion of Korea with the intent of conquering Chosŏn Korea and eventually Ming China. Landing at Pusan on May 23, the Japanese troops overwhelmed the scattered Korean defenders. The Japanese continued to route sparse Korean forces and within two weeks had captured Seoul and driven north past P'yŏngyang in two columns. The Korean king fled to Ŭiju, on the China–Korea border.

The initial Japanese success delighted Hideyoshi. That the Japanese saw this as a war over primacy in the international order is clear from his aims: Japan explicitly intended to replace China at the top of the international hierarchy. In May 1592, Hideyoshi wrote to his adopted son, Hidetsugu, outlining plans for the continent, which included some exceedingly revisionist aims:

1. Move the reigning Japanese emperor to the capital of China and enthrone him as the ruler of a new empire encompassing China, Japan, and Korea.

2. Assign Toyotomi Hidetsugu to be *kampaku*, or regent, of China. The regent of Japan would be either Toyotomi Hideyasu or Ukita Hideie.

3. Assign the imperial throne of Japan to one of two imperial princes.

4. Korea was to be under the charge of either Gifu Saisho or Bizen Saisho.

Hideyoshi further wrote, "it is not Ming China alone that is destined to be subjugated by us, but India, the Philippines, and many islands in the South Sea will share a like fate."[11]

Chosŏn pleaded for Ming support, and by February 1593 an initial Ming Chinese expeditionary force of 45,000 troops attacked the Japanese. The Ming forces captured P'yŏngyang in a single day and quickly drove the Japanese back past Seoul. The Japanese were also met with increasing Korean resistance. As the Japanese supply lines were extended, *ŭibyŏng*—"righteous soldiers" composed of irregular fighters and guerillas and accompanied by Buddhist monks—harassed their rear. Japanese ships were designed mostly for transport and fought by grappling. Korean ships, in contrast, were armored (the famous "turtle ships") and had longer-range and more powerful cannon. Korea also had a brilliant military tactician, Admiral Yi Sunsin, one of the greatest naval leaders in world history. Yi attacked Japanese ships mercilessly and repeatedly cut their transport and supply lines. He never lost a battle.

Japanese soldiers began to defect in large numbers, with reports of more than ten thousand Japanese having joined the Korean side. It soon became clear to both sides that Japan could not hope to conquer Korea, much less China.[12] The Japanese generals in Korea built a series of forts along the southeastern coast and prepared to negotiate with the Chinese.

In the negotiations between China and Japan (and, to a lesser degree, Korea) after the first burst of fighting, three things were unquestioned: the hierarchic nature of relations between all participants in the war; that status and role were the most important and legitimate issues to be resolved; and that how their subsequent relations would be negotiated and even about what they would call each other were critical to their appropriate sense of self and other. Where the participants disagreed was on the specifics of these roles, and where Japan fitted fit in the system. As Kim Youngjin concludes, the diplomacy and attempts to improve relative position were far more consequential to the outcome of the war than the military disposition on the battlefield itself.[13]

Hideyoshi began the war with exceedingly high ambitions. Centrally, many of those involved placing himself and Japan at the top of the hierarchy. As Ji-Young Lee writes,

> Perhaps one of the most striking examples of how tribute practices assumed the "self-evident and undisputed" quality of defining the socially possible is Japanese general Toyotomi Hideyoshi's plan to build a Japan-centered order through the tribute practices of gift exchange and investiture. Hideyoshi . . . revealed his vision to move the Japanese emperor to China's capital; to turn Korea, Ryukyu, Luzon (the Philippines), and Taiwan into Japan's tributary states; and to have one of his three sons invested as the ruler of Korea.[14]

As Arano Yasunori observes, Hideyoshi adopted "a Sinocentric rhetoric governing foreign relations with tributary states."[15]

By the time China and Japan began negotiating in 1593, the Japanese had reduced their ambitions considerably. As negotiations began, the Japanese made a series of seven demands.

1. The daughter of the Ming emperor to be given as consort to the emperor of Japan.
2. Licensed trade to be arranged.
3. Ministers of Japan and China to swear oaths of peace.
4. The capital of Korea and four provinces to be given over to Japan.
5. Korean hostages to be sent to Japan.

6. Two captured Korean princes to be returned to Korea.

7. The Koreans to swear never to attack Japan.[16]

The two main Japanese commanders, Kato Kiyomasa and Konishi Yukinaga, worked at cross purposes during the negotiations, neither coordinating with the other. Kato "argued for a permanent Japanese presence on the peninsula," while Konishi "angled for some type of trade relationship within the framework of the Ming tributary system."[17] The Japanese demands during negotiations were far more modest compared to Hideyoshi's grandiose vision during the early months of the war.

The Chinese would never acknowledge equality, but they did consider granting Japan investiture at a status similar to certain Mongol leaders and below that of Korea and Vietnam. Korea—and China—sent minor officials to negotiate with the Japanese because "the Koreans valued highly the tributary system and their place within the first rank of tributary states. As the Japanese held lower rank, the Koreans would have jeopardized their status had they sent royalty as envoys."[18] The Chinese were willing to invest Hideyoshi as "King of Japan" at a rank superficially equal to Chosŏn Korea, though in fact it was lower because they did not offer Japan the same trading rights that Korea enjoyed.

Three years after the initial negotiations, Ming emissaries arrived in Japan in the autumn of 1596, prepared to invest forty members of the Japanese court with official Ming ranks and titles. As to Hideyoshi himself, the Ming emperor wrote somewhat brusquely, "We hereby declare that you are invested as the king of Japan."[19] The absence of the normally flowery language that would accompany investiture from the Chinese emperor was not lost on the Japanese—nor was the condescension in the investiture itself.

Angered at the Chinese unwillingness to grant any of the Japanese demands, Japan launched a second invasion in 1597, which was much less effective than the first. By this time the Korean and Ming forces were more prepared and stronger, and the Japanese forces had been weakened. Fighting was vicious, but the Japanese made little progress despite destroying enormous swaths of Korea and killing hundreds of thousands of people. Swope estimates that perhaps 20 percent of the Korean population was killed during the war.[20] When Japanese ruler Hideyoshi suddenly died in 1598, the disorganized remnants of the Japanese forces retreated in chaos back to Japan.

Chinese forces were recalled to China almost immediately, leaving the Koreans to their own country. As for Japan, the new leader, Tokugawa Ieyasu, quickly made it clear that he had no designs on Korea and, as Swope points out, "could reasonably argue that he had nothing to do with it [the invasion of Korea]."[21] The Japanese invasion was thus blamed squarely on one leader's grandiose ambitions, not on Japan as a country itself. Chŏng Tuhŭi and Yi Kyŏng-sun conclude that no side actually won the war, since neither side was able to subdue the other. Instead, the diplomatic solution was the only way to end the hostilities.[22]

Japan–Korea relations were restored within a decade. Both sides claimed that it was superior to the other, a hybrid, "sort-of" solution that held up until the modern era. Both sides could show evidence that it was superior while claiming that the other side accepted inferior status. The Koreans were suspicious of the Japanese for centuries thereafter and restricted Japanese contact to one *waegwan* (왜관, compound for foreigners) in Pusan. The Koreans also did not allow the Japanese to send embassies to the capital, forcing them to remain at Pusan. Although that may have appeared insulting to the Japanese side, it also allowed the Japanese side to claim that it never was required to send embassies to Korea. For its part, Korea did send diplomatic embassies to Japan twelve times between 1610 and 1811. The Japanese interpreted this as an inferior's sending embassies to a superior, although the Koreans obviously felt differently. Trade between the two sides also began again.

As for China–Japan relations, there was considerable trade between the two sides, even though formal tributary relations were not restored. Some trade was done indirectly, through Ryukyu, while other trade was direct. For example, between 1685 and 1722, Ryukyu sent 110 tribute ships to China, and more than 2,500 private ships sailed between China and Japan during that same time.[23] Richard von Glahn writes that "Japanese trade with China grew substantially after the Tokugawa came to power in 1600. The Tokugawa *shogun* Ieyasu aggressively pursued foreign trade opportunities."[24] John Lee stresses the "undiminished importance of a trade relationship with China and, to a lesser extent, with Korea and the Ryukyu" during the Tokugawa period.[25] It is true that Japan remained officially outside the Qing order, but it did not challenge Chinese hegemony during the era of Tokugawa rule. Thus, Japan's sole attempt during its entire premodern history to challenge the hegemon ended in complete failure.

RELATIVE POWER

Rupture is often as instructive as success in providing insights into an international order, and Japan's challenge to China is one such example. An obvious power transition theory hypothesis is that the cause of Japan's invasion and attempted conquest of China must have been that Japan was close to an actual power transition as measured by relative power. To quote Chan, Japan superficially appears to be a "cocky upstart."[26] However, by any standard measure of power, there is no evidence that Japan had somehow begun to catch up with China.

Historical measures of gross domestic product (GDP) and population compiled by Angus Maddison serve as a useful starting point for examining whether power transitions occurred during the period before and after the Imjin War. We estimated China's state power in comparison to the other major powers by following Richard Ned Lebow and Benjamin Valentino, who multiplied each country's GDP by its total population. Lebow and Valentino argue that "for most of history . . . states with large populations can compensate for lower GDPs by fielding more troops; states with higher GDPs can compensate for lower populations by equipping their armies with more effective weaponry or hiring mercenaries."[27] In 1500, China had a population of 103 million and a GDP of $62 billion.[28] The size of China dwarfed any other political unit in either Asia or Europe. In comparison, Japan had a population of 15.4 million and a GDP of $8 billion. In 1600, that distribution of relative power remained unchanged, with Japan nowhere near approaching China's population or GDP (figure 5.1).

Not just far larger on conventional measures of power, Ming China was also a military behemoth. Swope notes that in the fifty years between 1570 and 1620,

the Ming managed to make peace with the Mongols, intervened in border disputes in Burma on multiple occasions, launched destabilizing raids and surgical strikes into Jurchen and Mongol territories . . . suppressed a major troop mutiny in . . . Ningxia, sent tens of thousands of troops on two occasions to oust the Japanese from Korea, mobilized another 200,000 plus troops to

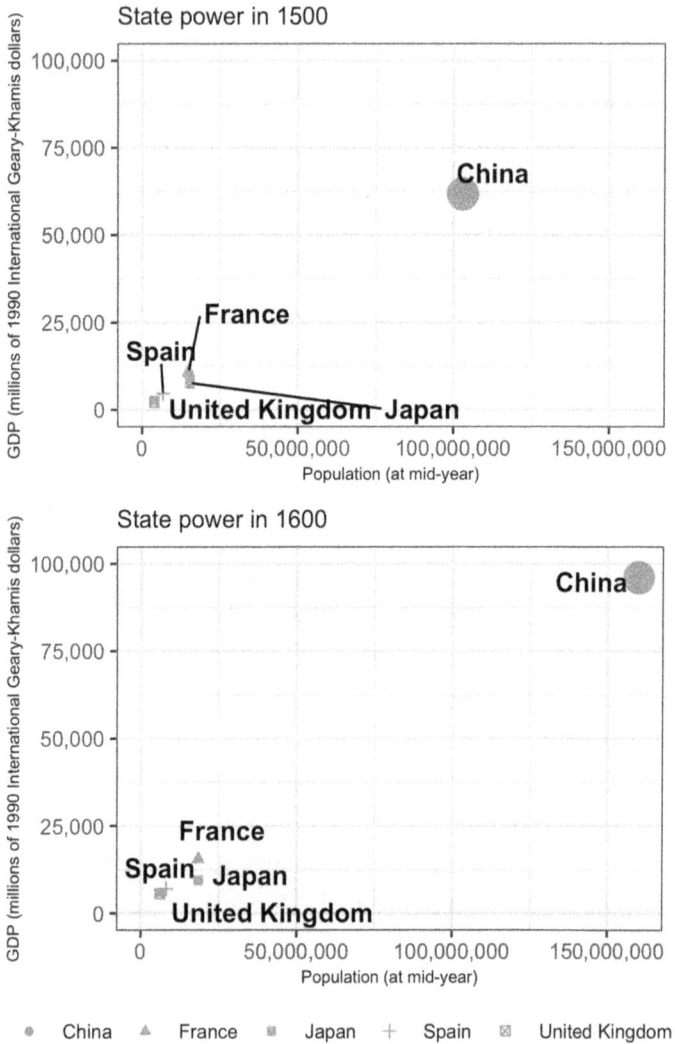

State power in 1500

GDP (millions of 1990 International Geary-Khamis dollars)

100,000 —

75,000 —

China

50,000 —

25,000 —
France
Spain

0 —
United Kingdom Japan

Population (at mid-year)

State power in 1600

GDP (millions of 1990 International Geary-Khamis dollars)

100,000 —
China

75,000 —

50,000 —

25,000 —
France
Spain Japan

0 —
United Kingdom

Population (at mid-year)

● China   ▲ France   ▪ Japan   + Spain   ⊠ United Kingdom

FIGURE 5.1 State power in 1500 and 1600.

Source: Maddison Database, version 2010.

crush an aboriginal uprising in Sichuan province, and conducted numerous other smaller military actions. . . . In the process the Ming retained its political, military, and economic primacy in East Asia.[29]

The Korean state also had the capacity to mobilize extraordinary military forces when necessary. During the Imjin War, Korea mobilized up to 84,500 troops along with 22,200 guerilla soldiers. The Japanese had invaded with a force of 281,840 troops, the initial invading contingent consisting of 158,700 men.[30]

Even more notably, there is no evidence from either the Chinese or Japanese archives of any assessment of the relative military capabilities or balance of power between the two sides. Ming officials evaluated the Japanese threat within the broader framework of its tributary commitments and defense needs around Asia, but there was virtually no discussion of Japan as a rising strategic threat at the time. Hideyoshi and his advisors made no assessment of the balance of power or any judgment that China was in decline and that Japan was rising. Yet this makes little sense given how Hideyoshi had waged war in Japan prior to this, with careful preparation and deliberate planning. He might have based his calculations on his "misreadings of scattered pirate campaigns conducted some thirty years earlier."[31] Mary Berry notes that Hideyoshi "knew little in detail about continental geography."[32] Real knowledge was sorely lacking, as were assessments based on that knowledge. As Swope notes, Hideyoshi "willfully ignored the warnings of the Koreans prior to the war and . . . was clearly unaware that the Ming was in the midst of a military revival under Emperor Wanli . . . that were designed to 'make the borders strong and the army fearsome once again.'"[33] Hideyoshi appears to have entertained a grandiose notion of his own powers and the strength of his armies—not unreasonable, given that he had managed to unify all of Japan. Hideyoshi wrote to his general before the war that the Ming was like "helpless women in their military spirit and fighting ability."[34]

As Berry observes, "there is no evidence that [Hideyoshi] systematically researched either the geographical problem or the problem of Chinese military organization."[35] Nam-lin Hur argues that Hideyoshi invaded Korea in order to consolidate his domestic rule.[36] In short, the central causal argument about power transitions—that rising and declining powers fear each other and identify each other as their primary threat—finds no support in the case of Japan's invasion of Korea in 1592. Japan's sole revisionist attempt to upset the hierarchy of the premodern tributary system ended in a disaster.

CAUSES OF THE JAPANESE INVASION

Why Hideyoshi decided to invade Korea remains inconclusive, but almost all evidence reinforces two themes of this book: the lack of a common conjecture and how internal challenges and motivations are often more important than external threats.

The ignorance and misinterpretation of initial warnings of invasion sent by Hideyoshi were particularly telling. The formation of a common conjecture requires constant interaction and communication. However, in an East Asia that centered on the Chinese dynasty, Japan had always appeared to be an outlier. The last time Japan received investiture was in 1402, when Emperor Yongle of the Ming dynasty gave Ashikaga Yoshimitsu, the third shogun of the Muromachi shogunate, the title "King of Japan." But that investiture was more motivated by the desire to hold official trade with the Ming dynasty rather than a genuine recognition of the Chinese dynasty as the Mandate of Heaven. From the Ming perspective, Emperor Yongle had just usurped the throne and urgently needed the approval of the "four barbarians." Since then, Japan and China begun trading intermittently in the name of "tribute," but the trade ended completely in the mid-sixteenth century.[37]

Japan's marginalized role in the tribute system led to a lack of direct communication among Japan, China, and China's vassal states, along with large-scale deceptions by intermediaries. The lord of Tsushima Island, the main operator of the Korea–Japan trade, had to play both sides, forging and tampering with official documents so that Japan and Korea could get by. In fact, as early as 1587, Hideyoshi sent a letter to Joseon through Sō Yoshitoshi (宗義智) asking Chosŏn to be a vassal state and a pioneer in attacking the Ming. Sō Yoshitoshi altered this letter to avoid offending Chosŏn so as to continue the trade, so Chosŏn was not even aware of the threat from Hideyoshi.[38] Also in 1589, Hideyoshi wrote a letter to Sō Yoshitoshi, demanding that he urge the king of Chosŏn to pay a visit to Kyoto. If the king did not come, Hideyoshi would send Konishi Yukinaga and Kato Kiyomasa with troops to Chosŏn. Chosŏn clarified that it was a vassal state of the Ming, so Hideyoshi's demand was unthinkable and unacceptable, since any official travel of the Chosŏn king to Japan would signify the intention of discontinuing the tribute relationship with the Ming. Later that year, the king of Chosŏn appointed Hwang Yun-gil (r. 1536–?) and Kim Seong-il (r. 1538–1593) as envoys to Kyoto. Chosŏn's purpose was to promote goodwill among the neighbors by talking about faith and friendship. However, owing to the purposeful misinterpretation of the lord of Tsushima Island, Hideyoshi thought that the visit of the Chosŏn envoys indicated Chosŏn's agreement to be a vassal state of Japan.[39]

On the other hand, there is almost no evidence that supports factors such as a changing distribution of relative power. Swope notes that Hideyoshi demanded a dynastic marriage with one of the Chinese emperor's daughters along with the resumption of tribute trade.[40] Gang Deng sees a Japanese desire to reenter into tribute status with China, writing that "Hideyoshi invaded Korea, a Ming vassal state, to force China to allow Japan to resume a tributary relationship, and threatened that a refusal would lead to invasion of China itself."[41] Samuel Hawley emphasizes continual war as a way for Hideyoshi to quell internal dissension among his followers.[42] As Ki-baek Lee notes, "Having succeeded in unifying the country, Hideyoshi sought to direct the energies of his commanders outward, thereby to enhance the solidarity and tranquility of Japan itself."[43]

It is true that Hideyoshi had incomplete control of Japan proper. Having unified Japan after decades of war, "Hideyoshi's rather unstable control of the Japanese islands led him to crave recognition from foreign rulers so as to legitimize his own hegemony."[44] He could hold the titles *kanpaku* (関白) and *taiko* (太閤), but he could never be *shogun* (将軍) because of his low-status birth. Engaging in war overseas would not only distract potential challengers to his power, but it would also weaken them militarily. If Hideyoshi lost, the *daimyo* (大名) would be weakened. If he won, there would be tremendous rewards to the *daimyo* and their soldiers in the conquered lands. Indeed, the Japanese invasion forces that went to Korea were composed "mainly of forces from the south, the region imperfectly crushed in 1587 by Hideyoshi."[45] Territory and wealth from occupying Korea would be an excellent way to divert the attention of the southern *daimyo* and to buy them off at the same time.

In line with Ki-baek Lee's earlier point, Chinese-language scholarship points to the severe domestic situation Hideyoshi faced as the major motivation for the initiation of the war. One of the key motivations was a need to strengthen control of the peasants and to repress peasant uprisings.[46] Prior to its unification by Hideyoshi, Japan experienced more than a hundred years of "Warring States," the *Sengoku jidai*. While the feudal ruling class was in civil strife, the peasants gradually formed independent economic forces and constantly launched peasant uprisings that were unprecedented in Japanese history—for example, the Yamashiro Uprising (1485–1493), and the Kaga Uprising (1473–1580). Hideyoshi implemented edicts such as "separation of soldiers and peasants," the "land survey" (太閤検地, *taikōkenchi*), and "confiscation of farmers' swords" (刀狩, *katanagari*) specifically to prevent the occurrence of peasant uprisings, which nevertheless mushroomed.[47]

As Wang Jiahua puts it, "[Hideyoshi] needs to look for new means to strengthen the control of the peasants as well as the territories controlled by independent *daimyos*. This external war became a continuation of internal politics."[48] Other motivations include the need to compensate the *daimyos* and samurai warriors that lost territory in the process of unification and the need to reward the merchants who had assisted Hideyoshi's unification by meeting their demand of monopolizing overseas trade.[49]

Though driven by domestic motivations, Hideyoshi clearly cared about Japan's relative position with respect to both China and Korea. This is what they negotiated over between 1593 and 1597—more about role, rank, and status than material benefits—and the chance for a settled peace was lost when Hideyoshi rejected the Ming offer of investiture at a rank lower than that of Korea. By that time, Japan clearly knew the military situation on the Korean Peninsula and the relative strength of Chinese, Japanese, and Korean forces. The second hostilities were thus not uninformed, but rather a result of incompatible views on relative role within the larger order.

What is also clear is that this attack is an exception rather than a convention. After all, as soon as the forces returned from Korea in 1598, within two years Tokugawa Ieyasu unified the country, and there was complete peace within Japan itself for 250 years. Tokugawa Ieyasu immediately sought to repair the relationship with the Ming. Specifically, a letter to the King of Ryukyu states that "China and Japan haven't traded for over thirty years till now. My general [Tokugawa Ieyasu] is deeply concerned and would like to have Iehisa Shimazu talk with your distinguished country [the Ryukyu Kingdom] so that ships in future years can dock at your distinguished country, while merchants from Ming and Japan can trade."[50] Tokugawa Ieyasu even swallowed his pride and pleaded the Ming with Mencius's idea of 以大事小 (*yi da shi xiao*) by labeling the Ming as "a great power" while humbly referring to Japan as "small."[51]

The Imjin War was an obvious moment of *potential* power transition that involved a massive conflict that dwarfed the scale of any war seen in contemporaneous Europe. This case might even be used to buttress the case for the likelihood of violence in contemporary power transitions. The fact that it does not come up suggests once again that if mainstream international relations scholars were to include the Imjin War, they would be obligated to think much more broadly and deeply about East Asian history in totality, not only because it might have something useful to say about China (certainly at least as much as Ancient Greece) but also because it might affect our understanding of international relations more broadly.

The lessons of the Imjin War strike at the heart of power transition theory. Most notably, this was an example of a relatively tiny country deciding to make an unprovoked attack on the unipolar hegemon which has been overwhelmingly understudied in the power transition literature. In reality, smaller countries often simply care more about an issue than a larger power, and then prevail or can challenge larger powers in ways that reflect many factors, not simply the distribution of capabilities.[52] In the case of historical East Asia, even a recently reunified Japan in 1592 was no possible military or economic equal of China. In 1600, China's economy was almost eight times that of Japan, and far more sophisticated. Japan may have started a war, but there is no possible way it was viewed as a power transition war between a rising and a declining power.

Moreover, the contours of the war and the aims and ambitions of all the participants cannot be explained without reference to the deep shared understandings and common conjecture that existed across East Asia. The hierarchy was unquestioned. That status and role were central to national identity was unquestioned. When there is no common conjecture due to the marginalized role of Japan in that system, war happens. When the common conjecture and the relative role and ranks are negotiated, peace obtains.

The dynamics between the countries involved at the time also worked the opposite to the way other structural theories would have predicted. For instance, in contrast to the balance of power theory, Japan and Korea—the two small powers—certainly never allied together to balance China, even if China deeply suspected that very possibility at the beginning of the Imjin War. It took three months of intense Korean diplomacy to convince Ming China that Korea was not conniving with Japan against China. Gari Ledyard writes that "many Chinese suspected the Koreans of somehow being in league with the Japanese, and doubted the early Korean reports."[53] An official Ming mission, headed by Huang Yingyang, visited Korea during the summer of 1592 and examined all reports and various documents assembled by the Koreans, including two letters from Konishi Yukinaga, then commander of the Japanese forces in P'yŏngyang. Finally convinced that the Japanese had actually invaded Korea and that their ultimate goal was to conquer China, Huang sent affirmative confirmation back to Beijing, which subsequently sent forces to support the Koreans.

In summary, the Imjin War provides further evidence that the notion that power transition theory is an enduring and inevitable phenomenon that applies universally around the globe and at all times warrants caution. It also shows the importance of domestic factors in causing war, rise, and decline and the relative unimportance of structural or external factors. Dynasties did rise and fall in historical East Asia, and although they fought occasionally, any explanation for their fighting and what they fought over must begin with the actual content and substance of their common conjecture and their shared understanding about what East Asian international relations should look like. Status and role were central issues, not a superficial gloss over more material aims. With this in mind, we now move to the next case, the Ming–Qing transition.

6

INTERNAL COLLAPSE

The Ming–Qing Transition, 1600–1680

The Japanese are a disease of the skin; domestic rebels are a disease of the heart.

—Chiang Kai-shek

Toyotomi Hideyoshi could not topple the Ming, and indeed he could not even conquer Korea. Yet a few decades later the Manchus replaced the Ming and ruled the Central Plain for over 250 years. The consensus among historians appears to be that the early Manchus originally had no intention of trying to conquer China. But as the Ming fell into greater internal disarray, and as eventually the Ming dynasty was toppled from within by rebels, the Manchus pushed on an open door. The rise of the Manchus and the fall of the Ming were separate events. While one had an influence on the other, they were not directly causally related.

Although she does not refer to it by name, Pamela Crossley points out that the Ming–Qing transition occurred almost nothing like power transition theory expects. As she writes, the standard narrative of Ming–Qing transition "is the assumption of a large power differential, which drives a schema of a weak

in situ entity being pierced and subdued by an external invading force." Yet, Crossley points out, "the problems with [this]
narrative are that it seriously understates the disunion of China
from the late sixteenth century on."[1] Indeed, as Timothy Brook
writes, "the greatest puzzle might well be to figure out how the
Ming remained standing for as long as it did."[2]

Although the Ming was the most powerful country on the
planet in 1600, it was weakening from within. For more than
two hundred years, the Ming had ruled China. They had stabilized relationships with most of their neighbors. The tribute
system was in use around the region. Japan's challenge in 1592—
from a small and peripheral, relatively backward country in the
eyes of the Chinese—had been dispatched with relative ease a
few years earlier. As Crossley notes, "arguments that [the reign
of the Wanli emperor, 1588–1620] was a period of economic or
even military decline are very difficult to validate."[3]

The structural causes of the Ming–Qing transition, such as
a changing balance of power, were not responsible for the fall of
the Ming and the rise of the Qing. Rather, the Ming collapsed
from within, and it was only in the wake of the collapse that the
Manchus moved in and began to build a new dynasty. Central
to their efforts was the strategic and intentional use of many
Ming institutions and norms, as well as the adoption of enduring Chinese ideas, such as the Mandate of Heaven legitimizing
their rule. Significantly, it was not at all clear to the Chinese
themselves or other regional actors that the Qing deserved to
rule China, and it was this issue more than their power that was
the core concern. The Qing quickly began engaging in the
regional common conjecture, using enduring East Asian and
Chinese ideas and institutions to rule China and in their relations with other countries. But this does not mean that the Manchus "assimilated" by any means: the Manchus retained many

of their own institutions and ideas as well as adopting Chinese rituals, institutions, ideas, and philosophies. The point, however, is that, in their relations with others and themselves, they used deeply enduring ideas that existed across the region. In this way, the fall of the Ming and the rise of the Qing is emblematic of the central themes of this book. Power transition theory has almost nothing to illuminate with respect to this episode. The regional conversation about role and responsibility was central to explaining the dynamics of the rise of the Qing; and internal challenges were more relevant than external relations.

DECLINE OF THE MING

Endemic skirmishing along the northern frontier had been a recurring nuisance throughout the reign of the Ming, but there had been no real threat to the Chinese homeland from the Central Asian steppe since the Mongols three centuries earlier. However, beneath this fairly stable surface cracks were beginning to show. Brook writes, "the fall of the Ming dynasty is many histories: the history of the expansion of the Manchu empire on its northeast border, the history of the most massive rebellions to wash over China since the fourteenth century, the history of the disintegration of the Ming state, and the history of a major climate episode."[4] Crossley writes that, "in 1450, the Ming empire occupied about 6.5 million square kilometers . . . by about 1640 they had lost nearly one-third [of that]."[5] The Ming dynasty in the early seventeenth century faced increasing internal rebellion and roving bands of regional bandits, especially in the northwest region. By the seventeenth century, the Ming were facing multiple rebellions throughout the empire. Swope notes that "on the whole it seems that the peasant rebels were deemed a more serious military threat by Emperor Chongzhen (1628–1644) because of their overt challenge to his domestic legitimacy and their ready ability to disappear into the countryside and hide among the people."[6]

The peasant rebellions slowly increased in frequency in the early seventeenth century as various rebellions arose and were crushed and yet others rose again. In fact, there were far more internal conflicts within the Ming itself than there were external conflicts between the Ming and other actors such as the Manchus. According to the Historical East Asian War dataset, version 3.0, there were sixty-seven instances of internal rebellion in Ming China between 1600 and 1644, and their frequency increased over that time as Ming internal control began to collapse (figure 6.1).

These internal conflicts also tended to be enormous in size, not simply riots—they were massive conflicts that involved huge numbers of troops on both sides. For example, a rebellion in the southwest, the She-An rebellion of 1621, was eventually crushed by the Ming, but at the cost of mobilizing almost one million troops, thirty-five million taels of silver (12,000/day), and two billion piculs of grain—that is, 132 million tons.[7]

The most consequential of these rebels was Li Zicheng. Born a peasant in Shaanxi province, by the late 1630s Li had begun to lead a major peasant uprising. He regularly commanded more than 100,000 troops during the early 1640s as he moved eastward from Shaanxi. As Wang Zaijin, the Pacification Commissioner of Shandong, observed, "Defending against Barbarians is easy but defending against Chinese is hard."[8] Li took the title "Prince of the New Discipline" in 1643, established a capital at Xi'an, Shaanxi Province, and marched on Beijing in April 1644 with 300,000 troops. He declared a new dynasty, the "Shun."

Another rebel, Zhang Xianzhong (1605–1647), also emerged in Shaanxi and Henan. After gaining control of parts of Hubei

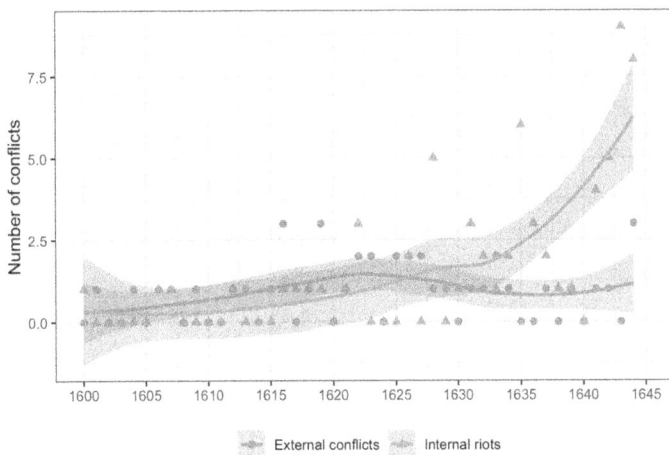

FIGURE 6.1 Internal and external conflicts in Ming China, 1600–1644. Total number of external conflicts: 40; total number of internal riots: 67.

Source: Historical East Asian War Dataset v. 3.0.

Province, he declared himself "King of the West." There was now chaos throughout the empire, with Ming officials joining various rebel groups or declaring their own pretender regimes. By the mid-1600s, at least eleven scattered regimes had emerged that all claimed to be the genuine Ming regime: in Yangzhou, Hangzhou, Shaoxing, Kuizhou, Wuchang, Fuzhou, Guilin, Zhaoqing, Xiamen, Jieyang, and Guangzhou.[9]

The Ming dynasty finally collapsed in April 1644, when rebels led by Li Zicheng took the capital without a fight—the gates having been opened from within—and the last Ming emperor hanged himself. The Chongzhen emperor had refused repeated appeals from his advisors to recall General Wu Sangui from the north to help defend Beijing and had refused appeals to move the court south to Nanjing. The Ming forces in the capital had dissolved, with most of the capital troops not having been paid for over a year. General Wu Xiang—father of General Wu Sangui—told the Chongzhen emperor that he had only around thirty thousand troops in Beijing, of which perhaps three thousand were elite and reliable.

The Ming collapse was hardly the result of powerful forces. Rather, a series of errors and seemingly small decisions wrote the final chapter of the Ming dynasty. As Mote writes, "the circumstances of Ming collapse—the capital's finding itself suddenly defenseless against a foreseeable and far from invincible military attack—were not brought about by any general disintegration of government and society. . . . Those fatal circumstances were brought about carelessly. . . . The fall of the Ming was, in short, caused by an accumulation of political errors."[10]

Swope provides a similar explanation: "One of the main conclusions of the present study is that imperial leadership after Wanli [emperor] failed in maintaining the appropriate balance between civil and military officials. . . . Simply put, they were commanders-in-chief and they made bad decisions given the information and resources at their disposal."[11]

The fall of the Ming was anything but mechanical and inevitable. That is, unlike Organski and Kugler's hypothesis that differential growth rates lead to war, even at the time of collapse the Ming were far superior in terms of material capabilities than either the various rebel groups or the Manchus. In fact, the Ming had "huge advantages in manpower, resources, and military technology. Yet they failed repeatedly."[12] The close historical work by Swope, Mote and others reaches the opposite of a materialist explanation: size by itself is useless without the proper use of that material advantage.

With the suicide of the last Ming emperor, Ming administration throughout the empire collapsed. General Wu Sangui, who was guarding the northwestern border—and who also commanded the largest Chinese force on the northern frontier—had actually been negotiating for years with the Manchus, and Wu's uncle and some other relatives had already joined the Manchus. Wu faced a choice: fight both the rebels under Li and also the Manchus, or to side with one against the other.

When Li Zicheng captured Beijing in the spring of 1644, Manchu forces were still months of travel away from the capital, in the northeast frontier region of Liaodong. Indeed, the Manchus showed no signs at that time of contemplating an attack on the Ming themselves. Wu eventually invited the Manchu forces to join him, and together they routed the rebels and .jointly entered Beijing in June 1644. The Manchus proclaimed a new dynasty, renaming themselves the Qing.

Although the Qing date the founding of the dynasty from June 1644, the subsequent transitional warfare lasted until 1683. Pirate king and Ming loyalist Zheng Chenggong created a base in Taiwan and fought for decades against the Qing, regularly conducting full-scale raids and engaging in pitched battles against the Qing along the Fujian coast. The Qing sent Wu Sangui himself to pacify Yunnan, in southwest China. As Wu established power in southwest China, he asked the Kangxi emperor (1662–1722) to allow his son to take on Wu's rulership in the south. Denied by the emperor, Wu rebelled and declared his own state of Zhou. Fighting continued into 1683, involving hundreds of thousands of troops on both sides. After the Qing finally destroyed the Zheng family regime, the Qing established control over Taiwan for the first time, administering it as a part of Fujian Province beginning in 1683.

As Swope notes, "the Ming state managed to hold out for decades against a dizzying array of military and environmental challenges. The fact that the Qing retained so many Ming

practices and institutions testifies to their continued viability."[13]
Ming loyalist regimes popped up everywhere, from Zheng
Chenggong on Taiwan to numerous polities in the southwest.
Various pieces of Ming China began breaking off in the late six-
teenth century—the Chahar khaghanate gained control of
northern Liaodong province, and portions of Shaanxi and Sich-
uan broke away as well. The rebel regimes of Li Zicheng and
Zhang Xianzhong took increasing power.

In short, it was "not a dynastic transition within a continuing
empire, nor displacement of one empire by another."[14] Rather,
the Ming collapsed, and into the vacuum came the Manchus.

THE RISE OF THE MANCHU STATE

The Manchus had arisen in the frontier regions to the northeast of China in the late sixteenth century, forming from a set
of seminomadic tribes that traced their lineage back to the
Jurchen Jin of the twelfth century. Manchuria was home to many
disparate peoples, languages, and cultures, and Crossley notes
that "the result was not the refinement of a homogenous people
and culture from heterogeneous sources, but the settlement of
the uneven terrain of the region by culturally diverse groups who
on occasion wove their lineages and federations together."[15] From
1583, a local warlord, Nurhaci (1559–1626), leading a few hundred
men of his tribe, began to unite a number of disparate tribes
under his banner. During the 1590s, Nurhaci introduced the
"banner system" whereby different fighting units were organized
according to a different colored military flag. Peter Perdue notes
that a predominant theme in studies of the rise of the Manchus
is "the transformation of the clan society of the Manchu tribes
into a centralized bureaucratic state."[16]

Nurhaci had accepted a Ming military appointment and had even offered to help Korea during the Imjin War. Using diplomacy, marriage, and coercion, Nurhaci quickly expanded his power base. "Nurhaci kept moving his capital farther westward and southward toward the Chinese border," and in 1616, after Nurhaci had brought many of the Mongol tribes under his banner, he declared himself "khan" of the Later Jin dynasty.[17]

Much of Nurhaci's expansion and growth was about economic control. Nicola Di Cosmo has found that the annual ginseng trade between Nurhaci and the Ming was as high as 100,000 *jin*, or "corresponded in value to approximately a quarter of the total foreign silver imported in China in a single year."[18] Thus, even the founding of the Manchu nation was not obviously about conquest or rejection of the existing international order. More prosaic needs were clearly more important to Nurhaci. Perdue notes, "as he defeated rival clan leaders . . . he incurred responsibilities for provisioning these troops . . . the urgent need for grain supplies became a major factor in the expansion of the state."[19] One of Nurhaci's first attacks on Ming frontier outposts, at Fushun in 1618, was prompted by heavy rains and the ruined harvests and starvation that Nurhaci's people were facing.[20] As Crossley writes of the creation of the Manchu state and declaration of war against the Ming in the early seventeenth century,

> It is probable that Nurgaci's declaration of war against the Ming was motivated less by the prospect of a dramatic increase in distributable wealth than by fears that the current levels would be constricted. . . . Because the conquest of Liaodong prepared the way for the creation of the Qing empire, we are often inclined to associate it with the unlimited energies, hopes, and ambitions that "birth" implies. . . . Yet there is no point at which either the

shape of his campaigns or his proclaimed reasons for them departs much from the consistent goal of protecting and enhancing the economic basis of the wealth his lineage had nurtured. . . . He achieved these ends, but there is no evidence that he was determined to do much more.[21]

Even as late as the 1640s, it was not clear that the Manchus had designs on conquering the Ming. The Manchus were not even that strong, nearly collapsing due to logistical problems. The Manchu state and its hold over its people were so precarious that Perdue concludes that the Manchus "were in danger of reverting to the old raid and extortion policy instead of creating a viable new state, let alone conquering a Chinese dynasty." Indeed, Perdue observes that the Manchus "nearly collapsed in the mid-seventeenth century" and avoided failure "only when the Ming court abandoned Beijing."[22]

The Qing were not as powerful as is often claimed. In 1644, the "Eight Banners" force was composed as much of managers, translators, accountants, and cooks as it was of actual fighting forces, and the actual troops totals were probably around 200,000. As Crossley notes about the Qing conquest, "the Qing unification of historical China in 1683 more resembles the Mongol Yuan unification of historical China in 1279 than it resembles, say, the transition from Sui to Tang, or even from Yuan to Ming. . . . The Mongols first seized part of north China in 1215, and then by slow succession fought for the Yangtze basin, and eventually completed the progression by securing Guangxi and Yunnan."[23]

Administration and control came by Qing adoption of existing Ming ideas and institutions. It is here that the common conjecture becomes important: ideas about proper role, conduct, and behavior were central. And this was true not just for domestic politics and society, but also in Qing foreign relations. It is true that the Qing themselves, like the Mongols before them, retained many of the customs that they brought with them from the steppe: the banner system.[24] For example, multiple languages, including Chinese and Manchu, were used in official communications. It has been too simplistic to say that the Qing were Sinified; that is a Chinese nationalist trope. Rather, they created a hybrid system of their own and Ming institutions and norms. Shi Zhan, an influential Chinese scholar, illustrates this point by using the example of the Mukden Palace, aka the Shenyang Imperial Palace, built by the Qing before they entered the Central Plain. Unlike the Forbidden City in Beijing, the Shenyang Imperial Palace has two administrative palaces. One is in the eastern section, which contains the Hall of Great Affairs (大政殿, *da zheng dian*), where emperors ascended the throne, enacted imperial edicts, and welcomed victorious generals and soldiers. A group of pavilions, known as the Ten Kings Pavilion (十王亭, *shi wang ting*), stand to its east and west, where emperors and leaders from the Eight Banners (八旗, *ba qi*) settled national affairs. This architectural style resembles the shape of a nomadic tent, while the coexistence of the Hall of Great Affairs and the Ten Kings Pavilion marked a stark representation of tribal relationships when Nurhachi was in power. The other administrative palace is the Phoenix Tower and Qingning Palace (崇政殿, *chong zheng dian*) in the middle section. Built by Nurhaci's son Abahai (Hong Taiji), the architectural style of this middle section resembles Han palaces, reflecting the embrace of Confucianism and the centralization of imperial power as opposed to the diffused power structure in the tribal system.[25]

It is also important to emphasize that the Manchu Qing were as deeply a part of the regional East Asia conversation about common conjecture as were any of the other countries; that is, they used many of the existing practices and norms to manage internal relations as well. Different modes of governance were adopted in different cultural-ecological-economic zones, where the Qing emperor took on different titles. The Central Plain and its provision of a large central treasury allowed the ruler of the Qing Dynasty to directly manage the Eight Banners, so the title of "emperor" was taken to maximize the centrality of the power. Manchuria and Mongolia denoted the security border. Cavalry from the grasslands was the most potent force in the era of cold weapons, so the title of "Great Khan" was taken here to mobilize militarily. In Tibet, the Qing emperor appeared as the reincarnation of Manjushri, and the similarity in the pronunciation of "Manchurian" and "Manjushri" was emphasized to provide further legitimacy.[26]

Crossley notes that "the Qing gained control over formerly Ming territory not by assimilating or rejecting Ming institutions or methods, but by converting them to their own uses. . . . Qing military conquest of China . . . came from Ming military power."[27] As we will see in chapter 7, Qing–Chosŏn relations were governed by these ideas long before the Qing completed their conquest of the Ming.

REGIONAL RELATIONS: WERE THE QING "CIVILIZED?"

As China fell into disarray, there was the potential for other countries of the region to attempt to take advantage and to further their own relative position. Yet most countries avoided rather than exploited the chaos in China. Perhaps most significantly, with the Ming collapse occurring less than fifty years after Hideyoshi's failed attempt to invade Korea, Japan could have tried again to conquer the mainland. Yet Japan under the Tokugawa shogunate had no interest in taking advantage of the turmoil on the Asian mainland in the early seventeenth century. Rather than seize an opportunity to attack China again, the Japanese—and Koreans—in the early seventeenth century remained almost completely out of the turmoil that gripped China. There is extensive evidence that the Japanese before and after Hideyoshi had no ambition or even thought to conquer China and displace it as the hegemon of the known world. Once again the key causal dynamics hypothesized in power transition theory appear to be almost completely absent in the minds of East Asian elites at the time.

What is perhaps most striking about the Ming–Qing transition is the absence of a regional power scramble. The other states of the region, rather than attempting to take advantage of Ming weakness, wanted to see who could rule all of China. Both Korea and Japan were concerned that the Manchus did not have the Mandate of Heaven to rule China. These were shared, unquestioned beliefs that existed around the region.

Japan did not take advantage of a window of opportunity to try to invade China. Furthermore, unlike John Mearsheimer's claims about the United Kingdom, Japan did not engage the continent as an offshore balancer to prevent the emergence of a hegemon.[28] Rather, the Japanese elites at the time of the Ming collapse were actually deeply concerned about whether the Manchus were "Chinese" enough to rule China. As Mizuno Norihito puts it,

When the news of the Manchu conquest of China was brought to Japan by Chinese merchants arriving in Nagasaki early in October 1644 (Kan'ei 寛永 21/9), indifference was not the response of the Tokugawa bakufu to the event on the East Asian mainland. . . . The Japanese, who had adopted the Chinese distinction of civilized and barbarian in viewing the self and others, perceived the Tatars as inferior barbarians. . . . Hayashi Gahō 林鵞鳳, Razan's son and the "rector of the Confucian college" (*daigaku no kami* 大学頭) did not recognize the emergence of the Manchu dynasty as an ordinary dynastic change of the sort China had undergone for the previous thousand years. Under the order of the bakufu, Gahō began in 1674 to compile information and documents regarding the events on the continent and gave his work the title, *Kai hentai* 華夷変態 (Metamorphosis from civilized to barbarian). Its preface reveals that he understood the Manchu conquest as China's transformation from "civilized" (*ka* 華) to "uncivilized" (*i* 夷).[29]

Indeed, Tokugawa Japan did nothing when the Ming began to crumble. The Tokugawa at the time, like Japan before Hideyoshi, was not an expansionist regime. It appears that Hideyoshi was the exception, not the norm, in how Japanese leaders viewed themselves and their relations with the rest of East Asia. After all, China, Japan, and Korea clearly had the military, logistical, organizational, and economic capabilities to conduct war across oceans on a massive scale. It was a political *choice* not to do so, not a material limitation. As Alex Roland observers, "The Tokugawa shogunate turned inward and gave up war, not the gun."[30] Swope writes, "because the Tokugawa maintained order in Japan, piracy was not the problem it had been in the past and the two states co-existed in relative peace until the late nineteenth century."[31]

Although Japan is often compared to the United Kingdom in its foreign relations, the reality is that the United Kingdom and

Japan had starkly different historical experiences with countries on their landmass. The British Isles have been regularly invaded from the mainland for at least two thousand years: this included the Romans, who built Hadrian's Wall; waves of Vikings and Danish raids and settlements; the Norman conquest of 1066; and the Spanish Armada of 1588. Furthermore, the English and British regularly involved themselves in wars on the continent, whether it was the Hundred Years' War (1337–1453), the War of the Spanish Succession (1701–1715), the French Revolutionary and Napoleonic Wars (1792–1815), and onward. Yet Japan never behaved the same way over the centuries with its Asian counterparts. The sole attempts to invade Japan in over 1,500 years were the Mongol invasions of 1274 and 1281. Furthermore, Japan involved itself in Asian wars only once after the seventh century: the abortive attempt to invade Korea in 1592. Thus we see literally centuries in which the Japanese did not act as an "offshore balancer preventing the rise of a continental hegemon," as Mearsheimer and Walt theorize about the United Kingdom.[32] Nor do we see either the Japanese or any Asian powers eyeing each other as possible areas for conquest.

As will be discussed in detail in chapter 7, the Koreans, for their part, were reluctant to accept the Manchus as legitimate rulers of China precisely because they were not necessarily "Confucian" enough. Chen Shangsheng has used *Yŏnhaengnok* (燕行錄, Travel Reports of Korean Envoys) to explore how the Koreans viewed the Ming–Qing transition. He finds extensive discussion about whether the Qing were civilized enough to earn the Mandate of Heaven.[33] Indeed, Sun Weiguo argues that although there was loyalty for Ming China among the Chosŏn ruling class, more significant was a deep-rooted antagonism toward the Manchu people, who were considered barbaric.[34]

Like Hideyoshi's invasion of Korea, the Manchu conquest of China appears to have been undertaken and accomplished with almost no attention to the balance of power. The Manchus had never approached the level of Ming military or economic power since their establishment. Although the exact size of the Manchu population and economy remains unknown, the number certainly would be insignificant in proportion to the extent of China; it could hardly be otherwise if we consider the conditions of nomad life. The Ming was aware of the new Manchu force, but it is not clear that they did a whole lot about it. Manchus were not even the cause of the toppling of the dynasty, as we have seen. Ming officials were certainly concerned about the Manchus, but the Chinese peasant rebels generally took precedence from the 1630s onward. It was somewhat akin to Chiang Kai-shek's assessment of Communists versus the Japanese: the peasant rebels were the "disease of the heart," whereas the Manchus were the "disease of the skin." Internal order trumped the external threat, at least for most of the Ming officials. The emperors tended to vacillate on this point. The most consequential dynastic transition in Asia over a period of half a millennium had almost nothing to do with the causal processes that any of our power transition models predict.

This is because East Asia's history was nothing like the European experience. East Asia historically was characterized by hegemony—a powerful, culturally influential China—as opposed to the routine bellicosity of balance of power Europe.[36] Had our international relations theories been derived from the Asian experience, it is quite likely that the focus of our theories would emphasize the centrality of shared understandings for explaining both war and peace.

7

HOW KOREA REMAINED
INDEPENDENT UNTIL 1910

The Common Conjecture Between
Small and Large States

中国人对于异族，历来只有两样称呼：一样是禽兽，一样是圣
上。从没有称他朋友，说他也同我们一样的。

Chinese people have always had only two terms of address for
foreigners: either "beasts" (禽兽, qinshou, 금수) or "majesties"
(圣上, shengshang, 성상). They have never been called friends,
nor said to be the same as us.

—Lu Xun (1919)

There is an obvious and important but often overlooked
pattern from the premodern East Asian world order:
Korea remained independent from the time of its emergence in the third to fifth centuries until 1910. There is a clear
lineage between the three Korean dynasties of Shilla (57 BCE—
935), Koryŏ (918–1392), and Chosŏn (1392–1910), and none of
them fell to external conquest until the Japanese imperial occupation of the modern era, in 1910. Yet Korean dynasties were also
always far smaller and weaker than their massive Chinese counterparts. Despite the episodic rise and fall of dominant Chinese
dynasties, Korea survived. Explaining how Korea managed its

relations with successive new Chinese dynasties leads to further insights into power transitions in East Asian history. Most notably, the common conjecture and shared understandings about appropriate and legitimate roles and behavior in the East Asian world order are far more important to explaining systematic patterns of diplomacy and violence than are relative material capabilities.

More than a generation ago, Gari Ledyard introduced an influential argument about the China–Manchuria–Korea triangle.[1] Ledyard identifies three cycles of Chinese expansion ("yang") and three cycles of Chinese contraction ("yin") and explores various patterns within these broad cycles. Here we focus more on how the Koreans dealt with rising Chinese dynasties. Ledyard argues that if the Manchurian region was unstable, China–Korea relations were unstable. Like Ledyard, Evelyn Rawski argues for "decentering China from the perspective of the periphery rather than from the core."[2] As we will see in detail, while emerging Chinese dynasties did expand in some directions, there were systematic patterns to their interactions and expansion. Significantly, Korea was always able to navigate these changes in Chinese power.

In East Asia, the closest example of a rising power came from the establishment of new dynasties. Although this is a bit of a caricature, from these transitions emerged new dynasties full of energy, hope, and vigor. Ledyard writes about new dynasties that, "each cycle begins with the launching of a major Chinese dynasty accompanied by a significant burst of Chinese expansion."[3] The dynasties would eventually grow weak and begin to decay from within. As disorder, rebellions, and social upheaval spread, the ruling elite would eventually crumble. Eventually, a new regime would emerge.

Within this overall pattern, however, and as we have emphasized throughout this book, it is important to note that this was not a "dynastic cycle" that endlessly repeated itself. Rather, there was considerable change and evolution in how these dynasties rose and fell over time, particularly in their relations to the surrounding political units. The most important changes to the entire system over the centuries were the gradual emergence, consolidation, and evolution of states other than China.[4] Before the third to fifth centuries CE, kingdoms in the Chinese Central Plain did not have any recognizable counterparts in the surrounding areas. First Korea and Japan, then later Vietnam rose and endured as states; other states such as Tibet, Ryukyu, and others came and went. As states became more stable and consolidated, China tended to craft enduring relations with them.

The Korean experience in dealing with successive rising Chinese dynasties offers an insightful view of rising powers' behavior toward smaller countries in East Asia. Over the past two millennia, Korean kingdoms had to navigate and craft relations with a number of Chinese dynasties, all of which were larger than their Korean counterparts. The overwhelming pattern has been one of continuity and stability: as a new Chinese dynasty rose, after an initial period of instability, the Korean kingdom would craft stable and enduring relations with it. The "common conjecture" was never obvious at the time—foreign relations were always being adapted, reconstructed, and revisited. This is the creation and recreation of the common conjecture over time.

Yet, significantly, relations were rarely based on deterrence or military power; instead, they were based on the enduring but constantly revisited East Asian common conjecture about mutually agreed roles and responsibilities as formalized through the diplomatic international tribute order of historical East Asia.

The Chinese side generally respected the Korean border and relations were stable. The few times the two sides had to negotiate over their long border precisely provide the detailed case studies that demonstrates how the two sides maintained and adjusted their relationship. Sixiang Wang writes:

> If ritual and rhetoric are conceived as able only to express (but not shape) ideology, then Chosŏn-Ming relations as they unfolded could only be the natural consequence of a shared Confucian culture. Within these parameters, only the stereotype that Korean elites aped Chinese high culture can prevail. But suppose imperial ideology and diplomatic norms are treated as open-ended and dynamic. In that case, Chosŏn diplomacy's ceremonial and inscriptional practices should be understood not as reflections of reality but as efforts to shape it.[5]

Furthermore, the experience of the Korean Peninsula illuminates a second theme of this book: Internal challenges are often far more consequential than external threats. Throughout its history, all three long-lasting Korean dynasties—Silla, Koryŏ, and Chosŏn—fell from within, not by external conquest until the arrival of the West and the fall of the Sinitic order in the early twentieth century.

Here we examine three key periods in China–Korea relations—all focused on how Korea crafted and negotiated its relations with a new and rising Chinese dynasty: relations between Koguryŏ and Shilla and the Tang dynasty of the mid-seventh century; Ming–Chosŏn relations of 1368–1392; and Qing–Chosŏn relations of 1626–1636. Each episode shows the ability of smaller powers to negotiate with and establish stable borders with the rising great power. In all three cases, after initial instability and negotiations, relations were stabilized between the two sides for extended periods of time, often centuries. Although over the years there were diplomatic and commercial issues to be resolved, an actual military threat was almost completely absent. The common conjecture was remarkably similar over time, and examining China–Korea relations across the centuries reveals a key element of the tribute system: If the two sides could craft a mutually agreed relative status, their relations were stable no matter how much one side was rising relative to the other.

The only significant fighting occurred in the first era, when the Korean states were transforming from a number of loose confederations of tribes into territorially defined, bureaucratic, and centralized states. Once relations and status were negotiated between China and Korea, they proved to be enduringly stable through the centuries. What might seem anomalous to theoretical approaches that emphasize material factors is that Korean survival was ensured through symbolic rhetoric and negotiations about relative responsibility and role. To Koreans and their counterparts, this symbolic role was a central motivating factor and a fundamental component of their philosophical worldview. Koreans were adept at foreign policy and were repeatedly able to secure their survival and security against giant odds.

SHILLA AND KOGURYŎ AND THE TANG DYNASTY IN THE SEVENTH CENTURY

The most churning among states occurred during the first few centuries CE, when states were emerging and had no history of relations with each other. As they negotiated and fought and crafted forms of interaction, relations stabilized. These were new states, with new relationships to each other and to the Tang. As Rawski notes, "the long-standing distinction between *hua* and *yi*, commonly known as the 'civilian–barbarian' discourse . . . was adopted by Korean and Japanese elites for use within a domestic context and also, on occasion, in diplomatic communication with other states."[6] China originated this distinction over two thousand years ago, perhaps as early as before 221 BCE, when it had few recognizable counterparts. It was possible for emergent states to become viewed as civilized as they developed in ways recognizable to existing states. Rawski notes that "faith in the ability of the peoples on the geographic and cultural periphery to adopt Chinese ways was a hallmark of Chinese frontier policy from ancient times onward."[7] This is precisely how Korean states evolved and learned to craft stable relations with successive Chinese dynasties.

When the Han dynasty collapsed from within in 220, it ushered in three centuries of divided rule in China. In these centuries, political order was just emerging on the Korean Peninsula and in Manchuria. During the third to sixth centuries, China was divided and posed no military threat to the peninsula or Japan.

By the beginning of the seventh century, three kingdoms had emerged on the Korean Peninsula: Koguryŏ, Paekche, and Shilla. All three Korean kingdoms emulated, copied, and learned from China. Jiang Weidong, for example, traces Koguryŏ's bureaucratic system back to the Han county-level bureaucracy.[8] All three Korean kingdoms were deeply influenced by Chinese culture and ideas; all had strained relations with each other; and to varying degrees all engaged in tribute relations with Chinese dynasties. The primary line of conflict was between Manchuria and the Chinese Central Plain; the Korean Peninsula was always an afterthought. Koguryŏ itself focused more on affairs in the Korean Peninsula than it did on expanding north or west, a main reason why modern Koreans claim Koguryŏ as a "Korean" predecessor.[9]

Three centuries of division on the Chinese Central Plain came to an end with the emergence of the Sui dynasty (581–618). The Sui attempted four times to conquer Koguryŏ. Koguryŏ fought Sui to a standstill. It is the cost and failures of these campaigns that are said to have contributed to the collapse of the Sui and the emergence of the Tang dynasty in 618. Wang Gaoxin writes,

> The Sui resorted to the use of force. Charging headlong on the basis of internal strength and wealth, and considering the large size of external territory, the arrogance [of Emperor Yang] triggered hatred [from Koguryŏ], as Emperor Yang launched the conquest out of temper. It is unheard of since ancient times that this behavior would not lead to a collapse of a country. In this case, how could we not deeply learn the lesson of handling different ethnic barbarians?[10]

The Tang dynasty (618–907) continued to contend with Koguryŏ, conducting four campaigns in the mid-seventh century. The most famous of these was the 642 Tang defeat at Ansi Fortress by Koguryŏ general Yang Munch'ŏn. Yet, after that initial spate of jockeying for position, there was only one war involving Korea, Japan, and China: the Korean War of Unification of 660–668. Over an eight-year period beginning in 660, Shilla allied with the Chinese Tang dynasty to crush Koguryŏ and Paekche, unifying the Korean Peninsula for the first time.

Yet the Korean unification war was not a regional war; it was a Korean war. Significantly, the two key power transition theory factors of dissatisfaction with the status quo and changing relative power seem absent in this situation. The direction of attention was from the Korean kingdoms toward the Tang, not from a newly powerful Tang dynasty expanding its ambitions into the Korean Peninsula. As Nadia Kanagawa describes it, "Efforts to draw the Tang into the conflicts on the Korean peninsula began early—in 626 both Paekche and Shilla sent envoys to the Tang complaining that Koguryŏ was preventing them from sending tribute and asking the Tang ruler to take action."[11] In 650, Shilla official Kim Ch'unch'u presented the Tang emperor with a poem written by Queen Chindŏk requested military aid against Paekche. Christina Lai's detailed study of these wars further emphasizes that point: "the Sui and Tang only had limited ambitions in occupying Koguryŏ and only asked that tribute be paid. . . . China's troops withdrew numerous times after victories and did not seize full control of Koguryŏ's territory."[12]

Also significant for power transition theory is that alliance dynamics did not involve the small states balancing together against the more powerful Tang. The conventional wisdom in the international relations scholarly literature would expect that the three small Korean kingdoms would balance against the most powerful unit in the system, Tang China, and that the more powerful Tang became, the more it would attempt to expand at the expense of the Korean kingdoms. Yet all three Korean kingdoms competed with each other to craft relations with China, not against it. Tang's ally Shilla ended in sole possession of most of the Korean Peninsula, and the two crafted enduring, stable relations. Han Sheng attributes the ability of Shilla and Tang to cooperate to the general Sinicization of Shilla, writing "Shilla's comprehensive implementation of the Tang's legal system had far-reaching implications on East Asia. . . .

Shilla succeeded in receiving the comprehensive support of the Tang dynasty, and cooperated with the Tang dynasty to destroy Paekche and Koguryŏ to unify the Korean Peninsula."[13]

In 660, Shilla and the Tang formed an alliance, and Shilla's envoy to the Tang, Kim Ch'unch'u, "obtained China's agreement that in the event the Shilla–T'ang allied army won the war against Koguryŏ, the territory south of P'yŏngyang would belong to Shilla."[14] The Tang–Shilla alliance first attacked Paekche.[15] The Korean annals *Samguk sagi* (삼국사기, History of the Three Kingdoms, written in 1145) recount that "[Tang] general Su Ting-fang said to [Shilla general] Yusin . . . 'My command allows me to exercise authority as conditions dictate, so I will now present to you as maintenance lands all of Paekche's territory that has been acquired, this as reward for your merit. How would that be?'"[16] Shilla and Tang then turned their attentions to Koguryŏ. In 668, the Tang–Shilla alliance defeated Koguryŏ, the gates to the Koguryŏ capital having been opened from within by a traitor.

After conquering Koguryŏ, the Tang and Shilla began to squabble about their relationship, in particular who should control the Korean Peninsula and where the border between the two countries should be. Tang and Shilla had agreed on a division of the peninsula, but after the successful war, the Tang "clearly wanted to control the entire peninsula," and proposed that Shilla become the "Great Commandery of Kyerim"—in essence, a Chinese territory. Shilla king Pŏmmin (r. 661–681) rejected the offer and instead moved forces into Tang-controlled territory. Wang Zhenping argues that "the conflict between China and Shilla was due to Emperor Gaozong's refusal to allow Shilla control of Paekche and areas south of P'yŏngyang, a promise his father had once made in exchange for Shilla's military collaboration in conquering the two countries."[17]

Yet, when the Tang and Shilla forces began to skirmish, "Gaozong . . . apparently did not want a prolonged campaign against Shilla. He pardoned [King] Pŏmmin and restored his Tang ranks and noble titles."[18] What is notable is that relations were reestablished based on the enduring common conjecture of the East Asian world order—war was avoided by working within the institutions of the tribute system—a clear hierarchy and acceptance of different roles.

The negotiation between Tang and Shilla resulted in an agreement that all the land south of the Taedong River near P'yŏngyang would belong to Shilla, and that Shilla would enter into subordinate tribute relations with the Tang. Ledyard writes, "From that time, Manchuria lay outside the limits of Korea's military power if not its political aspirations."[19] By 676, all Tang forces had withdrawn from the peninsula, "and the Korean peninsula (up to a line somewhere north of modern P'yŏngyang) was now unified."[20] As Kanagawa describes it,

> The *Samguk sagi* records suggest that Shilla leaders had long recognized that the Tang were both a potential threat and a potential ally. . . . By 679 CE the Tang had abandoned the peninsula, allowing Shilla to consolidate its control over the territory. Over the course of the 680s, Tang–Shilla relations would gradually improve, and Shilla would once again send regular envoys bearing tribute to the Tang court and receiving investiture from the Tang ruler.[21]

After the 670s, China–Korea relations were stable for more than two hundred years, with Shilla maintaining close tribute relations with the Tang. During that time, sixty-five Shilla envoys made tribute missions to the Tang court, an average of one every three years. Wang notes that "Shilla rulers, without exception, chose to act as part of the Chinese cultural and economic world for the benefit of their country. Shilla students and monks came to China to study and request books. Shilla maritime merchants traded extensively along the Chinese coasts."[22]

In short, power transition theory has little to say about the rise of the Tang and Silla and their relations. It is true that Tang and Sui before them fought bitterly with Koguryŏ for the first half of the seventh century. Yet, after combining to crush Koguryŏ, Silla and Tang crafted a remarkably enduring relationship based on inequality. Tang did not continue to try to crush Silla as well, even though Silla had unified the Korean Peninsula. Finally, both Tang and Silla fell for internal reasons, not from conquest. It was only Koguryŏ that fell from conquest, and the dynamics of dissatisfaction or changing relative power do not appear to be present. It is not a surprise that there was fighting as the states emerged from loose tribes and confederations. But as they became states and as they began to learn and engage in the regional common conjecture, relations stabilized.

MING-CHOSŎN RELATIONS, 1388-1392

Widely considered one of the most glorious of the traditional Chinese dynasties, the Ming rose in the fourteenth century out of the debris of a collapsing Yuan Mongol state. Claiming the Mandate of Heaven in 1368, the Ming (1368–1644) should be a particularly good case for power transition because the Ming were replacing what was considered an "alien" Mongol Yuan dynasty. A surge of Han nationalism could have justified extensive expansion or conquest. However, as with the Song, and the Jin and the Liao before it, the Ming made territorial concessions to Chosŏn in exchange for tribute relations. The rising power did not upend the order, but rather reestablished it. This required diplomacy on both sides, but resolution of relations occurred quite quickly, over a matter of a few years, considering that the relationship ultimately spanned 250 years.

As David Robinson points out, the fall of the Yuan left a gap in foreign relations, and it was not at all obvious at the time what would fill it. This is what we mean by a common conjecture: the time relations need to be established, defined, framed, and negotiated. This requires a shared cultural vocabulary, but it also requires selecting, emphasizing, and modifying elements of that vocabulary. Robinson writes:

> Patterns of interactions that developed between the Mongol and Goryeo courts directly influenced the Ming court's ideas about "normal" relations with the Goryeo court and its successor, the Chosŏn dynasty . . . in the face of shifting power and demands by both the Ming and Yuan dynasties, the Goryeo ruling elites turned to historical texts, historical memory, and personal experience for guidance in a rapidly changing and deeply uncertain world . . . the decades of Mongol rule's deterioration were defined by uncertainty . . . no one knew how long the decline might last or what road it might take. In the same way, no one knew which—if any—of the new regimes would last for how long or in what form . . . our knowledge that the Ming dynasty lasted until 1644 obscures the precariousness of the regime's early decades . . . there was nothing natural or automatic about Sino-Korean relations. Both sides evinced deep uncertainty about the form and substance.[23]

Sixiang Wang's argument is similar to our own—that Ming-Chosŏn relations were as much constructed as structural and involved both sides finding a common conjecture. Wang writes:

Chosŏn produced and reified the idea that a proper, moral empire also had to guarantee Korea's political integrity. Along with the trope of Korea's perpetual loyalty, the notion of moral empire framed what was within the realm of imperial possibility. Although these tropes have become emblematic of Chosŏn-Ming relations as a whole ... they emerged from Chosŏn's engagement with the rhetorical logic and ritual symbolism of empire.[24]

By the tenth century, Korea and China had established the Yalu River as their border, and it was affirmation of this border and Korean acceptance of tributary status in the fourteenth century that precluded a war between the new Ming Chinese and Chosŏn Korean dynasties. Korea's long northern border with China was the source of most of the tensions between the two sides over the millennia. The legitimate right of Korea to exist was almost never in question after Tang's desultory attempt to claim suzerainty over the Korean Peninsula in the seventh century; by the fourteenth and fifteenth centuries, the Chinese side was not even necessarily aiming to expand its territory. Rather, it was negotiation and disagreement over exactly where the border should be demarcated, and how to manage that border and the movement of people and goods across that border, that was the source of most of the negotiations. This occurred mainly because the Northeast Asian triangle of China, Korea, and Manchuria was not only a source of rich commercial and economic wealth but for centuries was also sparsely inhabited and very much an uncharted frontier zone.

In 1356, as the Yuan dynasty was collapsing, the Koryŏ king Kongmin sent fifty thousand troops to recover territory from the Yuan up to the Yalu River and also in the northeast, near the Tumen River. In 1362, Koryŏ again skirmished with remnants of

Yuan forces. Kongmin also sent troops to the Yalu to secure the Hamgyŏng region against Mongol or Jurchen incursions.

In 1368, Koryŏ fully severed tributary relations with the Yuan. In June 1369, the Koryŏ court stopped using the reign title of the Yuan dynasty and began using the Ming reign name. King Kongmin sent a tributary mission to the Ming capital. The king's memorial to the Ming Emperor Hongwu (founder of the Ming dynasty) declared: "Humbly residing in the east, your vassal [臣, *chen*] looks to the northern polar star. Although unable to participate in congratulation ceremonies, [your vassal] will always send tribute with sincerity."[25] In response, the emperor sent an envoy with a gold seal and imperial writ to invest King Kongmin as "king of Koryŏ," writing "I have sent an envoy with a seal to invest you as King of Koryŏ as before, allowing your propriety and institutions to follow local customs."[26] Emperor Hongwu asked for very little in terms of tribute. For example, in November 1372, he sent a letter to the Koryŏ saying, "It is proper to request that it follow the propriety of sending one big mission triennially and one small mission annually, and its tributary goods should be no more than ten bolts of locally produced cloth."[27]

The territory in Manchuria between Korea and China was disputed during this time. After pacifying Naghachu, a former Yuan general leading troops in Manchuria, in 1387, the Ming laid territorial claims to areas north, east, and west of Tieling (鐵嶺, 철령, Ch'ŏllyŏng). Hongwu claimed that these areas, previously part of the Mongol Kaiyuan district, now belonged to the Ming and began to incorporate them into its Liaodong garrison network.[28] Whether he also claimed territories south of the Yalu River is not clear, and historians disagree on the exact location of Tieling in 1388.[29] As the Ming gradually gained control over southern Liaodong, Zheng points out that "the emperor responded by warning Korea to accept the Yalu River as the border and to stop molesting the Chinese frontier," indicating that he actually did not want territories south of the Yalu.[30] Yet the Koryŏ court still seemed to have understood this as an attempt to define its northern border and decided to send an army north, into Liaodong.

Koryŏ decided to fight the Ming over the demarcation of the border. The Koryŏ regime sent General Yi Sŏnggye north with 38,830 soldiers and 11,600 support staff.[31] It was this campaign and General Yi's unwillingness to fight it (preferring negotiation) that led to the fall of Koryŏ and, three years later, the creation of a new dynasty, Chosŏn, headed by Yi. Instead of confronting the Ming in Liaodong, Yi gave "Four Reasons Why We Should Not Invade the Ming":

> There are four problems in raising an army at the present time. First, it is not advisable for a small country to challenge a large country. Second, it is also not a good idea to mobilize an army during the summer. Third, the Japanese will try to take advantage of the situation during our military campaign as we send our army to a far-off land. Fourth, since it is the rainy season now, the glue put on the bows will be loosened, and the soldiers will be exposed to epidemic disease.[32]

Ch'ŏllyŏng is accepted as the border area between Ming and Koryŏ/Chosŏn. But where is it? Scholars have consistently pointed to Ming's historical sources, such as the Geographical History of Ming, and the Mingshi (明实, Ming Records) excerpt that follows, among others. It is now generally accepted that Ch'ŏllyŏng was actually in Liaodong, north of the Yalu. Lands south of the Yalu were never disputed to begin with.

The location of Ch'ŏllyŏng does not change our main argument that there was a border dispute between the Ming and Koryŏ/Chosŏn, which was resolved peacefully when Yi Sŏnggye decided not to fight. But it bears clarifying where the border dispute area was, because it helps us understand the motivations of both sides. Yi immediately opened negotiations with China, and the Ming did indeed settle for Chosŏn's tributary status. Significantly, in exchange for entering into tribute status with China, Chosŏn Korea retained all territory previously held by Koryŏ, and relations between China and Korea were close and stable for 250 years, with the two sides exchanging numerous envoys and regularly trading. The day after Yi Sŏnggye was enthroned as King T'aejo and declared a new dynasty, he sent his envoy to the Ming capital for recognition of the new state. The name "Chosŏn" was selected by the Ming, and the Chosŏn restored the use of Ming era names and Ming attire.[33]

T'aejo died without ever receiving investiture from Emperor Hongwu. T'aejo, who was pro-Ming from before he established Chosŏn, returned Koryŏ's state seal to the Ming during the second year of his rule, in 1393, and two years later he requested the recognition of official investiture.[34] The Ming refused, saying that the content and expressions of the request were not polite enough.

Chŏngjong, T'aejo's third son and the second king of Chosŏn, also pursued pro-Ming policies and requested official investiture in September 1400.[35] The Emperor Jianwen of Ming agreed and sent his envoy with the official papers and seal to Chosŏn, but a few days later was notified that Chŏngjong had ceded the throne to his younger brother, T'aejong. Skeptical of Chosŏn's domestic political developments, Jianwen recalled his envoy. Thus, it was not until 1401 that T'aejong, the third king of Chosŏn, officially received investiture from the Ming.[36]

T'aejo had considered using force in 1398 to attempt to claim parts of Liaodong (요동지역), but ultimately he decided not to.

Even though Chosŏn considered using military force, the point is that diplomacy was ultimately used. By 1401, Chosŏn had received investiture, finalized the border, and established stable relations with the Ming. Significantly, despite worries in the Korean court that the Ming would use force against them, that never happened. There is no record in either Chinese or Korean annals of any clash between the two sides.[37]

King Sejong (r. 1419–1450) built six garrisons and demarcated four districts to designate the Yalu and Tuman rivers as the natural border of Korea. Between 1416 and 1443, Chosŏn established four counties (사군, *sagun*) on the upper Yalu: Yŏyŏn, Much'ang, Chasŏng, Uye.[38] In addition, Sejong established six garrisons (육진, *yukchin*) on the Tumen between 1434 and 1449, which were "strong and affluent; soldiers' horses are fast and tough. They may not be enough to raise armies, but they are good enough for defense."[39] Nothing in the historical record suggests actual Chinese intentions for conquest or Korean fears of invasion, despite Chosŏn reservations about possible Ming motives.[40] Everything is about demarcating and stabilizing the border and diplomacy. Jungshin Lee concludes that Ming "was focused less on territorial expansion and more on controlling the Jurchens."[41]

There are reasons to be skeptical of the Ming as an example of power transition, and reasons to see it as a power transition. "Power" is used in the sense of "state" as well as relative strength. Having risen, the Ming ostensibly could also have been a case for power transition theory. Having removed an alien conquering force of Mongols, returned a native, "Han Chinese" court, reaffirmed the Chinese and Confucian ways of doing things that had only been instrumentally and superficially used by the Mongol Yuan court, the Ming could easily have been a more expansionist, triumphal state that wanted to rule the world. Instead, this episode of Ming–Chosŏn relations shows the enduring influence of norms and values and identity. Rather than upend the traditional East Asian world order, the Ming embraced what it meant to be Chinese, claiming the Mandate of Heaven and working through the tribute system. This included reestablishing tributary ties with countries it regarded as Confucian, such as Korea.

The "common conjecture" between China and Korea appears vividly in how the two sides created a stable relationship. It is not immediately obvious how to understand, frame, and interpret another political actor—this is done through ritual, rhetoric, and interactions. As Sixiang Wang writes:

> When Chosŏn and Ming officials encountered one another in a diplomatic "trading zone," they operated through a shared imperial tradition with common conventions and precedents, but sharing each other's vision was not necessary for a diplomatic transaction to proceed. Chosŏn and Ming officials could, for instance, leave with different narratives, as long as the signs they used remained mutually legible and sufficient for "local coordination" when they reconvened; this was the role performed by the rhetorical and ritual practices described in this book. They made diplomacy possible.[42]

QING-CHOSŎN RELATIONS, 1626–1636

The final example of China–Korea relations comes 250 years later. As the Qing were growing powerful in Northeast Asia, they stabilized their relations with Korea even before setting their sights on China proper. As was briefly discussed in chapter 6, a key issue regarding the Manchus was whether or not they could claim the Mandate of Heaven and could be considered to be civilized.

We make two key points about Qing–Chosŏn relations. First, Chosŏn initially resisted establishing relations with the Qing because they did not believe that Qing deserved the Mandate of Heaven, viewing them as barbarians from Manchuria. Second, however, once relative status on the basis of shared understandings was established, there followed peace and commercial and diplomatic ties. This was never about conquest.

The key issue in Qing–Chosŏn relations was that the Koreans were deeply skeptical of a powerful non-Han state. As with the Mongols three centuries earlier, the Koreans widely despised the nascent Manchu state as being barbarian, having arisen not from the Central Plain in China but rather from the wilderness of Manchuria. As Seung Kye describes Korean views at the time, "even though the Manchus ruled China, the Chosŏn elites lived in an imaginary Ming order."[43] This conceptualization is evident in the *Chŏngjo Sillok* (정조실록, The Veritable Records of Chŏngjo's Rule) of 1779, long after the Qing had overtaken the Ming: "The barbarians have conquered the center, giving rise to the era of beasts."[44]

But significantly, although this period is remembered as a humiliating era in Korean history, it is quite clear that the Qing had no territorial ambitions against Korea. The Koreans felt humiliated because they did not uphold their tributary obligations to the Ming, not because the Qing treated Korea poorly.

By the early seventeenth century, a new state had arisen in East Asia: the Manchu state of Later Jin (후금, Hu Gŭm), proclaimed in 1616, with the name changed to Qing in 1636 (along with a change of their traditional ethnic identification from

"Jurchen" to "Manchu" in 1626). By any reckoning, this was much more than a barbarian conglomerate of scattered tribes. It had a stable government, with laws, bureaucratic structures, dependencies and alliances (primarily with Mongol groups), considerable territory (ethnic homelands plus lands formerly held and ruled by Ming), a well-organized military, and even a respectable industrial capacity for manufacturing arms and military supplies. This was clearly a new and rising power in East Asia.

However, it is far too facile to conclude that the Qing could not conquer Korea because they were busy with China. The Qing could always have conquered Korea before or after turning their attentions to the Ming. Significantly, there is no evidence at that the Qing even considered conquest of Korea. Three and a half centuries after the Mongols invaded Korea, peoples from the northern steppe once again moved against Korea. However, the aim of the steppe societies was not conquest but rather toward establishing stable hierarchic relations and removing Korea as an ally of the declining Ming Chinese dynasty. The Qing expeditions against the Korean Chosŏn dynasty in the early seventeenth century were aimed more at demarcation of borders and reestablishment of the tribute system than they were with conquest.[45] At the same time, Korean sources and much contemporary nationalist Korean historiography portrays the Manchu invasions as a humiliating defeat. Chosŏn leaders regularly referred to the Jurchen leaders as "barbarian" or "bandit," even after the Qing had become the rulers of China.

The Jin leader, Nurhaci (1559–1626), formally declared war on the Ming in 1618 by listing the "seven grievances." The Ming asked for Korean help to put down this threat, but the Korean king was not sure whom to support. Korea sent 13,000 men to the northwest to join with Ming forces, but they also took with them orders to wait and see which way the battle went.[46] When the Ming began to lose, the Korean forces surrendered without a fight, and the Jin released the soldiers back to Korea, requesting a resumption of their "brother" relationship of 500 years ago.

In the decades after the 1616 "war," the Manchus attacked Korea twice in order to secure their southern flank, known as the Chŏngmyohoran (정묘호란) of 1627 and the Pyŏngjahoran (병자호란) of 1636. By 1627, the Sŏin faction and their tool, King Injo, had allowed Ming troops into Korea; these had based themselves on offshore islands close to Manchu territory and were provoking hostilities. Jin leader Hong Taiji wanted to neutralize Korea before stepping up his campaign against Ming. After a three-month siege of King Injo at Namhansansŏng Castle, Injo was forced to surrender. He had to accept a Brotherhood Treaty (형제맹약, 兄弟盟約), which established the Jin as of equal status, and a nonaggression pact, and he had to open trade between Korea and the Jin.[47] Trade was particularly important to the Jin because they were not agricultural people and needed food to support the campaign against the Ming. At that time, Hong Taiji saw the territorial demarcation of the two countries as the key to their relationship, saying, "We two nations have now established peace. From today onward, let us each respect this agreement, each should observe the territories, and refrain from disputing small matters and excessive requirements."[48]

Ki-baek Lee notes that the invasion of 1627 "was of short duration, only a small part of Korea became a battlefield, and the damage suffered was relatively slight."[49] Indeed, the Jin could easily have conquered Korea, but its expeditions against the Korean Chosŏn dynasty were about Chosŏn's pro-Ming policies, which were seen to be hostile to the Manchus. This was particularly the case after the Sŏin's 1623 deposition of Prince Kwanghae, who had genuinely looked for room to maneuver between Ming and the Manchus, which the Manchus had understood and appreciated.[50] Chosŏn's royal cabinet (홍문관, Hongmun'gwan, Office of Advisors) told King Injo, "as a proud, civilized country, we cannot continue to be humiliated by these beast-like barbarians. . . . We must let these barbarians know they cannot continue to disrupt our land and customs."[51] This resulted in Chosŏn breaking off the Brotherhood Treaty and led to the Qing invasion in December 1636, the Pyŏngjahoran.

Of course, as time passed, there were people who disagreed. The Pukhakp'a/Sirhakp'a (북학파/실학파, 北學派/实學派, literally, "Let's learn from the North" or "Let's learn what's practical" faction) emerged, arguing that Chosŏn should be practical and learn from the technological and academic advances of the Qing (and the West). Yet even the Pukhakp'a/Sirhakp'a used the terms "beasts" and "barbarians." Hong Taeyong, a famous Pukhak/Sirhak scholar, wrote in 1776, "If you look down from the sky, there is no difference between the inside and outside. Each tends to its own people, reveres its own king, maintains its own customs. China (hua) and barbarians (yi) are the same."[52]

This debate over "is human nature the same as the nature of all other beings?" (or "is the Qing equivalent to the Ming?") became the key dividing issue between the two main political factions in Chosŏn during the 1700s.[53] This is called the Horangnonjaeng (호락논쟁, 湖洛論爭). The Horon (호론, 湖論) faction argued that beasts and humans are not the same (that is, Qing and Ming are fundamentally different). The Nangnon (낙론, 洛論) faction argued that beasts and humans are fundamentally the same (that is, Koreans should treat the Qing as equal to the Ming).

The 1637 invasion was much more serious than the 1627 expedition. The Sŏin had stuck to their pro-Ming stance despite their earlier promises to the contrary, and this time Hong Taiji did not fool around. He quickly extracted a humiliating treaty, had it carved on a huge stone in Manchu, Mongolian, and Chinese, erected it on the banks of the Han River, and took away three of King Injo's sons as hostages and most of the pro-Ming politicians as captives.[54] For most of them, the captivity lasted until the summer of 1644. All relations with Ming were now severed, never to be restored. However, the Chosŏn dynasty was left standing with Injo still on the throne and the Manchu troops gone, all that in a month or so.[55] Kenneth Lee notes that, "The [Qing] emperor was gentle in his treatment of Korea. [Qing] received sworn statements from the Korean king that [Qing] would be the 'elder brother.' [After pacifying Korea,] the [Qing] never interfered with Korean internal affairs and respected the country's independence until the end of the dynasty."[56] Sixiang Wang writes:

> Why did Hong Taiji not annex Korea when he had the chance? He certainly had the wherewithal. . . . On its face, Korea submitted willingly before imperial majesty. As a result, Hong Taiji magnanimously granted Chosŏn forgiveness for its transgressions, "unwilling to kill or harm [its people]," and thus "preserved [Korea's] ancestral temples" and "protected its living beings." Having so recently assumed the imperial title (and therefore eager to secure recognition for it), Hong Taiji perhaps saw more value in the idea of Korea's submission as a jewel in his crown than as a territory to be ruled as his dominion.[57]

As soon as tribute relations were established, all skirmishing ended (figure 7.1). Relations became commercial and diplomatic, about borders, trade, smuggling, and bandits. But more than the

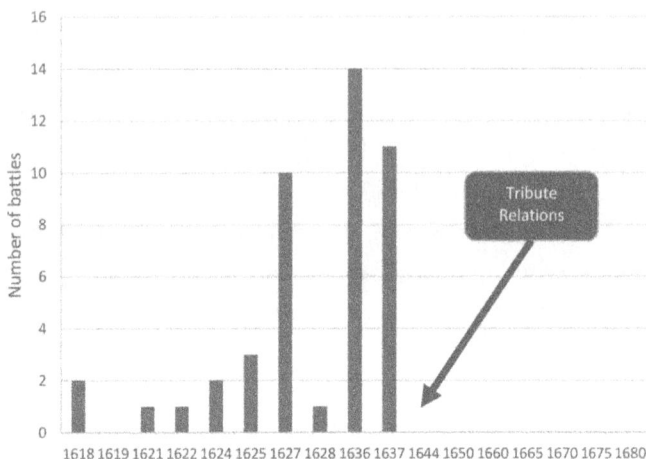

FIGURE 7.1 Qing–Chosŏn battles and skirmishes, 1616–1680.

Source: Historical East Asian War database, v.4.

practicalities, this was about the common conjecture and an appropriate relationship and expectations about the two sides. It was not conquest. Seonmin Kim notes that "it was the wild ginseng growing in the borderland that initiated the border demarcation between China and Korea."[58] He quotes Hong Taiji criticizing King Injo in 1631 for his trade policies, writing, "the ginseng prices used to be sixteen *liang* per *jin*, but you argued that ginseng is useless and fixed the price at nine *liang*. . . . I do not understand why you would steal such useless ginseng from us." This was not a simple commercial issue—the Manchurians viewed ginseng as a local product of the Manchus and a symbol of the Manchu people, not of Chosŏn.

The Koreans used the tribute system to their advantage. King Injo wrote to the Qing to do something about the soldiers and the disturbances of Qing officials, asking that

Chosŏn's territory be respected. He wrote, "Even though this small country [Chosŏn] is deemed by the great court [Qing] to be as close as a family, it is also true that each has its own territory. These days it is necessary to check people coming and going. . . . If [trespassers] are not firmly curbed now, territories will not be clearly fixed and the towns within them will not be stable."[59]

By the fifteenth century, Korea's long northern border along both the Yalu and Tumen rivers was essentially secure and peaceful, and these two rivers have formed the border between China and Korea ever since.

The three case studies in this chapter show that rising powers did not necessarily attempt to rewrite the international rules, nor did they necessarily attempt to expand in every direction possible. Largely they played by existing relationships and the enduring rules and norms of the East Asian international order. The last time Korea faced the possibility of actual conquest and national extinction from the Asian landmass was the Mongol depredations of the 1250s. Between 668 and 1259, there was no genuine existential threat to Korea. Put differently, between 668 and today, Korea has faced a sum total of one existential threat from the Asian landmass. China did not expand at the expense of Korea. Even the new energy of the new dynasties utilized and stabilized relations between the two sides based on an enduring common conjecture about the East Asian world order and each country's place in it.

To recap, part II of this book explored the contours of East Asian history and concluded that mainstream power transition theory generally does not explain much of East Asian history. The causes, factors, and patterns hypothesized by power transition theory are hard to identify in East Asian history. Instead, two different factors emerged as key: domestic political challenges and a shared common conjecture.

The collapse of the premodern East Asian international system and the arrival of the Western colonizing powers in the late nineteenth century, and in particular the collapse of the Qing dynasty in 1912, set off a half-century of chaos in East Asia. As Nicolas Tackett notes, "it was precisely in these years that an East Asian inter-state system long centered on China was finally abandoned to make way for the new world order based on a hegemonic Western European state system."[60]

Into the power vacuum of Qing decline came many Western imperial powers and, perhaps most notably, a rapidly rising Japan. In 1910, Japan once again attempted to colonize Korea. This time Japan succeeded where it had failed three centuries earlier, opening the chapter of the nineteenth-century Westphalian "harmonization" in the last part of the world that possessed "alternative and viably competitive, institutional, bureaucratic, and historical resources against the forces of empire."[61] War, civil war, colonization, and subsequent decolonization occupied the minds of political elites and peoples throughout East Asia during the twentieth century. The East Asian tribute system of international relations collapsed, never to return. All countries today—particularly China—view the world through the lens of the territorial sovereign Westphalian nation-state.[62] Given how much has changed, the key question is whether East Asia still operates on its own logic, or whether power transition theory—derived from the Western, European experience—is now a better lens to view contemporary East Asian regional relations. We now explore these questions in part III.

III

CONTEMPORARY U.S.-CHINA RELATIONS

8

EAST ASIAN POWER TRANSITIONS IN THE TWENTY-FIRST CENTURY

A forecast that Japan's economy will surpass America's by 2000 almost came true on April 19.

—*Los Angeles Times*, May 8, 1995

E arly in the twenty-first century, China completed a regional power transition by rapidly overtaking Japan. It did so astonishingly quickly, and it did so peacefully. China has returned to its position of central economic and perhaps diplomatic predominance in East Asia, even though it has not become a cultural or civilizational source of inspiration or innovation, as it had been in premodern times. Although a generation ago it was Japan that was by far the dominant country in East Asia, since the 1990s, China has caught up and surpassed Japan by almost any measure of power and wealth.

Whether the United States and China will trade places at the top of the global hierarchy is, in many ways, immaterial to actual East Asian regional security, and is also immaterial to U.S.–China relations. Overwhelmingly, U.S.–China relations will play out in a regional context, despite China's increasingly global role. Moreover, although the United States remains in some ways the dominant player, China has already engaged with the region more deeply than the United States in many dimensions.

THE DOMESTIC CAUSES OF JAPAN'S "LOST GENERATION"

Not so long ago, Japan was viewed as a potential cultural, economic, and political competitor to the United States—both different and dangerous. Japan was not just an economic challenge to American companies, but many viewed Japan as a potential national security threat to the United States itself. It may seem hard to remember today, but Japan in the late 1980s and 1990s was almost universally regarded as the most likely peer competitor to the United States. Yet within a decade Japan was no longer even in consideration as a possible competitor to the United States. The collapse of Japan's external and internal prominence came not from any power transition war or gigantic struggle with the United States. Rather, in an enduring theme of this book, Japan's eclipse came from a domestic cause: the collapse of its bubble economy and subsequent lack of economic response or reform.

We review at length some of the arguments of those who viewed Japan as an economic challenger and security threat to the United States to show both how wrong they were and that it is not possible to dismiss their fears about Japan as having been mild or restrained. In 1993, for example, three of the most influential and respected international relations theorists of their generation converged on the conclusion that Japan was a military, national security threat to the United States. Richard Betts wrote:

For a realist, a normally armed Japan, unless it is pinned down by a powerful common enemy, is a potential threat. It would be the strongest military power in Asia, and the second-ranking one in the world. The fact that Japan is democratic, in this view, does not bar it from conflict with other democracies (not to mention that some observers doubt whether Japan really is or will remain a democracy on western terms) . . . despite the unbalanced nature of Japan's power, its lopsided economic clout *already* gives it the weight of a hefty great power in a *multipolar* balance. In the near term, if Japan suddenly starts spending two to three times as much on defense and stocks up on nuclear weapons, it will be playing not a balancing role in the region, but a dominating one. . . . The key question Americans should ask themselves is: "How long are we prepared to be loyal allies of Japan and act as volunteer Hessians serving Japanese interests, without demanding genuine military reciprocity?" . . . The answer should be "As long as possible." . . . Once Japan starts spending blood as well as treasure to support international order, it will justifiably become interested in much more control over that order.[1]

Aaron Friedberg wrote:

Some American observers have speculated that the prospect of a militarily ascendant Japan might conceivably lead to a PRC–Korean mainland coalition to balance Japan's maritime position . . . those who have already begun to discount the future American role in Asia and to anticipate a rapid growth in all forms of Japanese power. One result would be an acceleration in the present East Asian arms buildup; another might be the coalescence of a regional coalition aimed at containing Japan. Faced with an increasingly hostile environment and

unable or unwilling to continue to rely for its security on the
United States, Japan would be forced to seek diplomatic reassur-
ance and military self-reliance . . . American power is the linch-
pin that holds Japan in place.[2]

And Kenneth Waltz wrote:

In discussing the likely emergence of new great powers, I con-
centrate on Japan as being by population and product the next
in line. . . . Much in Japan's institutions and behavior supports
the proposition that it will once again take its place among the
great powers. . . . Technical and economic advances accumulate. One technological breakthrough may lead to others. Economic growth rates compound. By projecting adjusted national
growth rates of GDP from the period 1950 to 1980 into the year
2010 using 1975 international dollars, William Baumol and his
associates arrived at any expected GDP per capita of $19,000 for
the United States and $31,000 for Japan. . . . Japan will lead the
east Asian bloc, now forming. . . . In March of 1988, Prime Minister Takeshita called for a defensive capability matching Japan's
economic power. A great power's panoply includes nuclear
weapons . . . Countries have always competed for wealth and security, and the competition has often led to conflict. Why should
the future be different from the past? . . . Given the expectation
of conflict, one may wonder how a state with the economic capability of a great power can refrain from arming itself with the
weapons that have served so well as the great deterrent.

Uncomfortable dependencies and perceived vulnerabilities
will lead Japan to acquire greater military capabilities. . . . In
recent years, the desire of Japan's leaders to play a more assertive
role has become apparent, a natural response to Japan's enhanced
economic standing. Again, the comparison with America at the

turn of the previous century is striking. . . . For a country to choose not to become a great power is a structural anomaly. For that reason, the choice is a difficult one to sustain. Sooner or later, usually sooner, the international status of countries has risen in step with their material resources. . . . Pride knows no nationality.[3]

These scholars, the most influential of their generation, appeared to be clear-eyed, hard-headed, and sober in their assessments of Japanese national security policy. Their conclusions about Japan seem so reasonable and obvious, built on "common sense" and the most intuitive understandings of how international relations ostensibly operates across time and space.

Yet these scholars were wrong. Thirty years later, Japan has still not decided to "take its place among the great powers," nor did it want "much more control over [the international] order."[4]

The Japanese threat was so palpable that it suffused popular culture, as well. A *Newsweek*/Gallup poll of September 1989 showed that 52 percent of Americans thought the economic power of Japan was a greater threat to the United States than the military power of the Soviet Union.[5] Movies, novels, and media during the 1980s and 1990s were rife with Orientalist images of an unknowable Japanese culture, different to capitalism from the West: dangerous, advanced but also timeless and secretive. Michael Crichton's 1992 novel and subsequent movie *Rising Sun* is about an inscrutable but technologically immensely sophisticated Japanese corporation threatening American business interests. Similarly, Tom Clancy's 1994 novel *Debt of Honor* begins with a Japanese stealth attack on American naval forces in the Pacific and concludes with a Japanese kamikaze attack on the White House. The 1980s and 1990s were rife with images of a dangerous, growing Japanese menace. There was a veritable genre of books published in the 1980s and 1990s about Japan's threat to the United States. Books such as *Blindside: Why Japan Is Still on Track to Overtake the U.S. by the Year 2000*; *Agents of Influence: How Japan's Lobbyists in the United States Are Manipulating Western Political and Economic Systems*; *The Second Pearl Harbor: Say No to Japan*; and *Japan as Number One: Lessons for America* became bestsellers.[6]

Yet three decades later Japan has almost completely vanished from any discussion about possible peer competitors to the United States, and indeed from any discussion about great powers. This resulted not from any titanic struggle between Japan and the United States, in which the United States valiantly overcame a Japanese challenge and remained the sole superpower. Rather, Japan's disappearance as a peer competitor came from internal causes within Japan itself. In an enduring theme of East Asian politics, Japan's domestic problems were the cause of its international slide from prominence.

It is widely agreed that Japan's economy, already one of the most productive in the world in the 1980s, entered a bubble phase in 1985. That was when Japan, the United States, and four other countries signed the "Plaza Accords" in New York, in which Japan agreed to depreciate the dollar against the yen. The goal was to increase U.S. exports by making them cheaper in Japan. What happened was that Japanese capital, now relatively much more valuable compared to foreign currencies, poured out of Japan and into foreign assets. Japan's banks, flush with cash, began to loan with abandon. Interest rates fell from 5 percent in 1985 to 2.5 percent by 1987.[7] Not only did this force up the value of Japanese real estate, but it also led to an outpouring of Japanese capital around the world.

In the United States, Japanese firms bought such famous landmarks as Pebble Beach Golf Club, the Rockefeller Center, and Columbia Pictures—the first foreign-owned movie studio in Hollywood history. It was widely reported in the late 1980s that the land of the Tokyo Imperial Palace was worth more than the entire real estate of California, for example. By late 1989, Japan's Nikkei 225 Stock Average had reached 39,000.

However, the stock market plummeted, losing more than $2 trillion in 1990. By 1992, the average closing price of Nikkei had fallen to 18,109, and in 2003 it reached a nadir of 9,311.[8] In the 2020s, the Nikkei was still consistently below 30,000. In 1990, Japan's GDP was $3.5 trillion (in constant 2015 U.S. dollars); in 2022, it was $4.5 trillion (figure 8.1). Although that might appear to be impressive economic growth, in reality that works out as an average annual growth rate of 1.0 percent. Over that same time span, China's economy grew from $1.03 trillion in 1990 to $16.3 trillion by 2022 (in constant terms). If Japan had grown at even the "normal" expectation of 3 percent annually, its GDP would be $9 trillion by 2022. In other words, Japan would be twice as wealthy as it is today. Put differently, Japan has forgone almost $5 trillion in national wealth because of its unwillingness to engage in needed economic reforms.

Despite obvious problems in the Japanese economy, three decades of leaders have not sought to radically change Japan's political economy. Voters in Japan seem perfectly content to muddle along. What had been called in the 1990s a "lost decade" of Japanese growth eventually became a "lost generation" of economic growth.

The Japanese political system showed almost no response to the bursting of the bubble. The Liberal Democratic Party (LDP) has held power virtually unchallenged since 1955, despite a brief period between 1993 and 1996, in which three different opposition prime ministers came and went, and between 2009 and 2012, when another three opposition prime ministers came and

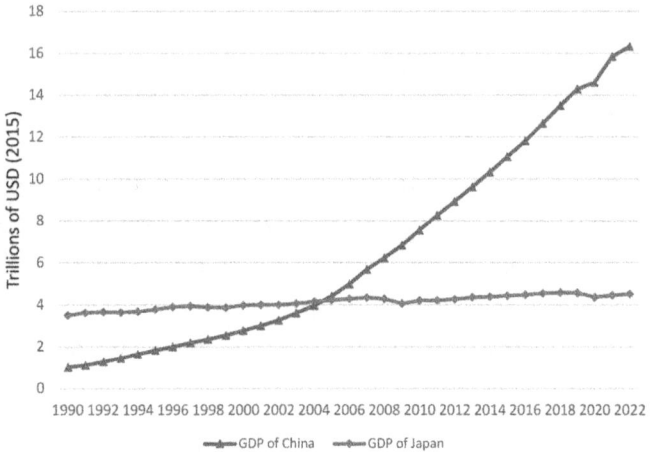

FIGURE 8.1 Gross domestic product of China and Japan, 1990–2022.
Source: World Development Indicators.

went. Yet even that LDP dominance was a sign of stasis, not innovation. During the twenty-three years between 1989, when the bubble burst started, and 2012, when Abe Shinzo took power, Japan had fifteen prime ministers. That is an average tenure of barely more than one year. After Abe's record tenure, in a return to past patterns, his first successor lasted little more than twelve months.

The LDP itself continued to hold power, but needed economic reforms did not come. Even Abe, the most dynamic Japanese prime minister in a generation, was unable to fundamentally change Japan's domestic or even foreign policy trajectories. He was seen as "tough on China," but the reality is that he neither radically increased Japanese defense spending, nor was he able to institute actual economic reforms that revitalized the economy. Brad Glosserman writes, "the inability of Abenomics to gain traction means that Tokyo's international influence is likely to be at its apogee, and will level off and eventually decline. Tokyo won't be irrelevant, but we may well be witnessing 'Peak Japan.'"[9] Furthermore, as T. J. Pempel wrote in 2015, "Japan is not back at all in regaining a commanding position within East Asia, in part due to its slow economic transformation, but due also to the atavistic positions taken by Abe's government on the historical interpretations of Japanese behavior in World War II."[10] Robert Dujarric writes about Japan that "stasis, lethargy, and fatalism, along with a pleasant lifestyle, best describe the archipelago in 2016."[11]

Japan's inward turn and lack of response to China's rise have taken place in society and culture, as well as in the military and economic realms. In 2000, there were 46,497 Japanese students studying in the United States, or 8.5 percent of the total foreign student population in the United States. By 2019, that number had dropped to 18,105, or 1.7 percent of the total foreign student population. That was a reduction of 28,000 Japanese students—a remarkable drop. In comparison, over the same time period the number of Chinese students studying in the United States increased from 59,939 students to 369,548 (33.7 percent of the total foreign student population in the United States).[12] Put differently, 300,000 more Chinese are studying in the United States today than there were in 2000. Put even more differently, there are now 350,000 more Chinese students than Japanese students studying in the United States.

Even South Korea sends three times as many students to study in the United States than Japan, despite having less than half the population. In 2019, there were 52,250 South Korean students in the United States compared to 18,105 Japanese students. By way of comparison, in 2018, there were also 70,540 South

Korean students studying in China, but only 13,595 Japanese students in China.[13] In 2011, South Korea sent 62,000 students to China, while Japan sent 17,961.

As to the military, Prime Minister Kishida in May 2022 pledged to increase Japan's defense spending, with the aim of reaching the NATO target level of 2 percent of GDP. There is more discussion that this time is different, and that Japan intends a sustained military buildup. It is true that SIPRI's figures for Japanese military budget in 2021 show a 7.3 percent increase since 2020 and an almost 18 percent increase over the decade 2012–2021. In comparison, China's military spending increased 72 percent over the decade of 2012–2021 (table 8.1).

Japan is investing more in its military after three decades. But this needs to be kept in context. Two years of 7 percent increases in military spending does not yet constitute an enduring trend. If the trend of increased Japanese defense spending continues over a number of years, Japan will have made a major increase in its investment in its military. At this point it is not conclusive that Japan intends to do that.

Moreover, Japan must continue large, perhaps even double-digit increases over a decade if not more simply to maintain the gap in spending with China. At the same time, Japan's economy must grow at a reasonable pace. This may be relatively difficult to achieve—the Fiscal System Council, which advises the finance minister, said in May 2022 that "there are no clever schemes or shortcuts . . . it is impossible to fulfill defense capabilities continuously and sufficiently without an economically, financially and fiscally strong macrostructure . . . [Japan] might lose without even fighting."[14] As Tom Le pointed out in 2023, even Kishida's attempts to increase defense spending will likely be modest in practice. Le writes, "Kishida's policy aspirations remain aspirations until they are fully funded and address Japan's

TABLE 8.1. JAPANESE AND CHINESE MILITARY EXPENDITURES, 2010–2021

	2012	2020	2021	% change, 2012–2021
Japan	47.45	51.97	55.77	17.5
China	156.97	257.97	270.01	72.0

Note: Figures are in constant (2020) billion U.S. dollars.

Source: SIPRI 2022.

most significant security liability, its aging and declining population. Changes to Japanese security policy will remain deliberate and incremental."[15]

The absence of a domestic Japanese reaction to its own economic stasis and the rise of China is even more obvious in comparison to Japan's response in the late nineteenth century and early twentieth century to the numerous international threats of the time. The arrival of Perry's "Black Ships" in 1853 jolted a complacent Japanese elite and populace into stunning reactions.[16] From the Meiji Restoration of 1868 to the rapid industrialization of the country in the subsequent decades and the startling Japanese triumph in the Russo-Japanese War of 1904–1905, Japan as a country engaged in an extraordinary mobilization of its people, economy, society, and politics in response to what it perceived to be numerous existential threats to its continued survival.

In the space of only a few decades, Japan in the early twentieth century became the first non-Western country to industrialize and the first non-Western country to defeat a Western great power in war. The Japanese response came about because of a clear threat to the survival of the Japanese state. The Western imperial powers were colonizing almost all of Asia—and Japan looked to be next in line. Such an overwhelming national response is what Japan does when its existence is threatened.

In contrast, the nonresponse by Japanese elites and population to China's return to centrality in the twenty-first century has a very clear cause: China is not a threat to Japan's continued survival or existence, and so Japanese people and leaders are not reacting as if it were. There are disagreements at the margins of China–Japan relations, such as on the precise demarcation of maritime borders around uninhabited islands and in the seas between them. But nobody seriously argues that China has any intention to invade and conquer Japan. Hence, Japan is not reacting as if it did.

CHINA HAS ALREADY COMPLETED A PEACEFUL REGIONAL POWER TRANSITION

The story of East Asia in the twentieth century was the story of Japan: its rise, ambitions, and failure to dominate East Asia. China was at best an afterthought in discussions of the future of East Asian security. Indeed, as recently as 1999, Gerald Segal wrote in *Foreign Affairs*, "Does China matter? . . . At best, China is a second-rank middle power that has mastered the art of diplomatic theater. . . . Only when we finally understand how little China matters will we be able to craft a sensible policy towards it."[17]

Scarcely two decades later, China had eclipsed Japan to the point that it seems impossible that we thought so highly of Japan and so little of China. As China came out of the twentieth century—a century of chaos, revolution, internal struggles, and self-inflicted planned economy—its return to the central position in East Asia was blindingly fast. In the space of thirty years, from 1990 to 2022, China's share of regional GDP grew from 16 percent to 60 percent, while Japan's share fell from 56 percent to 17 percent (figure 8.2).

China's share of regional trade, moreover, also increased at a similar, blindingly fast, pace. In 1996, China took 11 percent of total regional trade, while Japan accounted for 27 percent. By early 2000s, those lines crossed, with China now accounting for more trade than Japan (figure 8.3). By 2020, the latest year for which comprehensive data are available, trade with China comprised 39 percent of all regional trade, while Japan's share had

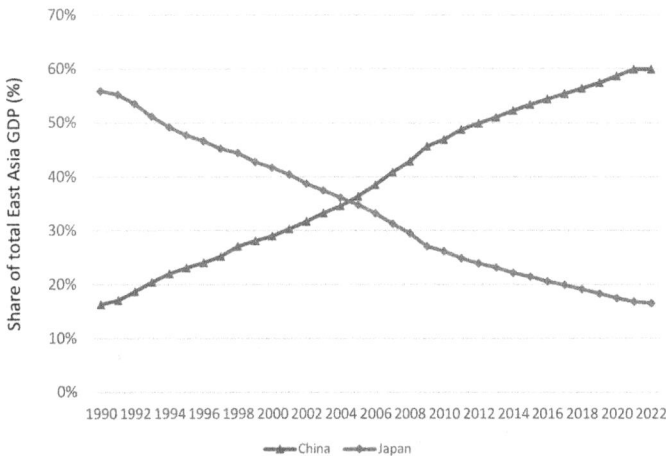

FIGURE 8.2 Chinese and Japanese shares of total East Asian gross domestic product, 1990–2022. The graph shows China's and Japan's GDP as a share of the total GDP of Australia, China, Indonesia, Japan, South Korea, Malaysia, the Philippines, Singapore, Thailand, and Vietnam.

Source: World Bank, World Development Indicators.

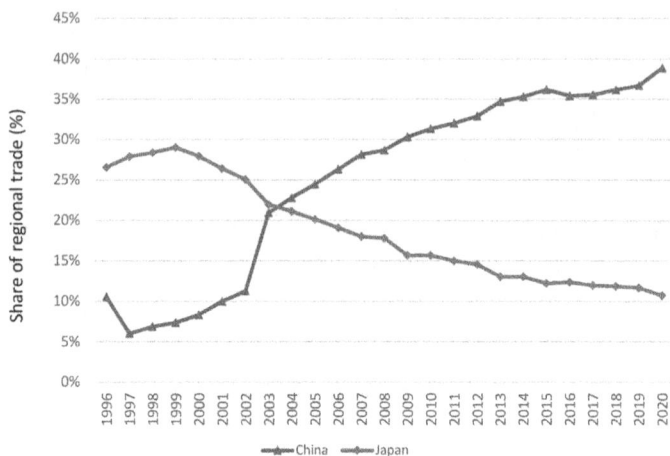

FIGURE 8.3 Chinese and Japanese shares of regional trade, 1996–2020. The region, East Asia and the Pacific, is as defined by the World Bank.

Source: World Integrated Trade Solution (WITS).

dropped to 11 percent. Not only the scale of the transition but also the speed at which this occurred in terms of both trade and overall economic size are remarkable.

Significantly, and in contrast to almost every power transition and balance of power theorist's predictions about East Asia, as China has grown richer and more integrated within East Asia itself, East Asian defense spending has steadily declined. Waltz, Betts, and Friedberg all confidently claimed that Japan not only had the capability to rearm but also that it would inevitably rearm and be the most powerful military power in East Asia. However, thirty years later, Japan had not responded in any meaningful way to China's return to power.

Overall in East Asia, no country has deemed it necessary to respond militarily to China's return to centrality. The proportion of the economy devoted to defense spending is now almost half of what it was in 1990 and shows no sign of increasing (figure 8.4). Specifically, the defense spending of nine main East Asian countries declined from an average of 2.88 percent of GDP in 1990 to an average of 1.5 percent in 2022.

These data tell an accurate, enduring, and often overlooked story about East Asia. China has already managed a head-spinningly fast regional power transition. The only question is how much larger the gap between China and its neighbors will become. Countries are rapidly increasing their economic ties with China and with each other, and East Asian countries apart from China have steadily reduced their defense spending, which

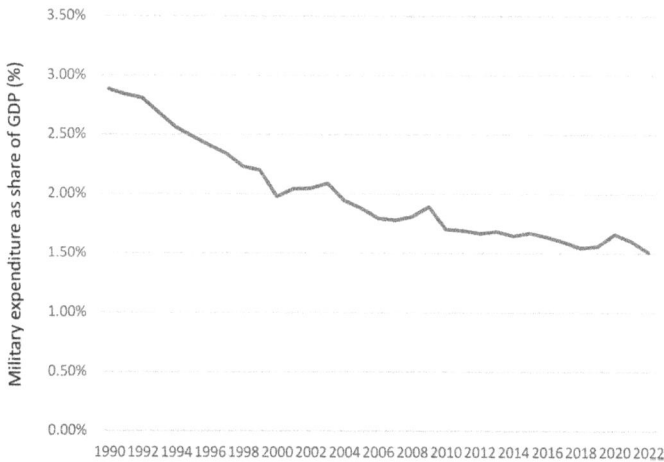

FIGURE 8.4 East Asian military expenditure as a share of gross domestic product, 1990–2022. Countries included are China, Japan, South Korea, Indonesia, Malaysia, the Philippines, Singapore, Taiwan, and Thailand. The figures for military spending as a share of GDP are calculated as the average of each country's military spending as a share of its GDP.

Source: SIPRI, 2022.

suggests that they do not think most of the region's unresolved issues are worth fighting over. All countries in the region have to coexist with each other; none are picking up and moving somewhere else. Countries are dealing with that reality and seeking diplomatic, commercial, and multilateral relations with each other and China, not primarily military strategies.

THE UNITED STATES AND CHINA IN EAST ASIA: A POWER TRANSITION?

As of 2022, China's GDP measured in constant US$2015 was $16.3 trillion, far behind the United States' $21 trillion. But as noted previously, the more practical question is not whether China will catch or overtake the United States on a global scale, but rather what is happening within the East Asian region? Here the picture is more mixed.

Of course, the United States retains a significant military advantage over China. Not only does the United States spend almost three times more on its military than does China, but it also has decades of established military alliances across the East Asian region. From Japan and South Korea to the Philippines and Australia, the United States has forward deployed military assets and numerous military bases around the region. The United States also regularly engages in military exchanges with countries around the region.

Yet China is far from isolated in military relations, and indeed in the past two decades has energetically engaged with countries around the region. Adam P. Liff, for example, argues that "joint exercises and training" are a "Waltzian categories of . . . external balancing" behavior.[18] Darren J. Lim and Zack Cooper also classify "routine joint training, exercises, or combat operations" as a "moderate alignment" signal that reveal secondary states' security interests shared with great powers.[19] Indeed, countries are increasingly engaging in joint military exercises with China, not just with the United States. As recently as 2000, China engaged in zero joint military exercises around the region. From 2000 to 2009, China engaged in twenty-three joint military exercises in the region; from 2010 to 2019, it engaged in 117 joint military exercises in the region. This measure is fairly strict, counting only times that "countries have participated by dispatching military personnel and/or military assets," and it does not count exercises where China was just an observer.[20]

Beyond military and security-related issues, a much more integrated, interactive region is emerging, a region in which countries want U.S. engagement but are also increasingly searching for alternative, complementary, institutional, economic, and diplomatic arrangements. China has rapidly increased its diplomatic and economic engagement with the region. Especially compared to a generation ago, China's position in the region has expanded rapidly. Diplomatically, China has normalized diplomatic relations with every country in the region. This seems obvious today, but it was less than thirty years ago that China normalized relations with many regional countries. Vietnam normalized relations with China in 1991, for example. China has rapidly expanded its diplomatic and economic relations around the region, from bridges built in Fiji to proposals for educational collaboration and development assistance across the Pacific.[71]

Economically, China rapidly became the top trade partner for every country in the region, including the United States. China is also the largest foreign investor in the Philippines, Indonesia, and Malaysia; the United States is the largest foreign investor in China itself, Australia, Japan, South Korea, and Singapore.[22]

China has signed nine bilateral or multilateral free trade agreements with regional partners; the United States has signed three. And China provided $36 billion of overseas development assistance within the region in 2017, the last year data is available, compared to $3 billion from the United States.

In multilateral regional institutions, and in contrast to the Chinese active and continuing efforts with the Asia-Pacific, the United States has pulled back from regional economic and diplomatic institutions in the past decade, not toward them. This is not simply a result of President Trump; President Biden has continued many of Trump's economic policies toward East Asia, and China in particular. The Biden administration has clearly signaled that it has no intention to rethink these policies. Secretary of State Antony Blinken said in March 2021, "Some of us previously argued for free trade agreements because we believed Americans would broadly share in the economic gains and that those deals would shape the global economy in ways that we wanted. . . . But we didn't do enough to understand who would be negatively affected."[23]

As for China, in November 2020 China and fourteen other East Asian states signed the Regional Comprehensive Economic Partnership (RCEP); Japan, Indonesia, Vietnam, the Philippines, and South Korea are among the signatories. Significantly, the United States chose not to participate. RCEP is the first trade agreement that includes all three of China, South Korea, and Japan. RCEP arose as a regional initiative of ASEAN in 2012 and is aimed at lowering tariffs, increasing investment, and allowing freer movement of goods around the region.

Another regional initiative is the Trans-Pacific Partnership (TPP). Originally a Japanese initiative, TPP was an extensive trade agreement that would have included the United States and eleven other North American, Latin American, and East Asian countries such as Vietnam and Singapore, but without South Korea or China. The original TPP was considered of higher quality than RCEP because in addition to trade and investment provisions, TPP was also to include provisions that emphasized labor rights, environmental and intellectual property protections, and dispute-resolution mechanisms. President Trump withdrew the United States from the agreement, and the other eleven countries continued to sign a modified agreement in March 2018, calling it the Comprehensive and Progressive Agreement for Trans-Pacific Partnership (CPTPP).

China applied to join the CPTPP in September 2021. This is significant but, as Alex Lin and Saori Katada argue, not new: Chinese leaders have consistently made aspirational statements about TPP entry since 2013.[24] A keynote speech given by Chinese Premier Li Keqiang at ASEAN in September 2013 was one of the first times a high-ranking Chinese official had openly said that they would entertain the TPP: "China is willing to join hands with ASEAN to advance talks of Regional Comprehensive Economic Partnership (RCEP), and discuss exchanges and interactions with frameworks such as Trans-Pacific Partnership (TPP) Agreement, so as to create an open, inclusive, and mutually beneficial climate to 'make two wheels of regional and global trade roll together.'"[25]

China's geo-economic endgame was always to engage with both RCEP and TPP. Again, Chinese rhetoric on this has been clear and consistent over the years. As an indication of intentions, China's application to join CPTPP is significant: China has changed domestically far more rapidly than anyone envisioned even a decade ago. Its domestic economic practices and institutions may not yet be sufficient to join CPTPP, but it is moving in that direction more rapidly than most had believed.

As for the United States, it is engaging in two contradictory tendencies. The first is to ignore the regional economic initiatives already in place, such as RCEP or CPTPP. The second is to proclaim loudly that the United States will present its own regional economic initiatives. But not only is there nothing concrete, the empty phrases explicitly rule out elements of trade expansion that are central to the concerns of East Asian countries. Claims of a "free and open Indo-Pacific strategy" have yet to be met with any concrete proposals. On May 23, 2022, the Biden administration revealed its "Indo-Pacific Economic Framework." Yet the IPEF was only twelve paragraphs long and contained no concrete proposals. In fact, the most telling line was "Today, we launch collective discussions toward future negotiations . . ."[26]

The Biden administration has clearly stated that it has no intention of applying to rejoin the CPTPP. Yet, in 2021, China applied to join the CPTPP. It is not clear whether China can meet the high standards of the pact at this point in time. However, as an indicator of Chinese intentions, it clearly aims to be capable of joining in the future. As another indicator of intentions, the United States is actively ignoring these regional trade pacts.

The U.S. approach contrasts with China's embrace of these multilateral institutions and open trading and investment regimes. The United States, as part of its general turn toward a hawkish approach to China, has embraced a trade dispute with it. Biden has left in place the tariffs on Chinese goods put there by Trump. Despite the imposition of tariffs on Chinese goods, the U.S. trade deficit with China actually expanded over the decade 2010–2022 (table 8.2). The Trump plan, put in place over the course of a few years, was an attempt to cause China problems by placing up to 25 percent tariffs on many imports from

TABLE 8.2. U.S.-CHINA TRADE, 2010-2022

Year	U.S.–China
2022 (Jan–Mar)	−101.0
2021	−355.3
2020	−310.2
2019	−345.2
2018	−419.0
2017	−375.2
2016	−346.8
2015	−367.3
2014	−344.8
2013	−318.7
2012	−315.1
2011	−295.2
2010	−273.0

Note: Figures are in billions of current U.S. dollars.

Source: U.S. Census, "Trade in Goods with China," https://
www.census.gov/foreign-trade/balance/c5700.html.

China. Yet the trade deficit with China remains stubbornly impervious to Trump's tariffs. Although the trade deficit with China shrank 11 percent between 2019 and 2020, that year is particularly difficult to interpret, given that the Covid-19 pandemic disrupted supply chains, travel, and economies around the world. As can be seen, in 2021 the trade deficit with China increased, and the first three months of 2022 show a year-on-year increase of 29 percent over the trade deficit for the first three months of 2021.

The reality, as Oxford Economics and the U.S.–China Business Council found in 2021, is that the United States lost 245,000 jobs directly as a result of the tariffs.[27] Samantha Vortherms and Jiakun Jack Zhang estimate that less than 1 percent of the increase in U.S. firms leaving China in 2018 and 2019 was due to U.S. tariffs. Comparatively, they find that U.S. firms were no more likely to divest from China than from Europe or the rest of Asia.[28] Indeed, in 2021, a survey of U.S. firms in China revealed that two-thirds of them remained optimistic about the Chinese market and planned to increase, not decrease, their investments in China.[29] In a survey by the American Chamber of Commerce in Shanghai, over half of U.S. businesses polled said that they were adopting the strategy of reorienting their China investments to serve Chinese consumers rather than international ones. In 2019, 61 percent of American firms surveyed were optimistic about the China market, and half expected their revenues to increase.[30] Many companies simply passed the cost of tariffs on to the American consumer in the form of higher prices. Econometric studies of the Trump tariffs on China found that "the full incidence of the tariff falls on domestic consumers, with a reduction in U.S. real income of $1.4 billion per month by the end of 2018."[31]

What is particularly perplexing about U.S. strategy on East Asia is that the clear worry about allowing China to become a regional hegemon explicitly concerns economic relations in the region. Elbridge Colby, a leading China hawk, claims that "if China could establish hegemony over Asia, it could then set up a commercial and trading bloc anchored in the world's largest market that would privilege its own and subordinates' economies while disfavoring America's."[32] But if the U.S. concern is prosperity, the United States could more actively engage in robust participation in East Asian trading pacts. Instead the United States actively retreats from those trade pacts while explicitly worrying about China excluding the United States from regional trade pacts.

In contrast to U.S. claims about Chinese intentions, what is largely absent in Chinese discourse about itself is regular statements of ambition to be a global or regional leader. That discourse—leader, hegemon, indispensable nation—is not a Chinese discourse. This is in clear contrast to the United States, where it is relatively unquestioned that the United States must be a global leader and must be a hegemon.

In fact, rhetoric about Chinese goals tends to be constrained, not grandiose or expanding. For example, the oft-used phrase "Chinese characteristics" is more than a catchphrase—it is a continual reminder that China is focused mainly on itself, not other countries: The phrase "Chinese characteristics" explicitly constricts Chinese ambitions and ideas to China itself. "Socialism with Chinese characteristics" is very difficult to export overseas—this is ideology and practice focused on China's own unique situation. This is clear when examining China's economic relations with the Global South—these are very different countries culturally, economically, and politically and China is not attempting to export its ideology or leadership to them. Rather, it tends to engage them economically but not with any larger expectations that other countries will mimic or learn Chinese ways.

Although there have been power transitions in East Asia, as defined by power transition theory, structurally, the countries have not behaved as predicted. Japan did not fight a preventive war against China to maintain its regional position; China did not fight a war against Japan. In the region itself, the past three decades have seen China clearly become a significant actor diplomatically, economically, and even militarily.

Moreover, despite decades of Western predictions to the contrary, it is by now widely admitted that East Asian states are not forming a balancing coalition against China out of fear of its rise. As Robert Jervis observed in 2019, "many observers thought that China's rise would call up a local counter-balancing coalition. These predictions did not come true, leading scholars to wonder whether balance of power theory was obsolete—or even wrong."[33] As Kishore Mahbubani, a former Singaporean ambassador to the United Nations, pointed out in 2019, "China is the only great power today that has not fired a single bullet across its borders in 30 years. By contrast, even under the peaceful American presidency of Barack Obama, the U.S. dropped 26,000 bombs on seven countries in 2016."[34]

American conjectures about East Asia are largely not shared in the region itself. There are at least three American consensus viewpoints about China and the region that are significant: that China has expansive ambitions and poses an indirect threat to the United States; that all countries in the region will join an American containment coalition against China; and that the United States must unquestionably be a global and regional leader.

In contrast to the aspirations that came from the American policymaking establishment, the reactions of East Asian countries were more restrained.[35] For instance, in a meeting between the Malaysian and Indonesia foreign ministers after the announcement of the AUKUS deal, Malaysian Foreign Minister Saifuddin Abdullah said that "Although [Australia] stated that these are nuclear-powered submarines and not nuclear-armed ones, both our governments expressed concern and disturbance."

Indonesian Foreign Minister Retno Marsudi added that the situation would "certainly not benefit anyone. . . . [Abdullah and I] both agreed that efforts to maintain a peaceful and stable region must continue and don't want the current dynamics to cause tension in the arms race and also in power projection."[36] Even on issues of Taiwan, when East Asian leaders do speak out, it is often to caution the United States from getting too far ahead of where even the Taiwanese themselves are. On November 4, 2021, Singaporean Defense Minister Ng Eng Hen said that for China, "Taiwan goes to the heart of the political legitimacy of the leader, of the party and it's a deep red line. I can think of no scenario [in] which there are winners if there is actual physical confrontation over Taiwan. . . . So, I would advise us to stay very far away from that."[37]

The United States does not share the understanding about China or its own role in East Asia that the East Asian countries share. East Asia in 2022 is more peaceful, richer, more stable, and more integrated than at any point in the past 150 years. This East Asian regional security complex has a set of shared understandings. None are as deep or full as those from the premodern era, but there are clearly elements of a contemporary common conjecture in the region.

IV

CONCLUSION

9

THE LESSONS OF HISTORY AND THE FUTURE OF EAST ASIA

The research in this book leads to a clear conclusion: Throughout East Asian history, the presence or absence of a common conjecture was more important to explaining war, stability, and peace than were power transitions between the units. If scholars began with East Asian history, they would never have developed a theory of power transitions, and indeed the theory does not appear to apply in the premodern East Asian context. Dynasties rose and fell over the centuries, but almost always for reasons of internal challenge, not external war or conquest. Time and again, when two units could negotiate over relative role and shared an understanding about each other's aims and about what comprised a legitimate concern, their relations were remarkably stable, sometimes for centuries—no matter what their relative balance of power. If two units could not find a common conjecture, their relations were unstable, no matter how powerful one was relative to the other. When there were disruptions to the system, the return to stability was almost always guided by shared understandings about how foreign relations should work and what was important in negotiating a relative hierarchy between the units. As Sixiang Wang sums up:

Over the centuries, Korean elites, as stakeholders rather than outsiders, helped shape the imperial tradition. The palpable irony
of all this is the myth of China's moral empire has persisted even
until today, partly because generations of Korean diplomats had
been repeating it to China's imperial forebears for centuries. . . .
But to come away with this conclusion is to forget why Korean
envoys and memorial drafters used the notion of moral empire
in the first place: it was to convince emperors and their agents
that behaving according to Korean expectations was the best way
to be imperial.[1]

The preceding quote focused on Korea, but this common conjecture was far wider. Liam Kelley prefers the term "manifest
civility" to distinguish the older Chinese concept of civilization
from the modern Western concept of civilization, and he writes:

To state that a kingdom was such a domain [of manifest civility]
indicated that it belonged to a category where it shared certain
governmental, ritual, educational, literary, intellectual, and social
practices with other members of this category, the proof of which
could be found in the existence of a body of "institutional records"
that recorded such practices, as well as the presence of "wise men"
who maintained these records. Furthermore . . . there was a dis-
cernible inequality in this respect, especially between Vietnam
and China.[2]

A key question for East Asian regional relations in the twenty-
first century that derives from the lessons identified in this book
is whether anything of the premodern common conjecture
remains. While all countries have embraced the Western state
system of international order, this does not mean that they have
completely forgotten their histories, their relations, and their

interactions, nor does it mean that all elements of their political and philosophical worldviews have been abandoned. To the extent that elements of a shared twenty-first-century understanding are identifiable, we would expect regional states to be better able to manage their relations than structural theories would expect. If, however, that common conjecture has been totally obliterated, then we might expect more instability.

Those traditional elements distilled from East Asian history provided a common vocabulary that allowed premodern states to understand and interact with each other over legitimate goals, ambitions, and the right to existence. Translated to modern times, the twenty-first-century common conjecture could be many things, but most centrally it revolves around whether East Asian states mutually accept the legitimate right of each to exist and a basic understanding of the ambitions and goals—often limited—of each state.

The countries in the region do not necessarily view China as benign—often China can be extremely pushy and a bully—but East Asian countries do not view China as a threat to their existence, and so they are not reacting as if it were. That is, despite the disruptions of the twentieth century and the massive changes that took place between the premodern and modern worlds, some elements of that premodern common conjecture remain. The countries in the region share a long history, many elements of philosophy, religion, and society—and there are elements of a shared understanding today, as well.

Another question for future stability in East Asia will be whether and to what extent the United States can develop a common conjecture with states in East Asia—or at least understand and apprehend the common conjecture that exists in East Asia. To the extent that it can do this, the United States will be able to more productively craft policies and relations with China and the region. Regional relations, U.S.–China relations, and indeed international security are going to depend much more on whether and how the United States and countries in East Asia are able to develop a shared common understanding about relative role and position in the region. At this point, it is an open question about how the United States perceives China and the region, and it is not clear whether the United States and East Asian states, including even U.S. allies, share the same understanding of how to develop their relations in the twenty-first century.

Indeed, U.S. relations with China have grown increasingly combative in the past few years, and many see U.S.–China relations as at their lowest historical point since normalization of ties began in the mid-1970s. Scholars on both left and right in the United States have begun to view China as an authoritarian power that has very different views and goals from the United States, and one that does not accept the U.S.-based rules-based international order. That the United States often ignores those same rules is not considered the issue. Rather, an enduring question that arises from our research is whether beliefs about what should be economic national strategy, institutional strategy, and diplomatic strategy are similar enough that there is room for compromise and adjustment, or whether China and American views of the international system are so different that they are incommensurate.

Is China trying to set up an alternative international economic order through its Belt and Road Initiative, or its creation of the Asian Infrastructure Investment Bank? Or are these simply Chinese-style economic institutions essentially similar to those of the United States? Answering those questions is not the focus of this book, but they are natural questions about the contemporary international order that would extend the arguments and theoretical ideas put forth here. Indeed, disagreements such as territorial disputes in East Asia may seem to conform to conventional causes, such as disagreements between authoritarian and democratic countries. But it is important to note that such disputes persist not only between authoritarian and democratic countries but even between democratic countries as well. Being democracies has not made it any easier for Korea and Japan to resolve their territorial disputes, nor has it helped the Philippines and Taiwan to do so either.

There is a second lesson that arises from studying East Asian history: Internal challenges are often far more consequential to the fate of nations than are external threats. Time and again throughout East Asian history, long-enduring dynasties and regimes crumbled from within. Only occasionally in East Asian history were countries overthrown by invasion and conquest. As lessons for the present, it is clear that both China and the United States face a host of domestic issues. Both countries have a political sphere that is far from stable; both economies have troubles; and both societies are undergoing cultural and social changes. Whether either China or the United States can handle these domestic and internal issues adequately will likely have a direct and lasting impact on their ability to handle their relations with each other and the wider world.

For China, managing a rapidly changing society that is grappling with a host of economic, political, and social issues is no easy task. Susan Shirk has argued that China is "strong abroad but fragile at home."[3] Minxin Pei has consistently argued that China's domestic political economy is trapped: it cannot reform without threatening the survival of the CCP, but without reform economic growth—a key source of CCP legitimacy—may falter.[4] David Shambaugh wrote in 2015 that "the endgame of Chinese communist rule has now begun, I believe, and it has progressed further than many think. . . . [The] party and political system . . . is extremely fragile on the inside. . . . China's economy—for all the Western views of it as an unstoppable juggernaut—is stuck in a series of systemic traps from which there is no easy exit. . . . We cannot predict when Chinese communism will collapse, but it is hard not to conclude that we are witnessing its final phase."[5] There is no question that the list of domestic challenges facing China is long, and many are intractable. Environmental concerns, a declining population, economic growth, inequality, corruption, political unrest, and rapid social change are causing strains on Chinese society.

Taking poverty alleviation as an example, what the West marveled at is the speed and scale at which China lifted people out of poverty. As Rob Schmitz puts it, "What China—its government and its people—have achieved is unprecedented in human history: Around 700 million Chinese have worked their way above the poverty line since 1980, accounting for three-quarters of global poverty reduction during that period."[6] However, a statement from China's former Premier Li Keqiang shocked the public and sparked a national debate on where China stands economically. In May 2020, during a press conference after the closing session of the National People's Congress, Li stated that while China's average per capita income is 30,000 yuan (US$4,200) per year, some 600 million low-to-middle-income Chinese—that is, nearly half of the Chinese population—live on a monthly income of 1,000 yuan (US$140), "a salary that cannot even allow them to rent a room in most Chinese cities. After the pandemic, livelihood issues (民生) should be prioritized."[7]

There is no fire without smoke. Chinese Business Network published an article describing Li's statement as an effective sobering-up aid for the public.[8] The statement also triggered multiple Chinese agencies to jump out as if to put out fires by explaining the complicated statistics behind Li's numbers.

The fact that this statement caught so much attention mirrors an almost schizophrenic view that the ordinary Chinese public holds regarding China's economy: on one hand, the government has painted this rosy picture of a rising China as the world's economic powerhouse; on the other hand, they—even the middle class—have been under an enormous financial burden, especially when it comes to housing. The soaring prices mean that affordable housing is out of reach of typical households, while low-income groups have been further hit by Covid-19. The phrase "*tang ping*" (躺平, lie flat) became the buzzword among the young generations, reflecting their frustration with a culture defined by longer hours, excessive ambition, and few rewards.

Again, we make no predictions as to whether the internal problems facing China will be solved. Rather, it is more important to point out that domestic issues may be more consequential for the future of China and for China's place in the world than any titanic struggle with the United States over global dominance would be.

Although it has become commonplace in U.S. policymaking circles to simply assert that China aims to replace the United States as the global hegemon, there is an argument to be made that China's primary strategic focus today—just as it was a millennium ago—is internal, not external. Chinese dreams of regional or even global influence and position will depend as much or perhaps more on how it manages the domestic social, environmental, economic, and political issues than it will on how China deals with its external relations. Although some American analysts see expansive Chinese goals, as Andrew Scobell points out, "it has long been conventional wisdom that the highest priority for the Politburo of the Chinese Communist Party (CCP) is 'regime survival.'"[9]

The United States also faces a myriad of domestic issues. Those domestic challenges may outweigh whatever issues China poses to the future security and prosperity of the United States. The issues are clear: from a deeply divided political landscape to widening economic disparities and deep social divisions, there are increasingly concerns about the strength and resilience of American society. As Andrew Bacevich observes, "To persist in illusions of reasserting U.S. global primacy will only accelerate American decline by deflecting attention from the imperative of repairing the social order here at home."[10]

Taken together, the applicability of power transition theory across time and space is far more truncated than is widely believed. The theory may be "right" or "wrong," but it does not apply in a vast geographic region over a remarkably long period. Yet power transition theory is largely considered to be a deductive and universal theory with an almost intuitive, self-evident logic to it.

Despite attempts by scholars to create an abstract, deductive theory of power transitions based on particular units and causal mechanisms, the application of power transition theory almost always proceeds by analogy, not theory. Scholars sometimes find a few factors that are similar and then look for whether they exist in another case. That is not an explicit theory with explicit causal processes being tested. For example, Betts references history to argue by analogy. He wrote about the post–Cold War system that "if the system were insecurely hierarchical, and edged toward bipolarity rather than wider balance, it might become more dangerous for the reasons Gilpin suggests in his interpretation of history as a series of hegemonic transitions. Or, if Waltz is correct, and the Cold War analogue is more appropriate than the Peloponnesian, bipolarity could make the structure stable."[11]

Referencing the Peloponnesian War or Thucydides is making an argument by analogy. Using Greek history to mine "lessons" is an implicit claim that the ideas of power transition are universal across time and space and do not depend on the particular type of political unit or international order. That is because Athens and Sparta were not "great powers" or "states" as conceived in the Westphalian international system that arose over the past five centuries. The ancient Greek city-states existed as different units in a different international order from the contemporary Westphalian order built on nation-states. The scholars who test power transition theory often use evidence from the past two hundred years, because they are making an argument about a particular order and the behavior of particular states. In that way, adducing evidence that these causal processes did not occur in East Asia should be falsifying to that argument, or at least evidence that these are truncated events and processes.

Having shown the limitations of power transition theory, perhaps we can question whether many of our other theories are more specific and more contingent than normally believed. If they are, carefully identifying those scope and boundary conditions will be a key element of future scholarship. Given the dramatically different contexts within which political regimes rose and fell in both European and East Asian history, it is also perhaps worth being more cautious about applying the "lessons of European history" to contemporary East Asian security dynamics.

Finally, we come to future research. Almost every chapter in this book could be expanded to become a full book of its own—we have surveyed an enormous swath of East Asian history and contemporary East Asian security. We have inevitably made generalizations that should probably be more nuanced, and we have ignored or missed issues that have a direct impact on our argument. Of all the issues that we have overlooked or treated too superficially, we believe there are two key intertwined areas for future research that derive directly from our argument: What is the most appropriate comparable case if we want to understand contemporary China or East Asia broadly? How does the obsession in material power confine our understanding of international relations?

It is by no means easy to identify comparable cases.[12] What makes the task more demanding is that the amount of variance with respect to crucial variables can often be hard to quantify but is of large significance. Many case studies of China differ from the narrow sense of case study in two important aspects: Inference deriving from case studies of China tends to be descriptive or even predictive in nature, instead of being causal; in addition, rather than using China to understand a larger class of similar units (a population), case studies of China aim to elucidate features specific to a particular case—China itself.[13]

The discussion here is not to dismiss the value of the idiographic analysis of China. Such studies are intrinsically valuable. Instead, we would like to point out a paradoxical and divisive situation when dealing with China: while China is often treated as an exception, the criteria for scholars to select cases comparable with such an "exceptional" China so as to derive predictions of its intentions are very vague. It is as if nothing can be compared to China and, at the same time, everything can be used to interpret China. For much of the power transition theory, such criteria have almost been reduced to one single bar, that is, "*rising*." Even scholars such as Barry Buzan and Michael Cox, who are mindful of Eurocentric bias, chose to compare contemporary China with the United States of the late nineteenth and early twentieth centuries.[14] If the problem of comparative endeavor identified by Giovanni Sartori is the loss of purpose, then this literature that compares China with European cases suffers from the opposite problem, that is, the existence of a narrowly predefined purpose.[15]

Finding the case most comparable to contemporary China is more than a methodological question: It is a question of how to define historical China in relation to today's China. Why compare? Ultimately, we care about a comparable case because we want to understand what a contemporary China wants, and we care about what happened centuries ago in East Asia because we believe that the ideas and events of the past affect the way we think and act in the present. Finding the case most comparable to contemporary China should not be a search "involving choice between equally unsatisfactory alternatives." In this way, we ask whether there are any historical roots to the way East Asians behave or believe today and how those roots might affect their contemporary foreign relations.

No matter how one answers that question, there are clearly important elements of the past that directly affect China's behavior today. It is clear that the PRC's main concerns—domestic, international, and regarding its borders—are transdynastic, and almost all of them date from the Qing dynasty in the nineteenth century or even before. China's residual border concerns—Taiwan, Tibet, Xinjiang—are all old, not new. Its maritime claims date from the twentieth century and before; the PRC did not first make these claims. Thus, although it may be possible to debate the nature and character of the ruling CCP, what is inarguable is that the main interests of the CCP were inherited from previous Chinese regimes.

Perhaps most likely, contemporary China may be partially like other countries and partially a function of its own past.[16]

After all, few countries have survived over millennia as recognizably the same country as have those in East Asia. Few single-party regimes can call upon the historical and cultural resources that the CCP can. Few countries are so massive and so centrally located in their regions. Directly researching what has changed from that long history and what China is like today would perhaps be a more useful starting point for explaining and predicting Chinese behavior and relations with the United States, rather than the generalizations many scholars make based on European historical experience.

As we have seen, one enduring challenge faced by historical China still stands out for today's China, constraining both its domestic and international policies: It is the pursuit of legitimacy. The Chinese Communist Party, since it has not won power by conventionally defined free election, needs to constantly establish and revive its legitimacy. That is a key difference from the Western democratic countries, whose administrations are endowed with legitimacy after each election. For instance, on multiple occasions Xi Jinping has emphasized that "Our people have an ardent love for life. They wish to have better education, more stable jobs, more income, greater social security, better medical and health care, improved housing conditions and a better environment. They want their children to have sound growth, have good jobs and lead a more enjoyable life. To meet their desire for a happy life is our mission."[17]

However, abstract comparative terms such as "better" and "improved" used in these statements create traps for the CCP. Such promises leave it with little room for error and launched it on a never-ending journey to prove that the nation under its rule is better than before. If it is not, then the party's legitimacy will be questioned.

The pursuit of legitimacy generates a constant process of defining and redefining legitimacy. In earlier decades, legitimacy was sought from economic achievement, and when that is done (or when it cannot be sustained in a pandemic era), legitimacy must be sustained in another way. As a result, aims such as the successful containment of Covid-19 or unification with Taiwan are declared not as a result of the CCP's belief in its rising power but as part of its effort to seek legitimacy with the domestic audience in mind. In other words, regime stability and internal challenges will continue to be the CCP's priority. As long as this focus on domestic legitimacy remains, contemporary China will resemble more a historical than a Westphalian one, and the lessons from historical East Asia matter more than Eurocentric theories in interpreting China.

A related question is how the past affects the present. Answering this question requires two steps in sequence. The first is to ask whether there is anything unique or distinctive about East Asia. The concept of East Asia itself is heteronomous in its origin. As Nianshen Song points out,

> Why are Europe and Asia divided into two "continents" while clearly belonging to the same continental plate? The Ural Mountains, the Caucasus Mountains, the Black Sea, and the Turkish Straits may constitute the decomposition of the Eurasian landscape. However, they do not separate the continent to the extent that the Himalayas do. They did not become a barrier to exchanges between the East and the West, either. . . . Asia is not a natural geographic unit, but a man-made cognitive unit. It is its neighbor, Europe, that creates the concept of Asia.[18]

Naoki Sakai summarizes,

> The word Asia was coined by the Europeans in order to distin-
> guish Europe from its eastern others . . . a term in the service of
> the constitution of Europe's self-representation as well as its
> distinction. . . . As the putative unity of Europe is inherently
> unstable and constantly changing, Asia has been defined and
> redefined according to contingent historical situations in
> which relationships between Europe and its others have under-
> gone vicissitudes.[19]

To see East Asia from its own historical tradition instead of as
an antithesis of Europe, we emphasize that East Asia changed
and evolved over the centuries as much as or more than any other
region of the world. There is no endless, stagnant "Chinese
dynastic cycle." Millward critiques arguments of continuity,
writing that, "the model of the Traditional Chinese World Order
(a term coined by John King Fairbank) . . . inaccurately, but
influentially, assumed an unchanging, continuous China-centered
international order and uniform Chinese diversity regime that
functioned from antiquity through the nineteenth century."[20] As
this book has shown, far from being an unchanging past, East
Asian history was vibrant, creative, and contingent. East Asia
grew, changed, evolved, and innovated as much or more than any
other region on the planet, and scholarship on state formation
should reflect that historical reality.

Yet avoiding the extreme of an unchanging China does not
mean that there is no continuity or that there is no pattern that
extends across time and space. Our task is to be sensitive to continuity as well as difference. And, as this book shows, countries
used remarkably consistent means to interact with each other
across more than a thousand years—and those shared understandings are key to explaining the longevity of some of the
participants in the system and key to explaining how they were

able to negotiate relations with each other. These understandings changed and evolved over time as well, even though there is a clear philosophical and cultural thread that ties them together. To that end, our argument is complementary with that of Victor Lieberman, who argues that Chinese administrative cycles, although roughly corresponding to integration and disintegration, are not cyclical, but linear: "each reintegrated state is stronger than its predecessor."[21]

The second step to take in examining whether the past affects the present is to ask: Have East Asian countries, peoples, and leaders completely internalized and been socialized into Western, Westphalian ideas? While a reasonable question, the Westphalian sovereign state, as a "universal" system, has existed for too short a time. We believe that the continuity of history, rather than its disruption, exert more influence on the processes of modernization and globalization and on the formation of national identities, and have more bearing on how East Asian leaders and people view and interact with each other. Rosemary Foot and Evelyn Goh characterize East Asia in the twenty-first century as "a hybrid of 'indigenous,' 'Western,' and 'global' norms, institutions, and practices fill the economic and security arenas."[22] How and to what extent the enduring conceptions of international order from both East Asia and Westphalia interact will be an important area for future research.[23] On this note, Lucian W. Pye's explicit observation in 1990 can still be instructive:

> The starting point for understanding the problem is to recognize that China is not just another nation-state in the family of nations. China is a civilization pretending to be a state. The story of modern China could be described as the effort by both Chinese and foreigners to squeeze a civilization into the arbitrary,

constraining framework of the modern state, an institutional invention that came out of the fragmentation of the West's own civilization.[24]

A second, and larger, background question is how to liberate our understanding of East Asia from the constraints of power-based theories and to get us out of that box of power-based theories in understanding East Asia. Excessive focus on measuring and quantifying power risk asking the wrong question when debating East Asia. As we have seen, scholars, even when not explicitly advocating for the power transition theory, have inadvertently operated within its paradigm. This inadvertently leads them to contemplate within the confines of this framework rather than commencing and concluding their analysis from East Asia's unique dynamics. If power transition does not lead to conflict or cooperation in the region but other factors do, then whether power transition happens in the region or not is irrelevant.

It is prohibitively difficult to make systematic and comparable measures to quantify power over more than two millennia, particularly in regions as vast, diverse, and complex as East Asia. For example, Korean historian Bak Yongun warns that any measure of the Koryo dynasty's population should "not be taken seriously," because surviving Koryo sources provide almost not insight into the demography of that era.[25] Ge Jianxiong, the leading authority on historical geography in China and the chief editor of the extensive six-volume *China Population History* spanning more than four thousand pages, explicitly states that "objectively, there are huge gaps in time and space in the historical sources, and not all periods of history or all regions can be found with sufficient primary sources, not even indirect, minimal historical sources. There is a lack of credible data on basic elements such as the production of agricultural products, the level of taxation, the size of the population. . . . How to convert the very rough records in historical materials into reliable data that can be accepted by Chinese and foreign scholars, and how to improve the accuracy of these data to an applicable unit of analysis . . . are all urgent issues that need to be solved."[26]

Moreover, the concept and measurement of power itself lacks broad acceptance and validity among scholars, even for measuring power in contemporary era. As Michael Beckley pointed out, even contemporary standard measurements of power such as GDP, military spending, or other index that incorporates urban population, iron and steel production, and energy consumption are logically unsound and empirically unreliable, severely mischaracterizing the balance of power in numerous cases in modern history. Measuring power by evaluating outcomes is not very useful, either, since even then researchers will know only the distribution of power regarding that particular event.[27] Given this, we welcome more efforts from scholars to reevaluate the reliance on power-based theories and explore more contextually relevant and appropriate theoretical frameworks that align with the region's unique historical dynamics.

Appendix

JOURNAL RANKINGS AND
JOURNAL ARTICLES ON
POWER TRANSITION

I n chapter 2, we argue that power transition literature suffers from a blind spot in its choice of empirical cases to test based on examination of fifty-three journal articles published in "top-tier journals." This appendix documents the details of the process of selecting these fifty-three articles.

The specific criteria we used to determine whether a journal is considered as "top-tier" is whether it has more than a thousand total citations in 2016, according to the InCites Journal Citation Report accessed through Web of Science. The standard of more than a thousand total citations might seem arbitrary, but we believe it suffices to cover a wide range of journals. We also cross-referenced the rankings of the journals with other indicators, such as journal impact factor, impact without journal self-citations, and five-year impact factor.

To get a list of articles on power transition, we used "power transition" as key words to search in ProQuest with "peer-reviewed journal" as an additional condition in October 2017. We then filtered the results by selecting articles that were published in the top-tier journals based on the criteria mentioned above. In addition, we included the nineteen results from the journal *International Interactions*. Although this journal did not have more than a thousand citations in 2016, it has published substantial contributions over the years on power transition by key power transition theorists such as Lemke, Tammen, and Kugler, thus making it worthwhile for us to examine.

In table A.1, we list the top-tier journals in the field of political science and international relations based on the Web of Science InCites Journal Citation Report. In table A.2, we list the articles on power transition that we examined.

TABLE A.1 JOURNALS BY RANK

Rank	Journal title	Total citations	Journal impact factor	Impact factor without journal self-citations	5-year impact factor
1	*American Political Science Review*	11,746	3.316	3.082	6.658
2	*American Journal of Political Science*	9,572	5.044	4.793	5.436
3	*Journal of Politics*	6,231	1.938	1.844	3.295
4	*Marine Policy*	5,436	2.235	1.654	2.532
5	*International Organization*	5,322	3.406	3.172	4.301
6	*Public Opinion Quarterly*	4,893	1.386	1.273	2.816
7	*Journal of Conflict Resolution*	3,900	2.947	2.876	3.258
8	*Annals of the American Academy of Political and Social Science*	3,827	2.118	2.018	2.293
9	*Comparative Political Studies*	3,676	2.481	2.382	3.291
10	*European Journal of Political Research*	3,659	2.891	2.674	3.458

(continued)

TABLE A.1 JOURNALS BY RANK (CONTINUED)

Rank	Journal title	Total citations	Journal impact factor	Impact factor without journal self-citations	5-year impact factor
11	*Public Choice*	3,501	0.788	0.640	1.214
12	*World Politics*	3,348	4.025	3.875	4.300
13	*Journal of Peace Research*	3,331	2.284	2.017	3.176
14	*Social Science Quarterly*	3,138	0.849	0.808	1.253
15	*International Studies Quarterly*	2,987	1.925	1.677	2.512
16	*British Journal of Political Science*	2,962	3.316	3.224	3.276
17	*Public Administration*	2,877	2.959	2.276	2.847
18	*Journal of European Public Policy*	2,822	2.982	2.644	2.732
19	*Political Analysis*	2,766	3.361	3.180	6.103
20	*Political Psychology*	2,616	2.760	2.587	2.766
21	*Foreign Affairs*	2,501	2.536	2.536	2.566

22	Annual Review of Political Science	2,483	2.804	2.667	4.777
23	Political Geography	2,441	2.410	1.860	3.318
24	Political Research Quarterly	2,406	1.053	1.008	1.816
25	JCMS–Journal of Common Market Studies	2,331	2.243	1.810	2.313
26	Electoral Studies	2,298	1.379	1.062	2.016
26	International Security	2,298	3.390	2.220	4.320
28	Journal of Democracy	2,236	1.631	1.359	1.931
29	West European Politics	2,187	2.512	1.856	2.663
30	Political Studies	2,175	1.200	1.164	1.900
31	World Economy	1,838	0.933	0.865	1.277
32	Philosophy & Public Affairs	1,782	2.182	1.864	3.446
33	Political Behavior	1,733	2.138	1.925	2.506
34	Party Politics	1,731	1.846	1.718	2.418
35	International Affairs	1,685	1.935	1.315	1.932

(continued)

TABLE A.1 JOURNALS BY RANK (CONTINUED)

Rank	Journal title	Total citations	Journal impact factor	Impact factor without journal self-citations	5-year impact factor
36	Political Communication	1,645	2.467	2.383	2.893
37	Environmental Politics	1,642	1.922	1.600	2.373
38	American Journal of International Law	1,612	1.851	1.500	1.449
39	PS–Political Science & Politics	1,559	0.950	0.824	1.012
40	Perspectives on Politics	1,513	3.234	2.727	3.680
41	Review of International Political Economy	1,510	3.452	2.976	2.822
42	Governance–An International Journal of Policy Administration and Institutions	1,508	2.603	2.569	3.326
43	Policy Studies Journal	1,492	2.153	1.814	3.412
44	European Journal of International Relations	1,474	2.277	2.096	2.702
45	Comparative Politics	1,468	1.469	1.449	1.959

46	New Left Review	1,447	1.770	1.770	1.520
47	Review of International Studies	1,265	1.264	1.126	1.135
48	European Journal of International Law	1,252	1.034	0.989	1.461
49	African Affairs	1,185	2.577	2.288	2.649
50	Politics & Society	1,105	1.659	1.561	2.408
51	Security Dialogue	1,069	2.692	2.369	3.155
52	Europe–Asia Studies	1,064	0.731	0.642	1.014
53	Legislative Studies Quarterly	1,058	1.114	1.000	1.776
54	Political Theory	1,046	0.746	0.678	0.935
55	European Journal of Political Economy	1,014	1.098	0.883	1.466
56	European Union Politics	1,012	2.052	1.672	2.627
57	Journal of Political Philosophy	1,000	2.182	2.114	1.912

Source: Web of Science InCites Journal Citation Report, October 16, 2017. Copyright © 2017 Clarivate Analytics.

TABLE A.2 JOURNAL ARTICLES ON POWER TRANSITION

Reference

1 Kugler, Jacek, and Frank C. Zagare. "The Long-term Stability of Deterrence." *International Interactions* 15, no. 3–4 (1990): 255–78.

2 Kugler, Jacek. "The War Phenomenon: A Working Distinction." *International Interactions* 16, no. 3 (1990): 201–13.

3 Geller, Daniel S. "Capability Concentration, Power Transition, and War." *International Interactions* 17, no. 3 (1990): 269–84.

4 Lemke, Douglas, and William Reed. "Regime Types and Status Quo Evaluations: Power Transition Theory and the Democratic Peace." *International Interactions* 22, no. 2 (1996): 143–64.

5 Rapkin, David, and William Thompson. "Power Transition, Challenge and the (Re)Emergence of China." *International Interactions* 29, no. 4 (2003): 315–42.

6 Lemke, Douglas, and Ronald L. Tammen. "Power Transition Theory and the Rise of China." *International Interactions* 29, no. 4 (2003): 269–71.

7 Efird, Brian, Jacek Kugler, and Gaspare M. Genna. "From War to Integration: Generalizing Power Transition Theory." *International Interactions* 29, no. 4 (2003): 293–313.

8 Kadera, Kelly M., and Gerald L. Sorokin. "Measuring National Power." *International Interactions* 30, no. 3 (2004): 211–30.

9 Quinn, David, Jonathan Wilkenfeld, Kathleen Smarick, and Victor Asal. "Power Play: Mediation in Symmetric and Asymmetric International Crises." *International Interactions* 32, no. 4 (2006): 441–70.

10 Hebron, Lui, Patrick James, and Michael Rudy. "Testing Dynamic Theories of Conflict: Power Cycles, Power Transitions, Foreign Policy Crises and Militarized Interstate Disputes." *International Interactions* 33, no. 1 (2007): 1–29.

11 Filson, Darren, and Suzanne Werner. "The Dynamics of Bargaining and War." *International Interactions* 33, no. 1 (2007): 31–50.

Reference

12 Danilovic, Vesna, and Joe Clare. "Global Power Transitions and Regional Interests." *International Interactions* 33, no. 3 (2007): 289–304.

13 Palmer, Glenn, and T. C. Morgan. "Power Transition, the Two-Good Theory, and Neorealism: A Comparison with Comments on Recent US Foreign Policy." *International Interactions* 33, no. 3 (2007): 329–46.

14 Benson, Michelle. "Status Quo Preferences and Disputes Short of War." *International Interactions* 33, no. 3 (2007): 271–88.

15 Zagare, Frank C. "Toward a Unified Theory of Interstate Conflict." *International Interactions* 33, no. 3 (2007): 305–27.

16 Toft, Monica Duffy. "Population Shifts and Civil War: A Test of Power Transition Theory." *International Interactions* 33, no. 3 (2007): 243–69.

17 Benson, Michelle. "Extending the Bounds of Power Transition Theory." *International Interactions* 33, no. 3 (2007): 211–15.

18 Weede, Erich. "The Capitalist Peace and the Rise of China: Establishing Global Harmony by Economic Interdependence." *International Interactions* 36, no. 2 (2010): 206–13.

19 Peterson, Timothy M., and Thomas Lassi. "Centers of Gravity: Regional Powers, Democracy, and Trade." *International Interactions* 43, no. 2 (2017): 326–48.

20 Houweling, Henk, and Jan G. Siccama. "Power Transitions as a Cause of War." *Journal of Conflict Resolution* 32, no. 1 (1988): 87–102.

21 Kim, Woosang. "Power, Alliance, and Major Wars, 1816–1975." *Journal of Conflict Resolution* 33, no. 2 (1989): 255–73.

22 Houweling, Henk, and Jan G. Siccama. "Power Transitions and Critical Points as Predictors of Great Power War Toward a Synthesis." *Journal of Conflict Resolution* 35, no. 4 (1991): 642–58.

(continued)

TABLE A.2 JOURNAL ARTICLES ON POWER TRANSITION (*CONTINUED*)

Reference

23 Huth, Paul, D. S. Bennett, and Christopher Gelpi. "System Uncertainty, Risk Propensity, and International Conflict Among the Great Powers." *Journal of Conflict Resolution* 36, no. 3 (1992): 478–517.

24 de Soysa, Indra, John R. Oneal, and Yong-Hee Park. "Testing Power-Transition Theory Using Alternative Measures of National Capabilities." *Journal of Conflict Resolution* 41, no. 4 (1997): 509–28.

25 Oneal, John R., Indra de Soysa, and Yong-Hee Park. "But Power and Wealth are Satisfying: A Reply to Lemke and Reed." *Journal of Conflict Resolution* 42, no. 4 (1998): 517–20.

26 Lemke, Douglas, and William Reed. "Power Is Not Satisfaction: A Comment on De Soysa, Oneal, and Park." *Journal of Conflict Resolution* 42, no. 4 (1998): 511–16.

27 DiCicco, Jonathan M., and Jack S. Levy. "Power Shifts and Problem Shifts: The Evolution of the Power Transition Research Program." *Journal of Conflict Resolution* 43, no. 6 (1999): 675–704.

28 Kim, Woosang. "Power Parity, Alliance, Dissatisfaction, and Wars in East Asia, 1860–1993." *Journal of Conflict Resolution* 46, no. 5 (2002): 654–71.

29 Moul, William. "Power Parity, Preponderance, and War Between Great Powers, 1816–1989." *Journal of Conflict Resolution* 47, no. 4 (2003): 468–89.

30 ——, "Erratum: 'Power Parity, Preponderance, and War Between Great Powers, 1816–1989.'" *Journal of Conflict Resolution* 47, no. 5 (2003): 1–706.

31 Sanjian, Gregory S. "Arms Transfers, Military Balances, and Interstate Relations: Modeling Power Balance Versus Power Transition Linkages." *Journal of Conflict Resolution* 47, no. 6 (2003): 711–27.

32 Bussmann, Margit, and John R. Oneal. "Do Hegemons Distribute Private Goods? A Test of Power-Transition Theory." *Journal of Conflict Resolution* 51, no. 1 (2007): 88–111.

Reference

33 Clark, Ian. "China and the United States: A Succession of Hegemonies?" *International Affairs* 87, no. 1 (2011): 13–28.

34 Taylor, Brendan. "Asia's Century and the Problem of Japan's Centrality." *International Affairs* 87, no. 4 (2011): 871–85.

35 Narlikar, Amrita. "Negotiating the Rise of New Powers." *International Affairs* 89, no. 3 (2013): 561–76.

36 Inoguchi, Takashi. "A Call for a New Japanese Foreign Policy: The Dilemmas of a Stakeholder State." *International Affairs* 90, no. 4 (2014): 943–58.

37 Yuan, Jingdong. "Averting US–China Conflict in the Asia-Pacific." *International Affairs* 92, no. 4: 977–86.

38 Womack, Brantly. "Asymmetric Parity: US–China Relations in a Multinodal World." *International Affairs* 92, no. 6: 1463–80.

39 Bueno De Mesquita, Bruce. "Pride of Place: The Origins of German Hegemony." *World Politics* 43, no. 1 (1990): 28–52.

40 Kim, Woosang. "Power Transitions and Great Power War from Westphalia to Waterloo." *World Politics* 45, no. 1 (1992): 153–72.

41 Ikenberry, G. J., Michael Mastanduno, and William C. Wohlforth. "Introduction: Unipolarity, State Behavior, and Systemic Consequences." *World Politics* 61, no. 1 (2009): 1–27.

42 Wohlforth, William C. "Unipolarity, Status Competition, and Great Power War." *World Politics* 61, no. 1 (2009): 28–57.

43 Nexon, Daniel H. "The Balance of Power in the Balance." World Politics 61, no. 2 (2009): 330–59.

44 Layne, Christopher. "The Waning of US Hegemony—Myth or Reality?" *International Security* 34, no. 1 (2009): 147–72.

45 MacDonald, Paul K., and Joseph M. Parent. "Graceful Decline? The Surprising Success of Great Power Retrenchment." *International Security* 35, no. 4 (2011): 7–44.

46 Kim, Woosang. "Alliance Transitions and Great Power War." *American Journal of Political Science* 35, no. 4 (1991): 833–50.

(continued)

TABLE A.2 JOURNAL ARTICLES ON POWER TRANSITION (*CONTINUED*)

Reference
47 Lemke, Douglas. "Power Politics and Wars Without States." *American Journal of Political Science* 52, no. 4 (2008): 774–86.
48 Lemke, Douglas, and Suzanne Werner. "Power Parity, Commitment to Change, and War." *International Studies Quarterly* 40, no. 2 (1996): 235–60.
49 Lemke, Douglas. "The Continuation of History: Power Transition Theory and the End of the Cold War." *Journal of Peace Research* 34, no. 1 (1997): 23–26.
50 Goldsmith, Benjamin E., and Baogang He. "Letting Go Without a Fight: Decolonization, Democracy and War, 1900–94." *Journal of Peace Research* 45, no. 5 (2008): 587–611.
51 Reed, William. "Information, Power, and War." *American Political Science Review* 97, no. 4 (2003): 633–41.
52 Sohn, Injoo. "After Renaissance: China's Multilateral Offensive in the Developing World." *European Journal of International Relations* 18, no. 1 (2012): 77–101.
53 Tingley, Dustin. "Rising Power on the Mind." *International Organization* 71, no. S1 (2017): S165–88.

NOTES

1. WHAT ARE THE LESSONS OF HISTORY?

1. Susan L. Shirk, *China: Fragile Superpower* (New York: Oxford University Press, 2007), 4.

2. Richard Ned Lebow and Benjamin Valentino, "Lost in Transition: A Critical Analysis of Power Transition Theory," *International Relations* 23, no. 3 (2009): 389.

3. Jacek Kugler and Douglas Lemke, eds., *Parity and War: Evaluations and Extensions of The War Ledger* (Ann Arbor: University of Michigan Press, 1996), 41; Steve Chan, *China, the U.S. and Power Transition Theory: A Critique* (London: Routledge, 2008), 24; Robert Ross and Zhu Feng, eds., *China's Ascent: Power, Security and the Future of International Politics* (Ithaca, NY: Cornell University Press, 2008), 32; G. John Ikenberry, "The Rise of China, Power Transitions, and Western Order," in *The Rise of China*, ed. Robert Ross (Ithaca, NY: Cornell University Press, 2008), 3, 106.

4. Richard Betts, "Wealth, Power, and Instability: East Asia and the United States After the Cold War," *International Security* 18, no. 3 (Winter 1993–1994): 69.

5. Steve Chan, *Thucydides's Trap? Historical Interpretation, Logic of Inquiry, and the Future of Sino-American Relations* (Ann Arbor: University of Michigan Press, 2020); Ian Chong and Todd Hall, "The Lessons of 1914 for East Asia Today: Missing the Trees for the Forest," *International Security* 39, no. 1 (Summer 2014): 7–43.

6. David C. Kang, *East Asia Before the West: Five Centuries of Trade and Tribute* (New York: Columbia University Press, 2010); Jiyoung Lee, *China's Hegemony: Four Hundred Years of East Asian Domination* (New York: Columbia University Press, 2016); Seo-Hyun Park, *Sovereignty and Status in East Asian International Relations* (New York: Cambridge University Press, 2017); and Feng Zhang, *Chinese Hegemony: Grand Strategy and International Institutions in East Asian History* (Stanford, CA: Stanford University Press, 2015).

7. A. F. K. Organski and Jacek Kugler, *The War Ledger* (Chicago: University of Chicago Press, 1980).

8. David C. Kang and Alex Yu-Ting Lin, "U.S. Bias in the Study of Asian Security: Using Europe to Study Asia," *Journal of Global Security Studies* 4, no. 3 (July 2019): 393.

9. J. C. Sharman, *Empires of the Weak: The Real Story of European Expansion and the Creation of the New World Order* (Princeton, NJ: Princeton University Press, 2019), 6.

10. Sixiang Wang, *Boundless Winds of Empire: Rhetoric and Ritual in Early Chosŏn Diplomacy with Ming China* (New York: Columbia University Press, 2023), 6–7.

11. Jean-Laurent Rosenthal and R. Bin Wong, *Before and Beyond Divergence: The Politics of Economic Change in China and Europe* (Cambridge, MA: Harvard University Press), 12–17.

12. Kenneth Swope, "Crouching Tigers, Secret Weapons: Military Technology Employed During the Sino-Japanese-Korean War, 1592–1598," *Journal of Military History* 69, no. 1 (2005): 11.

13. Kenneth Swope, "Perspectives on the Imjin War," *Journal of Korean Studies* 12, no. 1 (Fall 2007): 154.

14. We use anachronistic terms such as "Vietnam" and "China" for ease of use and continuity.

2. THE COMMON CONJECTURE IN WAR AND PEACE

1. Thucydides, *History of the Peloponnesian War*, translated by Richard Crawley (Dover Edition, 2017), 11, 269.

2. A. F. K. Organski and Jack Kugler, *The War Ledger* (Chicago: University of Chicago Press, 1980), 19–20.

3. Brian Efird, Jacek Kugler, and Gaspare Genna, "From War to Integration: Generalizing Power Transition Theory," *International Interactions* 29, no. 4 (2003): 294.

4. Organski and Kugler, *The War Ledger*, 61.

5. Organski and Kugler, *The War Ledger*, 42–45.

6. Steve Chan, "Exploring Puzzles in Power-Transition Theory: Implications for Sino-American Relations," *Security Studies* 13, no. 3 (2004): 103.

7. Jonathan M. DiCicco and Jack S. Levy, "Power Shifts and Problem Shifts: The Evolution of the Power Transition Research Program," *Journal of Conflict Resolution* 43, no. 6 (1999): 682.

8. Ronald L. Tammen et al., *Power Transitions: Strategies for the 21st Century* (New York: Chatham House, 2000), 31.

9. Robert Gilpin, *War and Change in World Politics* (New York: Cambridge University Press, 1981), 191–93.

10. DiCicco and Levy, "Power Shifts and Problem Shifts," 700.

11. Douglas Lemke and Suzanne Werner, "Power Parity, Commitment to Change, and War," *International Studies Quarterly* 40, no. 2 (1996): 235–60.

12. Woosang Kim, "Power, Alliance, and Major Wars, 1816–1975," *Journal of Conflict Resolution* 33, no. 2 (1989): 255–273; Woosang Kim and James Morrow, "When Do Power Shifts Lead to War?," *American Journal of Political Science* 36, no. 4 (1992): 896–922.

13. Bruce Bueno de Mesquita, "Pride of Place: The Origins of German Hegemony," *World Politics* 43, no. 1 (1990): 28–52; Daniel S. Geller, "Capability Concentration, Power Transition, and War," *International Interactions* 17, no. 3 (1992): 269–84; Suzanne Werner and Jacek Kugler, "Power Transitions and Military Buildups: Resolving the Relationship Between Arms Buildups and War," in *Parity and War: Evaluations and Extensions of The War Ledger*, ed. Jacek Kugler and Douglas Lemke (Ann Arbor: University of Michigan Press, 1996), 187–207; Woosang Kim, "Alliance Transitions and Great Power War," *American Journal of Political Science* 35, no. 4 (1991): 833–50.

14. Organski and Kugler, *The War Ledger*, 43–45.

15. Gilpin, *War and Change in World Politics*, 200.

16. Richard Ned Lebow and Benjamin Valentino, "Lost in Transition: A Critical Analysis of Power Transition Theory," *International Relations* 23, no. 3 (2009): 393.

17. See the appendix for the criteria and process used for selecting the journals.

18. The two exceptions, which both apply power transition theory to local hierarchies in South America, are Lemke and Werner, "Power Parity, Commitment to Change, and War," and Douglas Lemke, "Power Politics and Wars Without States," *American Journal of Political Science* 52, no. 4 (2008): 774–86.

19. William C. Wohlforth, "Unipolarity, Status Competition, and Great Power War," *World Politics* 61, no. 1 (2009): 42.

20. For instance, COW defines major powers as Austria–Hungary (1816–1918), Prussia/Germany (1816–1918; 1925–1945; 1991–2016), Russia/Soviet Union (1816–1917; 1922–2016), the United States (1898–2016), the United Kingdom (1816–2016), France (1816–1940; 1945–2016), Italy (1860–1943), Japan (1895–1945; 1991–2016), and China (1950–2016).

21. De Mesquita, "Pride of Place," 28–52; Kim, "Alliance Transitions and Great Power War," 840; Douglas Lemke and William Reed, "Regime Types and Status Quo Evaluations: Power Transition Theory and the Democratic Peace," *International Interactions* 22, no. 2 (1996): 158; William Moul, "Power Parity, Preponderance, and War Between Great Powers, 1816–1989," *Journal of Conflict Resolution* 47, no. 4 (2003): 478.

22. Woosang Kim, "Power Transitions and Great Power War from Westphalia to Waterloo," *World Politics* 45, no. 1 (1992): 153–72.

23. Woosang Kim, "Power Parity, Alliance, Dissatisfaction, and Wars in East Asia, 1860–1993," *Journal of Conflict Resolution* 46, no. 5 (2002): 654–71.

24. Lemke and Werner, "Power Parity, Commitment to Change, and War," 243, 256.

25. Lemke, "Power Politics and Wars Without States," 781.

26. Lebow and Valentino, "Lost in Transition," 401.

27. Barbara Geddes, "How the Cases You Choose Affect the Answers You Get: Selection Bias in Comparative Politics," *Political Analysis* 2 (1990): 131–50.

28. Lebow and Valentino, "Lost in Transition," 389.

29. Tammen et al., *Power Transitions*.

30. Aaron Friedberg, "Ripe for Rivalry: Prospects for Peace in a Multipolar Asia," *International Security* 18, no. 3 (Winter 1993–1994): 18.

31. John Mearsheimer, "Better to Be Godzilla Than Bambi," *Foreign Policy*, no. 146 (January–February 2005): 48.

32. Robert Art, "The United States and the Rise of China: Implications for the Long Haul," *Political Science Quarterly* 125, no. 3 (Fall 2010): 263.

33. Ian Chong and Todd Hall, "The Lessons of 1914 for East Asia Today: Missing the Trees for the Forest," *International Security* 39, no. 1 (Summer 2014): 7–43.

34. Steve Chan, *Thucydides's Trap? Historical Interpretation, Logic of Inquiry, and the Future of Sino-American Relations* (Ann Arbor: University of Michigan Press, 2020).

35. Jingdong Yuan, "Averting US–China Conflict in the Asia–Pacific," *International Affairs* 92, no. 4 (2016): 977.

36. Chan, *Thucydides's Trap?*. For Chan's criticism of Allison's interpretation, see chap. 2. For direct quotes, see p. 149, 8, and 190.

37. Yuan-kang Wang, "Roundtable on Steve Chan, *Thucydides Trap?*," ISSF Roundtable XII-2, 2020: 28.

38. Chong and Hall, "The Lessons of 1914 for East Asia Today," 9.

39. Lebow and Valentino, "Lost in Transition," 401.

40. Xinru Ma and David Kang, "Why Vietnam is not Balancing China: Vietnamese Security Priorities and the Dynamics in Sino-Vietnam Relations," *Journal of East Asian Studies* 23, no. 3 (2023): 367.

41. David Kang, "International Relations Theory and East Asian History: An Overview," *Journal of East Asian Studies* 13, no. 2 (2013): 187.

42. Ji-young Lee, "Diplomatic Ritual as a Power Resource: The Politics of Asymmetry in Early Modern Chinese-Korean Relations," *Journal of East Asian Studies* 13, no. 2 (2013): 310.

43. James D. Fearon, "Rationalist Explanations for War," *International Organization* 49, no. 3 (1995): 405–6.

44. Kenneth A. Schultz and Henk E. Goemans, "Aims, Claims, and the Bargaining Model of War," *International Theory* 11, no. 3 (2019): 345. The quote cites Kalevi J. Holsti, *Peace and War: Armed Conflicts and International Order, 1648–1989* (New York: Cambridge University Press, 1991), 14; Raymond Aron, *Peace and War* (London: Weidenfeld & Nicolson, 1966), 8; John J. Mearsheimer, *The Tragedy of Great Power Politics* (New York: W. W. Norton, 2001), 2.

45. Robert Jervis, "T.V. Paul. 'Restraining Great Powers: Soft Balancing from Empires to the Global Era.'" ISSF Roundtable, June 2019, https://issforum.org/ISSF/PDF/ISSF-Roundtable-10-29.pdf.

46. David Kang, "International Relations Theory and East Asian History," 197.

47. Schultz and Goemans, "Aims, Claims, and the Bargaining Model of War," 344.

48. David Kang, "International Relations Theory and East Asian History," 184.

49. Sixiang Wang, *Boundless Winds of Empire: Rhetoric and Ritual in Early Chosŏn Diplomacy with Ming China* (New York: Columbia University Press, 2023), 7.

50. James Fearon and Alexander Wendt, "Rationalism v. Constructivism: A Skeptical View," in *Handbook of International Relations Theory*, ed. Walter Carlsnaes, Thomas Risse, and Beth A. Simmons (London: Sage Publications, 2002), 55, 59.

51. Fearon, "Rationalist Explanations for War," 379–414.

52. Robert Powell, "Bargaining Theory and International Conflict," *American Review of Political Science* 5, no. 1 (2002): 17–18.

53. Powell, "Bargaining Theory and International Conflict," 17–18.

54. Quoted in Powell, "Bargaining Theory and International Conflict," 21.

55. Stacie Goddard, *Indivisible Territory and the Politics of Legitimacy: Jerusalem and Northern Ireland* (Cambridge: Cambridge University Press, 2010), 24.

56. Beth A. Simmons, Frank Dobbin and Geoffrey Garrett, "Introduction: The International Diffusion of Liberalism," *International Organization* 60, no. 4 (2006): 799.

57. Emanuel Adler and Vincent Pouliot, "International Practices," *International Theory* 3, no. 1 (February 2011): 7.

58. Bridget Coggins, *Power Politics and State Formation in the Twentieth Century: The Dynamics of Recognition* (Cambridge: Cambridge University Press, 2014), 3.

59. Ji-Young Lee, *China's Hegemony: Four Hundred Years of East Asian Domination* (New York: Columbia University Press, 2016); Feng Zhang, *Chinese Hegemony: Grand Strategy and International Institutions in East Asian History* (Stanford, CA: Stanford University Press, 2015);

Seo-Hyun Park, *Sovereignty and Status in East Asian International Relations* (Cambridge: Cambridge University Press, 2017).
60. Lee, *China's Hegemony*, 64–65.

3. THE LESSONS OF EAST ASIAN HISTORY, 500-1900

1. Joseph MacKay, "The Nomadic Other: Ontological Security and the Inner Asian Steppe in Historical East Asian International Politics," *Review of International Studies* 42, no. 3 (July 2016): 474.
2. Yuri Pines, *The Everlasting Empire: The Political Culture of Ancient China and Its Imperial Legacy* (Princeton, NJ: Princeton University Press, 2012), 2–3.
3. Walter Scheidel, "Roman Population Size: The Logic of the Debate," working paper, Princeton/Stanford Working Papers in Classics Paper no. 070706, July 2007, 8.
4. Chin-Hao Huang and David C. Kang, "State Formation in Korea and Japan, 400–800 CE: Emulation and Learning, Not Bellicist Competition," *International Organization* 76, no. 1 (2022): 1–31.
5. David Kang, "International Order in Historical East Asia: Tribute and Hierarchy beyond Sinocentrism and Eurocentrism." *International Organization* 74, no. 1 (2020): 78.
6. Mark Dincecco and Yuhua Wang, "Violent Conflict and Political Development over the Long Run: China versus Europe." *Annual Review of Political Science* 21 (2018): 341–58.
7. David Kang, "International Order in Historical East Asia," 67–68. See also David Kang and 夺赴音, "Response: Theory and Empirics in the Study of Historical East Asian International Relations," *Harvard Journal of Asiatic Studies* 77, no. 1 (2017): 113.
8. Keith Taylor, *A History of the Vietnamese* (Cambridge: Cambridge University Press, 2013), 183.
9. Dincecco and Wang, "Violence Conflict and Political Development Over the Long Run," 342.
10. Chiu Yu Ko, Mark Koyama, and Tuan-Hwee Sng, "Unified China and Divided Europe," *International Economic Review* 59, no. 1 (February 2018): 289.

11. David C. Wright, "The Northern Frontier," in *A Military History of China*, ed. David A. Graf and Robin Higham (Lexington: University Press of Kentucky, 2012), 57.

12. David C. Kang, *East Asia Before the West: Five Centuries of Trade and Tribute* (New York: Columbia University Press, 2010), 10.

13. Kang, *East Asia Before the West*, chap. 5.

14. Fu Zhongxia 傅仲侠, ed., 中国历代战争年表 (Chronology of Wars in China Through Successive Dynasties), 2 vols. (Beijing: Jiefangjun chubanshe [People's Liberation Army Press], 2003).

15. Institute of Military History (ROK), 한민족 전쟁통사 (Chronology of Wars of the Korean People) (Seoul: IMH, 1996); Thanh Giản Phan, ed., 欽定越史通鑑綱目 (The Imperially Ordered Annotated Text Completely Reflecting the History of Viet) (Taipei: National Library, 1969); David C. Kang, Ronan Tse-min Fu, and Meredith Shaw, "Measuring War in Early Modern East Asia: Introducing Chinese and Korean Language Sources," *International Studies Quarterly* 60, no. 4 (December 2016): 766–77; David C. Kang, Dat Nguyen, Meredith Shaw, and Ronan Tse-min Fu, "War, Rebellion, and Intervention Under Hierarchy: Vietnam–China Relations, 1365–1841," *Journal of Conflict Resolution* 63, no. 4 (2019): 839–1105.

16. Bruce Batten, *To the Ends of Japan: Premodern Frontiers, Boundaries, and Interactions* (Honolulu: University of Hawai'i Press, 2003), 30, 236.

17. Batten, *To the Ends of Japan*, 147.

18. John Mearsheimer, *The Tragedy of Great Power Politics* (New York: W. W. Norton, 2001), 237–38.

19. Abbey Steele, Christopher Paik, and Seiki Tanaka, "Constraining the Samurai: Rebellion and Taxation in Early Modern Japan," *International Studies Quarterly* 61, no. 2 (June 2017): 352.

20. Liam Kelley, "Convergence and Conflict: Dai Viet in the Sinic Order," in *Sacred Mandates: Asian International Relations Since Chinggis Khan*, ed. Timothy Brook, Michael van Walt van Praag, and Miek Boltjes (Chicago: University of Chicago Press, 2018), 83.

21. James Anderson, "Distinguishing Between China and Vietnam: Three Relational Equilibriums in Sino-Vietnamese Relations," *Journal of East Asian Studies* 13, no. 2 (2013): 271.

4. THE MONGOL CONQUEST OF THE THIRTEENTH CENTURY AND THE SONG-YUAN TRANSITION

The epigraph has very different meanings for Chinese in the Central Plain than for Koreans. The Koreans, who did not experience enduring incursions from steppe equestrians, intend the term as a pleasant reference to harvest seasons with beautiful weather. However, for settled peoples in the Central Plain, the horses of nomadic peoples are well fed by autumn, and nomadic warriors may pour into the Central Plain to loot supplies for the winter, thus rendering the term a harbinger of coming dangers of border conflicts. For more details, see Victor Mair, "Sky High Horse Fat," *Language Log,* May 2, 2012, https://languagelog.ldc.upenn.edu/nll/?p=3931.

1. Thomas Allsen, *Culture and Conquest in Mongol Eurasia* (Cambridge: Cambridge University Press, 2001), 4.

2. Marie Favereau, *The Horde: How the Mongols Changed the World* (Cambridge, MA: Harvard University Press, 2021), 6.

3. Yao Guangxiao 姚廣孝 et al., eds., 明太祖實錄 (Veritable Records of the Ming Emperor Taizu) (1418), juan 25.

4. Quoted in Yao Dali 姚大力, 追寻"我们"的根源:中国历史上的民族与国家意识 (Tracing the Roots of "Us:" Ethnic and National Consciousness in Chinese History) (Beijing: 生活读书新知三联书店 [SDX Joint Publishing Company], 2018), 212.

5. Peter St. Onge, "How Paper Money Led to the Mongol Conquest: Money and the Collapse of Song China," *Independent Review* 22, no. 2 (Fall 2017): 225.

6. St. Onge, "How Paper Money Led to the Mongol Conquest," 227.

7. Thanks to Richard von Glahn for these points.

8. Harold M. Tanner, *China: A History* (Indianapolis: Hackett, 2009), 214–15; Harry Miller, *State Versus Gentry in Late Ming Dynasty China* (New York: Palgrave, 2008), 11.

9. Li Tao 李燾, 續資治通鑑長編 (Extended Continuation to the Comprehensive Mirror in Aid of Governance) (Beijing: 中华书局 [Zhonghua Book Company], 1995), 19:436.

10. Quoted in Gao Hongqing, 高红清, 燕云十六州 (The Sixteen Prefectures of Yanyun) (Beijing: 北京燕山出版社有限公司 [Beijing Yanshan Publishing Company], 2018], 132.

11. Jing-shen Tao, "Barbarians or Northerners: Northern Sung Images of the Khitans," in *China Among Equals: The Middle Kingdom and Its Neighbors, 10th-14th Centuries,* ed. Morris Rossabi (Berkeley: University of California Press, 1983), 69.

12. Tao, "Barbarians or Northerners," 70.

13. Peter Lorge, *The Reunification of China: Peace Through War Under the Song Dynasty* (Cambridge: Cambridge University Press, 2015), 7.

14. Li, 續資治通鑑長編, 137:3,285–86.

15. Hongqing Gao, 燕云十六州 (The Sixteen Prefectures of Yanyun) (Beijing: 北京燕山出版社有限公司 [Beijing Yanshan Publishing Company], 2018), 233.

16. Nicolas Tackett, *The Origins of the Chinese Nation: Song China and the Forging of an East Asian World Order* (Cambridge: Cambridge University Press, 2017), 1.

17. Timothy Brook, *The Troubled Empire: China in the Yuan and Ming Dynasties* (Cambridge, MA: Harvard University Press, 2013), 79.

18. Peter Lorge, *War, Politics, and Society in Early Modern China, 900–1795* (London: Routledge, 2005), 18.

19. Devin Fitzgerald and Maura Dykstra, "Shi Jie, On China," *Books and the Early Modern World,* https://chinesecourses.voices.wooster.edu/confucianism/.

20. Gao, 燕云十六州, 285–86.

21. Ge Zhaoguang 葛兆光, "宋代 '中国' 意识的凸显——关于近世民族主义思想的一个远源" (The Prominence of the Consciousness of "China" in the Song Dynasty—A Distant Source of Modern Nationalism), 文哲史 (Journal of Literature, History, and Philosophy) (2004): 5–12.

22. Liu Pujiang 刘浦江, "德运之争与辽金王朝的正统性问题" (Debates on the Cycle of the Five Virtuous Elements and Legitimacy of the Liao and Jurchen Jin Dynasties), 中國社會科學 (Social Sciences in China) 2 (2004): 191–92.

23. Hu Lin, "A Tale of Five Capitals: Contests for Legitimacy Between the Liao and its Rivals," *Journal of Asian History* 44, no. 2 (2010): 117, 122.

24. Quoted in Tackett, *The Origins of the Chinese Nation,* 143.

25. Tackett, *The Origins of the Chinese Nation,* 144.

26. Gari Ledyard, "Yin and Yang in the China–Manchuria–Korea Triangle," in *China Among Equals: The Middle Kingdom and Its Neighbors,*

10th–14th Centuries, ed. Morris Rossabi (Berkeley: University of California Press, 1983), 344.

27. Song and the Jurchen Jin were geographically separated by the Khitan Liao, so negotiations were carried out at sea, hence the name.

28. Ye Longli 叶隆礼, 契丹国志 (Records of the Khitan State), juan 9 (Shanghai: 上海古籍出版社 [Shanghai Ancient Books Publishing Company], 1985), 95.

29. Lorge, *War, Politics, and Society in Early Modern China*, 50.

30. Lorge, *War, Politics, and Society in Early Modern China*, 58.

31. Morris Rossabi, "The Reign of Khubilai Khan," in *The Cambridge History of China*, vol. 6, *Alien Regimes and Border States, 907–1368*, ed. Herbert Franke and Denis Twitchett (Cambridge: Cambridge University Press, 1994), 429.

32. Herbert Franke, "The Chin Dynasty," in Franke and Twitchett, *The Cambridge History of China*, 6:248.

33. Lorge, *War, Politics and Society in Early Modern China*, 73.

34. Charles Peterson, "Old Illusions and New Realities: Sung Foreign Policy, 1217–1234," in Rossabi, *China Among Equals*, 230.

35. Jung-Pang Lo, *China as a Sea Power, 1127–1368: A Preliminary Survey of the Maritime Expansion and Naval Exploits of the Chinese People during the Southern Song and Yuan Periods* (Singapore: National University of Singapore Press, 2012), 186–206.

36. Lo, *China as a Sea Power, 1127–1368*, 183–84, 211.

37. John Man quoted in Carrie Gracie, "Kublai Khan: China's Favourite Barbarian," BBC News, October 9, 2012, https://www.bbc.com/news/magazine-19850234.

38. Sugiyama Masaaki 杉山正明, 忽必烈的挑战: 蒙古帝国与世界历史的大转向 (The Challenge of Kublai: The Mongol Empire and the Great Turn of World History), trans. Junyv Zhou 周俊宇 (Beijing: 社会科学文献出版社 [Social Sciences Academic Press], 2017), 160–63.

39. Victor Cunrui Xiong and Kenneth James Hammond, eds., *Routledge Handbook of Imperial Chinese History* (London: Routledge, 2019), 226.

40. Lorge, *War, Politics, and Society in Early Modern China*, 71.

41. Thomas Allsen, "The Rise of the Mongolian Empire and Mongolian Rule in North China," in Franke and Twitchett, *The Cambridge History of China*, 6:358.

42. Franke, "The Chin Dynasty," 259.

43. Chen Zhen 陈振, 宋史 (History of the Song Dynasty) (Shanghai: 上海人民出版社 [Shanghai People's Publishing Company], 2020), 541.

44. Allsen, "The Rise of the Mongolian Empire," 372.

45. Steve Chan, *Thucydides's Trap?: Historical Interpretation, Logic of Inquiry, and the Future of Sino-American Relations* (Ann Arbor: University of Michigan Press, 2020), 31.

46. A. F. K. Organski, *World Politics* (New York: Knopf, 1958), 333.

47. Ronald L. Tammen et al., *Power Transitions: Strategies for the 21st Century* (New York: Chatham House, 2000), 21.

48. Philip D. Curtin, *Cross-Cultural Trade in World History* (Cambridge: Cambridge University Press, 1984), 109.

49. Peter Lorge, "Military Institutions as a Defining Feature of the Song Dynasty," *Journal of Chinese History* 1, no. 2 (2017): 270, 273.

50. Patricia Ebrey and Anne Walthall, *East Asia: A Cultural, Social, and Political History*, 3rd ed. (Boston: Cengage Learning, 2013), 130.

51. Pamela Kyle Crossley, *Hammer and Anvil: Nomad Rulers at the Forge of the Modern World* (Lanham, MD: Rowman & Littlefield, 2019), 133; Stephen Broadberry, "Accounting for the Great Divergence" (working paper, London School of Economics, July 13, 2015), 28.

52. Rossabi, "The Reign of Khubilai Khan," 430.

53. Charles Holcombe, *A History of East Asia: From the Origins of Civilization to the Twenty-First Century* (Cambridge: Cambridge University Press, 2010), 35.

54. Crossley, *Hammer and Anvil*, 137.

55. Allsen, *Culture and Conquest in Mongol Eurasia*, 5.

56. Yuri Pines, "The Limits of All-Under-Heaven: Ideology and Praxis of 'Great Unity' in Early Chinese Empire," in *The Limits of Universal Rule: Eurasian Empires Compared*, ed. Yuri Pines, Michal Biran, and Jörg Rüpke (Cambridge: Cambridge University Press, 2021), 79.

57. Brantly Womack, *China Among Unequals: Asymmetric Foreign Relations in Asia* (Singapore: World Scientific, 2010), 154.

58. Peter Frankopan, *The Silk Roads: A New History of the World* (New York: Vintage Books, 2015), 155.

59. Crossley, *Hammer and Anvil*, 101.

60. Allsen, *Culture and Conquest in Mongol Eurasia*, 17.

61. Ruth Dunnell, "The Hsi Hsia," in Franke and Twitchett, *The Cambridge History of China*, 6:183.
62. Hsiao Ch'i-Ch'ing, "Mid-Yüan Politics," in Franke and Twitchett, *The Cambridge History of China*, 6:501.
63. Brook, *The Troubled Empire*, 30. Biran agrees, concluding that riders could cover 200–250 miles (350–400 km) a day. Michael Biran, "The Mongol Imperial Space: From Universalism to Glocalization," in Pines, Biran, and Rüpke, *The Limits of Universal Rule*, 234.
64. Hsiao, "Mid-Yüan Politics," 558.
65. Weiwen Yin, "Climate Shocks, Political Institutions, and Nomadic Invasions in Early Modern East Asia," *Journal of Conflict Resolution* 64, no. 6 (2020): 1049.
66. Crossley, *Hammer and Anvil*, 125.
67. Favereau, *The Horde*, 8.
68. Biran, "The Mongol Imperial Space," 222.
69. Ayşe Zarakol, *Before the West: The Rise and Fall of Eastern World Orders* (Cambridge: Cambridge University Press, 2022).

5. THE SMALL ATTACK THE LARGE

1. Frederick W. Mote, *Imperial China 900–1800* (Cambridge, MA: Harvard University Press, 2003), 783.
2. Richard von Glahn, *An Economic History of China: From Antiquity to the Nineteenth Century* (Cambridge: Cambridge University Press, 2016).
3. James Palais, *Confucian Statecraft and Korean Institutions* (Seattle: University of Washington Press, 1996), 78.
4. Kenneth Swope, "Crouching Tigers, Secret Weapons: Military Technology Employed During the Sino-Japanese-Korean War, 1592–1598," *Journal of Military History* 69, no. 1 (2005): 13.
5. John Mearsheimer, *The Tragedy of Great Power Politics* (New York: W. W. Norton, 2001), 237.
6. Kenneth Swope, "Perspectives on the Imjin War," *Journal of Korean Studies* 12, no. 1 (Fall 2007): 154.
7. James B. Lewis, "Introduction," in *The East Asian War, 1592–1598: International Relations, Violence and Memory*, ed. James B. Lewis (London: Routledge, 2014), 6.

8. Eugene Park, "War and Peace in Premodern Korea: Institutional and Ideological Dimensions," in *The Military and South Korean Society*, Sigur Center Asia Papers no. 26, ed. Young-Key Kim-Renaud, Richard Grinker, and Kirk W. Larsen (Washington, DC: George Washington University, 2006), 6.

9. Kenneth Lee, *Korea and East Asia* (Westport, CT: Greenwood, 1997), 99.

10. Ki-baek Lee, *A New History of Korea* (Cambridge, MA: Harvard University Press, 1984), 210.

11. Mary Elizabeth Berry, *Hideyoshi* (Cambridge, MA: Harvard University Press, 1982), 211.

12. Samuel J. Hawley, *The Imjin War: Japan's Sixteenth-Century Invasion of Korea and Attempt to Conquer China* (Seoul: Royal Asiatic Society–Korea Branch, 2005), 409.

13. Kim Youngjin 김영진, *임진 왜란: 2년 전쟁 12년 논쟁* (Imjin War: 2-Year War, 12-Year Contest) (Seoul: 성균관대학교출판부 [Sungkyunkwan University Press], 2021).

14. Ji-Young Lee, *China's Hegemony: Four Hundred Years of East Asian Domination* (New York: Columbia University Press, 2016), 52.

15. Arano Yasunori, "The Formation of a Japanocentric World Order," *International Journal of Asian Studies* 2, no. 2 (2005): 185.

16. Berry, *Hideyoshi*, 214.

17. Kenneth Swope, "Ming Grand Strategy During the Great East Asian War, 1592–1598," in *East Asia in the World: Twelve Events that Shaped the Modern International Order*, ed. Stephan Haggard and David C. Kang (Cambridge: Cambridge University Press, 2020), 111.

18. Kenneth M. Swope, "Deceit, Disguise, and Dependence: China, Japan, and the Future of the Tributary System, 1592–1596," *International History Review* 24, no. 4 (2002): 780.

19. Berry, *Hideyoshi*, 232.

20. Swope, "Ming Grand Strategy During the Great East Asian War," 113.

21. Swope, "Ming Grand Strategy During the Great East Asian War," 128.

22. Chŏng Tu-hŭi 정두희 and Yi Kyŏng-sun 이경순, *임진왜란: 동아시아 삼국전쟁* (A Transnational History of the Imjin Waeran, 1592–1598: The East Asian Dimension) (Seoul: 휴머니스트 [Humanist], 2007).

23. David C. Kang, *East Asia Before the West: Five Centuries of Trade and Tribute* (New York: Columbia University Press, 2010), 107–38.

24. Richard von Glahn, "Myth and Reality of China's Seventeenth Century Monetary Crisis," *Journal of Economic History* 56, no. 2 (1996): 429–54.

25. John Lee, "Trade and Economy in Preindustrial East Asia, c. 1500–1800," *Journal of Asian Studies* 58, no. 1 (February 1999): 7.

26. Steve Chan, *Thucydides's Trap? Historical Interpretation, Logic of Inquiry, and the Future of Sino-American Relations* (Ann Arbor: University of Michigan Press, 2020), 8.

27. Richard Ned Lebow and Benjamin Valentino, "Lost in Transition: A Critical Analysis of Power Transition Theory," *International Relations* 23, no. 3 (2009): 396.

28. Jutta Bolt and Jan Luiten van Zanden, "The Maddison Project: Collaborative Research on Historical National Accounts," *Economic History Review* 67, no. 3 (2014): 627–51.

29. Kenneth M. Swope, *A Dragon's Head and Serpent's Tail* (Norman: University of Oklahoma Press, 2009), 15.

30. Palais, *Confucian Statecraft and Korean Institutions*, 82, 78.

31. Swope, "Ming Grand Strategy During the Great East Asian War," 108.

32. Berry, *Hideyoshi*, 213

33. Swope, "Ming Grand Strategy During the Great East Asian War," 108.

34. Lee, *China's Hegemony*, 107.

35. Berry, *Hideyoshi*, 278.

36. Nam-lin Hur, "Japan's Invasions of Korea in 1592–98 and the Hideyoshi Regime," in *The Tokugawa World*, ed. Gary Leupp and De-Min Tao (Routledge, 2021), 23–45.

37. Song Nianshen 宋念申, 发现东亚 (Finding Asia) (Beijing: 新星出版社 [New Star Press], 2018), 30.

38. Song, 发现东亚, 34–35.

39. Luo Lixin 羅麗馨, "豐臣秀吉侵略朝鮮" (Toyotomi Hideyoshi's Invasion of Korea), 國立政治大學歷史學報 (Journal of History of National Chengchi University) 35 (2011): 55.

40. Swope, *A Dragon's Head and Serpent's Tail*, 188.

41. Gang Deng, "The Foreign Staple Trade of China in the Pre-Modern Era," *International History Review* 19, no. 2 (1997): 254.

42. Hawley, *The Imjin War*, 22–24, 76.

43. Lee, *A New History of Korea*, 210.

44. Swope, "Ming Grand Strategy During the Great East Asian War," 117.

45. L. M. Cullen, *A History of Japan, 1582–1941: Internal and External Worlds* (Cambridge: Cambridge University Press, 2003), 27.

46. Wang Jiahua 王家骅, "略论丰臣秀吉侵朝战争的原因" (A Brief Discussion on the Reasons for Toyotomi Hideyoshi Invading Korea), 日本研究 (Japanese Studies) 3 (1985): 37.

47. Wang, "略论丰臣秀吉侵朝战争的原因," 37. See also Zong Huiyu 宗惠玉 and Jin Rongguo 金荣国, "也论丰臣秀吉侵朝战争的原因" (Discussion of Toyotomi Hideyoshi's Invasion of Korea), 东疆学刊哲学社会科学版 (Dongjiang Journal of Philosophy and Social Sciences) 4 (1993): 53–57.

48. Wang, "略论丰臣秀吉侵朝战争的原因," 37.

49. Wang Zhen 王臻, "朝鲜壬辰战争诸问题再探讨" (On the Issues of the Imjin War), 求索 (Seek) 2 (2016): 26–30.

50. Quoted in Wang Laite 王来特, "朝贡贸易体系的脱出与日本型区域秩序的构建" (The Disengagement of the Tribute Trade System and the Construction of a Japanese-Type Regional Order), 日本学刊 (Journal of Japanese Studies) 6 (2012): 140.

51. Zhao Gang 赵刚, "德川幕府对外关系史料考" (Historical Examination of Tokugawa Shogunate's Foreign Relations), 日本学刊 (Journal of Japanese Studies) 1 (2006): 158.

52. Todd S. Sechser, "Goliath's Curse: Coercive Threats and Asymmetric Power," *International Organization* 64, no. 4 (2010): 627–60.

53. Gari Ledyard, "Confucianism and War: The Korean Security Crisis of 1598," *Journal of Korean Studies* 6 (1989): 84.

6. INTERNAL COLLAPSE

1. Pamela Crossley, "The Qing Unification, 1618–1683," in *East Asia in the World: Twelve Events That Shaped the Modern International Order*, ed. Stephan Haggard and David C. Kang (Cambridge: Cambridge University Press, 2020), 129, 130.

2. Timothy Brook, *The Troubled Empire: China in the Yuan and Ming Dynasties* (Cambridge, MA: Harvard University Press, 2013), 243.

3. Crossley, "The Qing Unification," 136.

4. Brook, *The Troubled Empire*, 254.

5. Crossley, "The Qing Unification," 131.

6. Kenneth Swope, *The Military Collapse of China's Ming Dynasty, 1618–44* (London: Routledge, 2014), 6.

7. Swope, *The Military Collapse of China's Ming Dynasty*, 44.

8. Swope, *The Military Collapse of China's Ming Dynasty*, 26.

9. Crossley, "The Qing Unification," 138.

10. Frederick W. Mote, *Imperial China 900–1800* (Cambridge, MA: Harvard University Press, 2003), 802.

11. Swope, *The Military Collapse of China's Ming Dynasty*, 3.

12. Swope, *The Military Collapse of China's Ming Dynasty*, 6.

13. Swope, *The Military Collapse of China's Ming Dynasty*, 7.

14. Crossley, "The Qing Unification," 132.

15. Pamela Kyle Crossley, *The Manchus* (Oxford: Blackwell, 1997), 17.

16. Peter Perdue, *China Marches West: The Qing Conquest of Central Eurasia* (Cambridge, MA: Harvard University Press, 2005), 109.

17. Perdue, *China Marches West*, 111.

18. Nicola Di Cosmo, "The Manchu Conquest in World-Historical Perspective: A Note on Trade and Silver," *Journal of Central Eurasian Studies* 1 (2009): 54.

19. Perdue, *China Marches West*, 117.

20. Swope, *The Military Collapse of China's Ming Dynasty*, 12.

21. Crossley, *The Manchus*, 69–74.

22. Perdue, *China Marches West*, 120–21.

23. Crossley, "The Qing Unification," 142, 143.

24. Mark Elliot, *The Manchu Way: The Eight Banners and Ethnic Identity in Late Imperial China* (Stanford, CA: Stanford University Press, 2001).

25. Shi Zhan 施展, 枢纽: 3000年的中国 (The Hub: 3000 Years of China) (Guilin: 广西师范大学出版社 [Guangxi Normal University Press], 2018), 75.

26. Shi, 枢纽, 271.

27. Crossley, "The Qing Unification," 143.

28. John Mearsheimer, *The Tragedy of Great Power Politics* (New York: W. W. Norton, 2001), 237.

29. Mizuno Norihito, "China in Tokugawa Foreign Relations: The Tokugawa Bakufu's Perception of and Attitudes Toward Ming–Qing China," *Sino-Japanese Studies Journal* 15 (2003): 136–37.

30. Alex Roland, "*Firearms: A Global History to 1700* by Kenneth Chase," *Journal of Interdisciplinary History* 35, no. 4 (2005): 617–19.

31. Kenneth Swope, "Deceit, Disguise, and Dependence: China, Japan, and the Future of the Tributary System, 1592–1596," *International History Review* 24, no. 4 (2002): 781.

32. John Mearsheimer and Stephen Walt, "The Case for Offshore Balancing: A Superior U.S. Grand Strategy," *Foreign Affairs* 95, no. 4 (July–August 2016): 70–83.

33. Chen Shangsheng 陈尚胜, 朝鲜王朝对华观的演变 (Changes in the Korean Perception of China) (Jinan:山东大学出版社 [Shandong University Press], 1999).

34. Sun Weiguo 孙卫国, 大明旗号与小中华意识: 朝鲜王朝尊周思明问题研究 (1637–1800) ("Great Ming" and "Little China"—Studies of the Chosŏn Period Trend of Revering the Zhou and Longing for the Ming, 1637–1800) (Beijing: 商务印书馆有限公司 [Commercial Press], 2007).

7. HOW KOREA REMAINED INDEPENDENT UNTIL 1910

1. Gari Ledyard, "Yin and Yang in the China–Manchuria–Korea Triangle," in *China Among Equals: The Middle Kingdom and Its Neighbors, 10th–14th Centuries*, ed. Martin Rossabi (Berkeley: University of California Press, 1983), 313.

2. Evelyn Rawski, *Early Modern China and Northeast Asia: Cross-Border Perspectives* (Cambridge: Cambridge University Press, 2015).

3. Ledyard, "Yin and Yang," 313.

4. Chin-Hao Huang and David C. Kang, *State Formation Through Emulation: The East Asian Model* (New York: Cambridge University Press, 2022).

5. Sixiang Wang, *Boundless Winds of Empire: Rhetoric and Ritual in Early Chosŏn Diplomacy with Ming China* (New York: Columbia University Press, 2023), 9–10.

6. Rawski, *Early Modern China and Northeast Asia*, 188.

7. Rawski, *Early Modern China and Northeast Asia*, 190.

8. Jiang Weidong 姜维东, 高句丽历史编年 (The Chronicle of Koguryŏ History) (Beijing: 科学出版社 [Science Press], 2016), 505.

9. Ledyard concludes, "Koguryŏ involves itself principally in Korean, not Chinese affairs, and in the end develops a peninsular outlook, which continues. . . . Its descendants in northern Korea create in Koryŏ a state that henceforth accepts its confinement to the land south of the Yalu." Ledyard, "Yin and Yang," 339.

10. Wang Gaoxin 汪高鑫, 二十四史的民族史撰述研究 (Studies on the Ethno-Historical Recounts in Twenty-Four Histories) (Hefei: 黄山书社 [Huang Shan Book Club], 2016), 199.

11. Nadia Kanagawa, "East Asia's First World War, 643–668 CE," in *East Asia in the World: Twelve Events That Shaped the Modern International Order*, ed. Stephan Haggard and David C. Kang (Cambridge: Cambridge University Press, 2020).

12. Christina Lai, "Realism Revisited: China's Status-Driven Wars Against Koguryŏ in the Sui and Tang Dynasties," *Asian Security* 17, no. 2 (2021): 140, 153.

13. Han Sheng 韩昇, 东亚世界形成史论 (Studies on the Formation of East Asian World) (Beijing: 中国方正出版社 [China Fangzheng Press], 2015), 68.

14. Peter Lee and Theodore de Bary, *Sources of Korean Tradition*, vol. 1, *From Early Times Through the Sixteenth Century* (New York: Columbia University Press, 1997), 57.

15. Patricia Ebrey and Anne Walthall, *East Asia: A Cultural, Social, and Political History*, 3rd ed. (Boston: Cengage Learning, 2013); Brett L. Walker, *A Concise History of Japan* (Cambridge: Cambridge University Press, 2015); Michael J. Seth, *A Concise History of Korea*, 2nd ed. (Lanham, MD: Rowman & Littlefield, 2016); Kyung Moon Hwang, *A History of Korea* (New York: Palgrave Macmillan, 2017)—none of these even mention Japan in their descriptions of the Shilla unification of the peninsula.

16. *Samguk sagi*, 41:394, from Lee and de Bary, *Sources of Korean Tradition*, 60.

17. Wang Zhenping, *Tang China in Multi-polar Asia* (Honolulu: University of Hawai'i Press, 2013), 81.

18. Wang, *Tang China in Multi-polar Asia*, 84.

19. Gari Ledyard, "Cartography in Korea," in *Cartography in the Traditional East and Southeast Asian Societies*, ed. J. B. Harley and David Woodward (Chicago: University of Chicago Press, 1994), 238.

20. Charles Holcombe, *A History of East Asia: From the Origins of Civilization to the Twenty-First Century* (Cambridge: Cambridge University Press, 2010), 111.

21. Kanagawa, "East Asia's First World War," 79.

22. Wang, *Tang China in Multi-polar Asia*, 84, 85.

23. David M. Robinson, *Korea and the Fall of the Mongol Empire: Alliance, Upheaval, and the Rise of a New East Asian Order* (Cambridge: Cambridge University Press, 2023), 4, 16, 252–53.

24. Wang, *Boundless Winds of Empire*, 273.

25. Wu Han 吴晗, 朝鮮李朝實錄中的中國史料 (China Materials in the Veritable Records of Korea's Yi Dynasty, 1354–1374) (Beijing: 中華書局 [Zhonghua Book Company], 1980), 1:14, 15.

26. Feng Zhang, *Chinese Hegemony: Grand Strategy and International Institutions in East Asian History* (Stanford, CA: Stanford University Press, 2015), 60.

27. Zhang Peiheng 章培恒 and Yu Suisheng 喻遂生, 二十四史全译: 明史 (Full Translation of the Twenty-Four Histories: The History of the Ming Dynasty) (Shanghai: 汉语大词典出版社 [Hanyu Da Cidian Publishing Company], 2004), 6,672; Liu Jinghua 刘菁华, Xu Qingyu 许清玉, and Hu Xianhui 胡显慧, 明实录朝鲜资料辑录 (A Compilation of Korea Materials from the Veritable Records of the Ming Dynasty) (Chengdu: 巴蜀书社 [Bashu Publishing House], 2005), 24.

28. Donald Neil Clark, "Autonomy, Legitimacy, and Tributary Politics: Sino-Korean Relations in the Fall of Koryŏ and the Founding of the Yi" (PhD diss., Harvard University, 1978), 91.

29. Zhang, *Chinese Hegemony*, 65; Zhang and Yu, 二十四史全译, 6,672.

30. Kyŏngin Publishing Editorial Department, 국역 고려사: 우왕 14년 (1388) 무진년 (History of Koryŏ: The 14th Year of King U (1388), the Year of Mujin) (Seoul: 경인문화사 [Kyŏngin Publishing], 2006), vol. 3, https://terms.naver.com/entry.naver?docId=1624407&cid=62131&categoryId=62161.

31. Kim, "Koryŏ, wŏnŭi yŏngt'ojŏngch'aek, in'gujŏngch'aeng yŏn'gu."

32. Byonghyon Choi, *The Annals of King T'aejo: Founder of Korea's Chosŏn Dynasty* (Cambridge, MA: Harvard University Press, 2014), 57.

33. Pak describes how once T'aejo (이성계) decided to change Koryŏ's name he ended up with two final candidates: Chosŏn (朝鮮) and the

old name of his birth town, Hwaryung (和寧). T'aejo then sent an envoy to the Ming, displaying an attitude of humility by requesting the Ming emperor choose the final name. The Ming emperor replied, "the name Chosŏn is beautiful and also comes from a long tradition, which should be inherited," designating the name "Chosŏn." Pak Wŏnho, "Myŏnggwaŭi kwan'gye" (Relations with the Ming), Han'guksa (History of Korea) 22 (1995).

34. *T'aejo Sillok* (Veritable Records of King Taejo), Year 2 March 9, http://sillok.history.go.kr/id/kaa_10203009_002; Year 4 November 11, http://sillok.history.go.kr/id/kaa_10411011_002; Year 5 March 29, http://sillok.history.go.kr/id/kaa_10503029_003

35. *Chŏngjong Sillok* (Veritable Records of King Jeongjong), Year 2 September 19, http://sillok.history.go.kr/id/kba_10209019_002.

36. *T'aejong Sillok* (Veritable Record of King Taejong), Year 1 March 6, http://sillok.history.go.kr/id/kca_10103006_001.

37. David C. Kang, Ronan Tse-min Fu, and Meredith Shaw, "Measuring War in Early Modern East Asia: Introducing Chinese and Korean Language Sources," *International Studies Quarterly* 60, no. 4 (December 2016): 766–77.

38. O Chongnok, *Chosŏnch'ogi yanggyeŭi kunsajedowa kukpang* (Military Institutions and Dynastic Defense in Northern and Eastern Borders in Early Chosŏn) (Seoul: Kukhak Charyowŏn, 2014).

39. *Sejong Sillok* (Veritable Records of King Sejong) (Sŏul si: Sejong Taewang Kinyŏm Saŏphoe, 1991): 116:9b.

40. Yu Chaech'un, "15 segi Myŏng-ŭi Tongp'alch'am chiyŏk chŏmgŏ-wa Chosŏn-ŭi taeŭng" (Ming's occupation of the Tongp'alch'am region in the 15th century and Chosŏn's reaction), *Chosŏn sidaesa hakbo* (Journal of Chosŏn Dynasty History) 18 (2001): 7.

41. Jungshin Lee, "Koreans' Perception of the Liaodong Region During the Chosŏn Dynasty," *International Journal of Korean History* 21, no. 1 (2016): 47–84.

42. Wang, *Boundless Winds of Empire*, 281.

43. Seung B. Kye, "Huddling Under the Imperial Umbrella: A Korean Approach to Ming China in the Early 1500s," *Journal of Korean Studies* 15, no. 1 (2010): 59.

44. *Chŏngjo Sillok* (The Veritable Records of King Chŏngjo's) (Seoul: National Institute of Korean History), February 14, 1779.

45. Han Myŏngki, *Imjinwaeran'gwa hanjunggwan'gye* (The Imjin Intervention and Sino-Korean Relations) (Seoul: Yŏksa pip'yŏngsa, 1999).

46. Lee, *A New History of Korea*, 215.

47. Lee, *Korea and East Asia*, 112.

48. Seonmin Kim, *Ginseng and Borderland: Territorial Boundaries and Political Relations Between Qing China and Choson Korea, 1636–1912* (Oakland, Calif.: University of California Press, 2017), 10.

49. Lee, *A New History of Korea*, 216.

50. Kenneth Lee, *Korea and East Asia* (Westport, CT: Greenwood, 19), 112; Ch'oe Soja, *Myŏngch'ŏngshidae chunghan'gwan'gyesa yŏn'gu* (Study on Sino-Korean Relations During Ming–Qing Periods) (Seoul: Ewha Womans' University Press, 1997).

51. *Injo Sillok* (Veritable Records of King Injo), Year 14 February 21, https://sillok.history.go.kr/id/kpa_11402021_003.

52. Hong Taeyong (洪大容), "Catechism of Eusan Mountain (Ŭisanmundap, 의산문답, 醫山問答)," in *Tamhŏnsŏ* 湛軒書 (1776); 〔국역담헌서〕 (Minjok Munhwa Chujinhoe, 1974).

53. 호락논쟁 ("about human nature theory") is one of the three most famous political debates in Chosŏn, the other two being the sixteenth-century "사단칠정(四端七情) 논쟁" (about humanity, evil, and between Mencian and Confucian views of the world) and the seventeenth-century "예송(禮訟)논쟁" (about succession and how many years that certain practices should be performed).

54. Ch'oe Soja, *Ch'ŏng wa Chosŏn: Kŭnse tong ashia ŭi sangho inshik* (Qing and Chosŏn: Mutual Perceptions in Premodern Asia) (Seoul: Hyean, 2005).

55. Han, *Imjinwaeran'gwa hanjunggwan'gye*.

56. Lee, *Korea and East Asia*, 113.

57. Wang, *Boundless Winds of Empire*, 279.

58. Seonmin Kim, "Ginseng and Border Trespassing Between Qing China and Chosŏn Korea," conference paper, annual meeting of the Association for Asian Studies, San Diego, CA, April 6–9, 2006.

59. "The 10th day of the first month (正月十日), *Taizong Wen Huangdi shilu* 54 (太宗文皇帝實錄卷之五十四)." In *Qing shilu* (清實錄), 722:2–723:1. Beijing: Zhonghua shuju, 1986. Scripta Sinica Database 漢籍全文資料庫).

60. Nicolas Tackett, *The Origins of the Chinese Nation: Song China and the Forging of an East Asian World Order* (Cambridge: Cambridge University Press, 2017), 3.

61. Saeyoung Park, "The Death of Eastphalia, 1874," in Haggard and Kang, *East Asia in the World*, 257.

62. Allen Carlson, *Unifying China, Integrating with the World: Securing Chinese Sovereignty in the Reform Era* (Stanford, CA: Stanford University Press, 2005).

8. EAST ASIAN POWER TRANSITIONS IN THE TWENTY-FIRST CENTURY

1. Richard Betts, "Wealth, Power, and Instability: East Asia and the United States After the Cold War," *International Security* 18, no. 3 (Winter 1993–1994): 56, 59.

2. Aaron Friedberg, "Ripe for Rivalry: Prospects for Peace in a Multipolar Asia," *International Security* 18, no. 3 (Winter 1993–1994): 30, 32.

3. Kenneth Waltz, "The Emerging Structure of International Politics," *International Security* 18, no. 2 (Fall 1993): 55–56.

4. Betts, "Wealth, Power, and Instability," 59.

5. Waltz, "The Emerging Structure of International Politics," 60.

6. Pat Choate, *Agents of Influence: How Japan's Lobbyists in the United States Are Manipulating Western Political and Economic Systems* (New York: Knopf, 1990); Michael A. Cusumano, *Japan's Software Factories: A Challenge to U.S. Management* (New York: Oxford University Press, 1991); Edward A. Feigenbaum and Pamela McCorduck, *The Fifth Generation: Artificial Intelligence and Japan's Computer Challenge to the World* (Reading, MA: Addison-Wesley, 1983); Eamonn Fingleton, *Blindside: Why Japan Is Still on Track to Overtake the U.S. by the Year 2000* (Boston: Houghton Mifflin, 1995); George Friedman and Meredith LeBard, *The Coming War with Japan* (New York: St. Martin's Press, 1991); Sam Jameson, "Economic Superpowers at Odds," *Los Angeles Times*, May 8, 1995, https://www.latimes.com/archives/la-xpm-1995-05-08-fi-63836-story.html; Chalmers Johnson, *MITI and the Japanese Miracle: The Growth of Industrial Policy, 1925–1975* (Stanford, CA: Stanford University Press, 1982); Ira C. Magaziner and Robert B.

Reich, *Minding America's Business: The Decline and Rise of the American Economy* (New York: Harcourt Brace Jovanovich, 1982); T. Boone Pickens, Pat Choate, and Christopher Burke, *The Second Pearl Harbor: Say No to Japan* (Washington, DC: National Press Books, 1992); J. J. Servan-Schreiber, *The World Challenge* (New York: Simon & Schuster, 1980); Ezra F. Vogel, *Japan as Number One: Lessons for America* (Cambridge, MA: Harvard University Press, 1978).

7. R. Taggart Murphy, *The Weight of the Yen: How Denial Imperils America's Future and Ruins an Alliance* (New York: W. W. Norton, 1997).

8. "Nikkei 225 Index—67 Year Historical Chart," Macrotrends, https://www.macrotrends.net/2593/nikkei-225-index-historical-chart-data.

9. Brad Glosserman, "The Regional Implications of 'Peak Japan,'" *Strategist*, March 31, 2016, http://www.aspistrategist.org.au/the-regional-implications-of-peak-japan/.

10. T. J. Pempel, "Back to the Future? Japan's Search for a Meaningful New Role in the Emerging Regional Order," *Asian Perspective* 39, no. 3 (July 2015): 361–80.

11. Robert Dujarric, "Japan Without Ambition," *Diplomat*, January 22, 2016, http://thediplomat.com/2016/01/japan-without-ambition/.

12. Institute of International Education (IIE), *2019 Open Doors: Report on International Educational Exchange* (New York: IIE and U.S. Department of State, Bureau of Educational and Cultural Affairs, 2019).

13. China Power Team, "Is China Both a Source and a Hub for International Students?" *China Power*, September 26, 2017, updated September 4, 2020, https://chinapower.csis.org/china-international-students/.

14. "Kishida Wants to Boost Defense Spending, but How to Fund It Remains a Question," *Japan Times*, May 26, 2022.

15. Tom Le, "A Japanese Security Sea Change? Let's See Change First," *Critical Asian Studies* 54, no. 4 (January 4, 2023).

16. Alexis Dudden, "Matthew Perry in Japan, 1852–1854," in *East Asia in the World: Twelve Events That Shaped the Modern International Order*, ed. Stephan Haggard and David C. Kang (Cambridge: Cambridge University Press, 2020), 188–205.

17. Gerald Segal, "Does China Matter?" *Foreign Affairs* 78, no. 5 (September–October 1999): 24.

18. Adam P. Liff, "Whither the Balancers? The Case for a Methodological Reset," *Security Studies* 25, no. 3 (2016): 436.

19. Darren J. Lim and Zack Cooper, "Reassessing Hedging: The Logic of Alignment in East Asia," *Security Studies* 24, no. 4 (2015): 704.

20. Kyuri Park, "Goldilocks' Signal for Cooperation in East Asia: China's Rise, Hedging, and Joint Military Exercises," manuscript, Stanford University, 2022.

21. Damien Cave, "Why China Is Miles Ahead in a Pacific Race for Influence," *New York Times*, May 31, 2022.

22. All data come from the "Asian Power Index, 2021 Edition," Lowy Institute, Australia.

23. Quoted in Yuka Hayashi, "Japan Wants U.S. Back in the TPP: It Will Likely Have to Wait," *Wall Street Journal*, April 16, 2021.

24. Alex Yu-Ting Lin and Saori Katada, "Striving for Greatness: Status Aspirations, Rhetorical Entrapment, and Domestic Reforms," *Review of International Political Economy* 29, no.1 (2022): 175–201.

25. Quoted in Lin and Katada, "Striving for Greatness."

26. "Statement on Indo-Pacific Economic Framework for Prosperity," White House, May 5, 2023, https://www.whitehouse.gov/briefing-roo m/statements-releases/2022/05/23/statement-on-indo-pacific-econo mic-framework-for-prosperity/.

27. David Lawder, "U.S.–China Trade War Has Cost up to 245,000 U.S. Jobs: Business Group Study," *Reuters*, January 14, 2021.

28. Samantha Vortherms and Jiakun Jack Zhang, "Political Risk and Firm Exit: Evidence from the US–China Trade War," research paper, University of California San Diego, 21st Century China Center, Research Paper no. 2021-09 (September 1, 2021), 2.

29. American Chamber of Commerce in China, "2021 American Business in China White Paper," May 11, 2021.

30. Tom Hancock, "US Companies in China More Pessimistic About Revenue Outlook," *Financial Times*, September 11, 2019.

31. Mary Amiti, Stephen J. Redding, and David Weinstein, "The Impact of the 2018 Trade War on U.S. Prices and Welfare," working paper, National Bureau of Economic Research (NBER) Working Paper no. 25672, March 2019, http://www.nber.org/papers/w25672.

32. Elbridge Colby, *The Strategy of Denial: American Defense in an Age of Great Power Conflict* (New Haven, CT: Yale University Press, 2021), 10.

33. Robert Jervis, "Roundtable on T. V. Paul, *Restraining Great Powers: Soft Balancing from Empires to the Global Era*," ISSF Roundtable 10–29, 2019, https://issforum.org/ISSF/PDF/ISSF-Roundtable-10-29.pdf, 2..

34. Quoted in Lee Jeong-ho, "US Using Trade War to stop China Overtaking It: Ex-Singapore Diplomat Kishore Mahbubani," *South China Morning Post*, September 4, 2019.

35. Andrew Erickson, "Australia Badly Needs Nuclear Submarines," *Foreign Policy*, September 20, 2021.

36. Sebastian Strangio, "Indonesia and Malaysia Reiterate Concerns about AUKUS Pact," *Diplomat*, October 19, 2021, https://thediplomat.com /2021/10/indonesia-and-malaysia-reiterate-concerns-about-aukus-pact/.

37. Aqil Haziq Mahmud, "US Should 'Stay Very Far Away' from Physically Confronting China Over Taiwan: Ng Eng Hen," *Channel News Asia*, November 4, 2021, https://www.channelnewsasia.com/singapore /taiwan-china-us-tension-ng-eng-hen-2290256.

9. THE LESSONS OF HISTORY AND THE FUTURE OF EAST ASIA

1. Sixiang Wang, *Boundless Winds of Empire: Rhetoric and Ritual in Early Chosŏn Diplomacy with Ming China* (New York: Columbia University Press, 2023), 284.

2. Liam Kelley, "Vietnam as a 'Domain of Manifest Civility' (Van Hien Chi Bang)," *Journal of Southeast Asian Studies* 34, no. 1 (February 2003): 68.

3. Susan L. Shirk, *China: Fragile Superpower* (New York: Oxford University Press, 2007), 1.

4. Minxin Pei, *China's Trapped Transition: The Limits of Developmental Autocracy* (Cambridge, MA: Harvard University Press, 2008).

5. David Shambaugh, "The Coming Chinese Crackup," *Wall Street Journal*, March 6, 2015.

6. Rob Schmitz, "Who's Lifting Chinese People out of Poverty?," National Public Radio, January 17, 2017.

7. Zhou Xin, "Is China Rich or Poor? Nation's Wealth Debate Muddied by Conflicting Government Data," *South China Morning Post*, May 29, 2020.

8. "'6亿人月入1000元'是最有效的清醒剂" ("600 Million People Earn $1,000 a Month" Is the Most Effective Sobering Agent), 第一财经 (China Business Network), June 3, 2020.

9. Andrew Scobell, "China and Grand Strategy: Does the Empire Have a Plan? A Review Essay," *Political Science Quarterly* 137 (2022): 156.

10. Andrew Bacevich, "Who Lost Fiji?" *American Conservative*, June 8, 2022.

11. Richard Betts, "Wealth, Power, and Instability: East Asia and the United States After the Cold War," *International Security* 18, no. 3 (Winter 1993–1994): 69.

12. Arend Lijphart, "The Comparable-Cases Strategy in Comparative Research," *Comparative Political Studies* 8, no. 2 (1975): 163.

13. For more detailed discussion on different types of case and case study, see Jason Seawright and John Gerring, "Case Selection Techniques in Case Study Research: A Menu of Qualitative and Quantitative Options," *Political Research Quarterly* 61, no. 2 (2008): 294–308.

14. Barry Buzan and Michael Cox, "China and the US: Comparable Cases of 'Peaceful Rise?'" *Chinese Journal of International Politics* 6, no. 2 (2013): 109–32.

15. Giovanni Sartori, "Comparing and Miscomparing," *Journal of Theoretical Politics* 3, no. 3 (1991): 243–57.

16. Elizabeth Perry, "Chinese Conceptions of "Rights:" From Mencius to Mao—and Now," *Perspectives on Politics* 6, no. 1 (March 2008): 37–50.

17. "Xi Leads Top Leadership, Meeting Press," Chinese Ministry of Foreign Affairs, November 16, 2012.

18. Nianshen Song, 发现东亚 (Finding Asia) (Beijing: 新星出版社 [New Star Press], 2018), 10.

19. Naoki Sakai, "'You Asians': On the Historical Role of the West and Asia Binary," *South Atlantic Quarterly* 99, no. 4 (2000): 791.

20. James Millward, "Qing and Twentieth-Century Chinese Diversity Regimes," in *Culture and Order in World Politics*, ed. Andrew Phillips

and Christian Reus-Smit (New York: Cambridge University Press, 2020), 73.

21. Victor Lieberman, *Strange Parallels: Southeast Asia in Global Context, c.800–1830* (Cambridge: Cambridge University Press, 2003), as described by Peter Perdue, "Strange Parallels Across Eurasia," *Social Science* 32, no. 2 (2008): 266.

22. Rosemary Foot and Evelyn Goh, "The International Relations of East Asia: A New Research Prospectus." *International Studies Review* 21, no. 3 (2019): 401.

23. David Kang, "International Order in Historical East Asia," 86.

24. Lucian W. Pye, "China: Erratic State, Frustrated Society," *Foreign Affairs* 69, no. 4 (1990): 58.

25. Bak Yongun, *Goryeo sidae Gaegyeong yeongu* (Research on Koryo Era Capital) (Seoul: Iljisa, 1996), 3.

26. Ge Jianxiong 葛剑雄, and Hua Linfu 华林甫, "Ershi shiji de zhongguo lishi dili yanji" 二十世纪的中国历史地理研究 (Studies in Chinese Historical Geography in the Twentieth Century), 历史研究 3 (Historical Research) (2002): 152, 165.

27. Michael Beckley, "The Power of Nations: Measuring What Matters." *International Security* 43, no. 2 (2018): 8–9.

BIBLIOGRAPHY

Adler, Emanuel, and Vincent Pouliot. "International Practices." *International Theory* 3, no. 1 (February 2011): 1–36.

Allsen, Thomas. *Culture and Conquest in Mongol Eurasia*. Cambridge: Cambridge University Press, 2001.

——. "The Rise of the Mongolian Empire and Mongolian Rule in North China." In Franke and Twitchett, *Alien Regimes and Border States, 907–1368*, 321–413.

American Chamber of Commerce in China. "2021 American Business in China White Paper." May 11, 2021.

Amiti, Mary, Stephen J. Redding, and David Weinstein. "The Impact of the 2018 Trade War on U.S. Prices and Welfare." Working paper, National Bureau of Economic Research (NBER) Working Paper no. 25672, March 2019. http://www.nber.org/papers/w25672.

Anderson, James. "Distinguishing Between China and Vietnam: Three Relational Equilibriums in Sino-Vietnamese Relations." *Journal of East Asian Studies* 13, no. 2 (2013): 259–80.

Aron, Raymond. *Peace and War*. London: Weidenfeld & Nicolson, 1966.

Art, Robert. "The United States and the Rise of China: Implications for the Long Haul." *Political Science Quarterly* 125, no. 3 (Fall 2010): 359–91.

"Asian Power Index, 2021 Edition." Lowy Institute, Australia.

Bacevich, Andrew. "Who Lost Fiji?" *American Conservative*, June 8, 2022.

Bak, Yongun. *Goryeo sidae Gaegyeong yeongu* (Research on Koryo Era Capital). Seoul: Iljisa, 1996.

Batten, Bruce. *To the Ends of Japan: Premodern Frontiers, Boundaries, and Interactions.* Honolulu: University of Hawai'i Press, 2003.

Beckley, Michael. "The Power of Nations: Measuring What Matters." *International Security* 43, no. 2 (2018): 7–44.

Berry, Mary Elizabeth. *Hideyoshi.* Cambridge, MA: Harvard University Press, 1982.

Betts, Richard. "Wealth, Power, and Instability: East Asia and the United States After the Cold War." *International Security* 18, no. 3 (Winter 1993–1994): 34–77.

Biran, Michael. "The Mongol Imperial Space: From Universalism to Glocalization." In Pines, Biran, and Rüpke, *The Limits of Universal Rule*, 220–56.

Bolt, Jutta, and Jan Luiten van Zanden. "The Maddison Project: Collaborative Research on Historical National Accounts." *Economic History Review* 67, no. 3 (2014): 627–51.

Broadberry, Stephen. "Accounting for the Great Divergence." Working paper, London School of Economics, July 13, 2015.

Brook, Timothy. *The Troubled Empire: China in the Yuan and Ming Dynasties.* Cambridge, MA: Harvard University Press, 2013.

Buzan, Barry, and Michael Cox. "China and the US: Comparable Cases of 'Peaceful Rise?'" *Chinese Journal of International Politics* 6, no. 2 (2013): 109–32.

Carlson, Allen. *Unifying China, Integrating with the World: Securing Chinese Sovereignty in the Reform Era.* Stanford, CA: Stanford University Press, 2005.

Chan, Steve. *China, the U.S. and Power Transition Theory: A Critique.* London: Routledge, 2008.

——. "Exploring Puzzles in Power-Transition Theory: Implications for Sino-American Relations." *Security Studies* 13, no. 3 (2004): 103–41.

——. *Thucydides's Trap? Historical Interpretation, Logic of Inquiry, and the Future of Sino-American Relations.* Ann Arbor: University of Michigan Press, 2020.

Chen, Shangsheng 陈尚胜. 朝鲜王朝对华观的演变 (Changes in the Korean Perception of China). Jinan: 山东大学出版社 Shandong University Press, 1999.

Chen, Zhen 陈振. 宋史 (History of the Song Dynasty). Shanghai: 上海人民出版社 (Shanghai People's Publishing Company), 2020.

China Power Team. "Is China Both a Source and a Hub for International Students?" *China Power*, September 26, 2017, updated September 4, 2020. https://chinapower.csis.org/china-international-students/.

Chinese Ministry of Foreign Affairs. "Xi Leads Top Leadership, Meeting Press." November 16, 2012. http://vienna.china-mission.gov.cn/eng/zt /zggcdsbd/201211/t20121115_8878899.htm.

Choate, Pat. *Agents of Influence: How Japan's Lobbyists in the United States Are Manipulating Western Political and Economic Systems*. New York: Knopf, 1990.

Ch'oe, Soja. *Myŏngch'ŏngshidae chunghan'gwan'gyesa yŏn'gu* (Study on Sino-Korean Relations During the Ming–Qing Periods). Seoul: Ewha Women's University Press, 1997.

——. Ch'ŏng wa Chosŏn: Kŭnse tong ashia ŭi sangho inshik (Qing and Chosŏn: Mutual Perceptions in Premodern Asia). Seoul: 혜안 (Hyean), 2005.

Choi, Byonghyon. *The Annals of King T'aejo: Founder of Korea's Chosŏn Dynasty*. Cambridge, MA: Harvard University Press, 2014.

Chong, Ian, and Todd Hall. "The Lessons of 1914 for East Asia Today: Missing the Trees for the Forest." *International Security* 39, no. 1 (Summer 2014): 7–43.

Chŏng, Tu-hŭi and Yi Kyŏng-sun. Imjinwaeranr tongashia samgukchŏnjaeng (*A Transnational History of the Imjin Waeran, 1592–1598: The East Asian Dimension*). Seoul: Humanist, 2007.

Chŏngjo Sillok. (The Veritable Records of Chŏngjo's Rule). Seoul: National Institute of Korean History.

Chŏngjong Sillok. (Veritable Records of King Jeongjong). Seoul: National Institute of Korean History.

Clark, Donald Neil. "Autonomy, Legitimacy, and Tributary Politics: Sino-Korean Relations in the Fall of Koryŏ and the Founding of the Yi." PhD diss., Harvard University, 1978.

Coggins, Bridget. *Power Politics and State Formation in the Twentieth Century: The Dynamics of Recognition*. Cambridge: Cambridge University Press, 2014.

Colby, Elbridge. *The Strategy of Denial: American Defense in an Age of Great Power Conflict*. New Haven, CT: Yale University Press, 2021.

Crossley, Pamela Kyle. *Hammer and Anvil: Nomad Rulers at the Forge of the Modern World*. Lanham, MD: Rowman & Littlefield, 2019.

——. *The Manchus*. Oxford: Blackwell, 1997.

——. "The Qing Unification, 1618–1683." In Haggard and Kang, *East Asia in the World*, 129–49. Cambridge: Cambridge University Press, 2020.

Cullen, L. M. *A History of Japan, 1582–1941: Internal and External Worlds*. Cambridge: Cambridge University Press, 2003.

Curtin, Philip D. *Cross-Cultural Trade in World History*. Cambridge: Cambridge University Press, 1984.

Cusumano, Michael A. *Japan's Software Factories: A Challenge to U.S. Management*. New York: Oxford University Press, 1991.

de Mesquita, Bruce Bueno. "Pride of Place: The Origins of German Hegemony." *World Politics* 43, no. 1 (1990): 28–52.

Deng, Gang. "The Foreign Staple Trade of China in the Pre-Modern Era." *International History Review* 19, no. 2 (1997): 253–85.

Di Cosmo, Nicola. "The Manchu Conquest in World-Historical Perspective: A Note on Trade and Silver." *Journal of Central Eurasian Studies* 1 (2009): 43–60.

DiCicco, Jonathan M., and Jack S. Levy. "Power Shifts and Problem Shifts: The Evolution of the Power Transition Research Program." *Journal of Conflict Resolution* 43, no. 6 (1999): 675–704.

Dincecco, Mark, and Yuhua Wang. "Violence Conflict and Political Development Over the Long Run: China Versus Europe." *Annual Review of Political Science* 21 (2018): 341–58.

Dudden, Alexis. "Matthew Perry in Japan, 1852–1854." In Haggard and Kang, *East Asia in the World*, 188–205.

Dujarric, Robert. "Japan Without Ambition." *Diplomat*, January 22, 2016. http://thediplomat.com/2016/01/japan-without-ambition/.

Dunnell, Ruth. "The Hsi Hsia." In Franke and Twitchett, *Alien Regimes and Border States, 907–1368*, 154–214.

Ebrey, Patricia, and Anne Walthall. *East Asia: A Cultural, Social, and Political History*, 3rd ed. Boston: Cengage Learning, 2013.

Efird, Brian, Jacek Kugler, and Gaspare Genna. "From War to Integration: Generalizing Power Transition Theory." *International Interactions* 29, no. 4 (2003): 293–313.

Elliot, Mark. *The Manchu Way: The Eight Banners and Ethnic Identity in Late Imperial China*. Stanford, CA: Stanford University Press, 2001.

Erickson, Andrew. "Australia Badly Needs Nuclear Submarines." *Foreign Policy*, September 20, 2021.

Favereau, Marie. *The Horde: How the Mongols Changed the World*. Cambridge, MA: Harvard University Press, 2021.

Fearon, James. "Rationalist Explanations for War." *International Organization* 49, no. 3 (1995): 379–414.

Fearon, James, and Alexander Wendt. "Rationalism v. Constructivism: A Skeptical View." In *Handbook of International Relations Theory*, ed. Walter Carlsnaes, Thomas Risse, and Beth A. Simmons, 52–72. London: Sage Publications, 2002.

Feigenbaum, Edward A., and Pamela McCorduck. *The Fifth Generation: Artificial Intelligence and Japan's Computer Challenge to the World*. Reading, MA: Addison-Wesley, 1983.

Fingleton, Eamonn. *Blindside: Why Japan Is Still on Track to Overtake the U.S. by the Year 2000*. Boston: Houghton Mifflin, 1995.

Fitzgerald, Devin, and Maura Dykstra. "Shi Jie, On China." *Books and Early Modern World*. https://chinesecourses.voices.wooster.edu/confucianism/.

Franke, Herbert. "The Chin Dynasty." In Franke and Twitchett, *Alien Regimes and Border States, 907–1368*, 215–320.

Franke, Herbert, and Denis Twitchett, eds. *The Cambridge History of China*, vol. 6, *Alien Regimes and Border States, 907–1368*. Cambridge: Cambridge University Press, 1994.

Frankopan, Peter. *The Silk Roads: A New History of the World*. New York: Vintage Books, 2015.

Friedberg, Aaron. "Ripe for Rivalry: Prospects for Peace in a Multipolar Asia." *International Security* 18, no. 3 (Winter 1993–1994): 5–33.

Friedman, George, and Meredith LeBard. *The Coming War with Japan*. New York: St. Martin's Press, 1991.

Foot, Rosemary, and Evelyn Goh. "The International Relations of East Asia: A New Research Prospectus." *International Studies Review* 21, no. 3 (2019): 398–423.

Fu, Zhongxia 傅仲侠, ed. 中国历代战争年表 (Chronology of Wars in China Through Successive Dynasties), 2 vols. Beijing: 解放军出版社 (People's Liberation Army Press), 2003.

Gao, Hongqing 高红清. 燕云十六州 (The Sixteen Prefectures of Yanyun). Beijing: 北京燕山出版社有限公司 (Beijing Yanshan Publishing Company), 2018.

Ge, Jianxiong 葛剑雄, and Hua Linfu 华林甫. "Ershi shiji de zhongguo lishi dili yanji" 二十世纪的中国历史地理研究 (Studies in Chinese Historical

Geography in the Twentieth Century). 历史研究 3 (Historical Research) (2002): 145–65.

Ge, Zhaoguang 葛兆光. "宋代 '中国' 意识的凸显——关于近世民族主义思想的一个远源" (The Prominence of the Consciousness of "China" in the Song Dynasty—A Distant Source of Modern Nationalism). 文哲史 (Journal of Literature, History, and Philosophy) (2004): 5–12.

Geddes, Barbara. "How the Cases You Choose Affect the Answers You Get: Selection Bias in Comparative Politics." *Political Analysis* 2 (1990): 131–50.

Geller, Daniel S. "Capability Concentration, Power Transition, and War." *International Interactions* 17, no. 3 (1992): 269–84.

Gilpin, Robert. *War and Change in World Politics.* New York: Cambridge University Press, 1981.

Glosserman, Brad. "The Regional Implications of 'Peak Japan.'" *Strategist*, March 31, 2016. http://www.aspistrategist.org.au/the-regional-implications-of-peak-japan/.

Goddard, Stacie. *Indivisible Territory and the Politics of Legitimacy: Jerusalem and Northern Ireland.* Cambridge: Cambridge University Press, 2010.

Gracie, Carrie. "Kublai Khan: China's Favourite Barbarian." *BBC News*, October 9, 2012. https://www.bbc.com/news/magazine-19850234.

Haggard, Stephan, and David C. Kang, eds. *East Asia in the World: Twelve Events That Shaped the Modern International Order.* Cambridge: Cambridge University Press, 2020.

Han, Myŏngki. *Imjinwaeran'gwa hanjunggwan'gye* (The Imjin War and Sino-Korean Relations). Seoul: Yŏksa pip'yŏngsa, 1999.

Han, Sheng 韩昇. 东亚世界形成史论 (*Studies on the Formation of East Asian World*). Beijing: 中国方正出版社 (China Fangzheng Press), 2015.

Hancock, Tom. "US Companies in China More Pessimistic about Revenue Outlook." *Financial Times*, September 11, 2019.

Hawley, Samuel J. *The Imjin War: Japan's Sixteenth-Century Invasion of Korea and Attempt to Conquer China.* Seoul: Royal Asiatic Society–Korea Branch, 2005.

Hayashi, Yuka. "Japan Wants U.S. Back in the TPP: It Will Likely Have to Wait." *Wall Street Journal*, April 16, 2021.

Holcombe, Charles. *A History of East Asia: From the Origins of Civilization to the Twenty-First Century.* Cambridge: Cambridge University Press, 2010.

Holsti, Kalevi J. *Peace and War: Armed Conflicts and International Order, 1648–1989.* New York: Cambridge University Press, 1991.

Hong, Tae-yong. 洪大容. "醫山問答 (Ŭisanmundap, "Catechism of Eusan Mountain"). In *Gukyeok Tamhŏnsŏ* 湛軒書 1776. Seoul: Minjok Munhwa Ch'ujinhoe, 1974–1975.

Hsiao, Ch'i-Ch'ing. "Mid-Yüan Politics." In Franke and Twitchett, *Alien Regimes and Border States, 907–1368,* 490–560.

Huang, Chin-Hao, and David C. Kang. "State Formation in Korea and Japan, 400–800 CE: Emulation and Learning, Not Bellicist Competition." *International Organization* 74, no. 1 (2022): 1–31.

——. *State Formation Through Emulation: The East Asian Model.* New York: Cambridge University Press, 2022.

Huang, Haifeng. "From 'the Moon is Rounder Abroad' to 'Bravo, My Country': How China Misperceives the World." *Studies in Comparative International Development* 56, no. 1 (2021): 112–30.

Hur, Nam-lin. "Japan's Invasions of Korea in 1592–98 and the Hideyoshi Regime." In *The Tokugawa World,* ed. Gary Leupp and De-Min Tao, 23–45. London: Routledge, 2021.

Hwang, Kyung Moon. *A History of Korea.* New York: Palgrave Macmillan, 2017.

Ikenberry, G. John. "The Rise of China, Power Transitions, and Western Order." In *China's Ascent: Power, Security, and the Future of International Politics,* ed. Robert Ross and Zhu Feng, 89–114. Ithaca, NY: Cornell University Press, 2008.

Injo Sillok (Veritable Records of King Injo). Year 14 February 21. National Institute of Korean History, https://sillok.history.go.kr/id/kpa_11402021_003.

Institute of International Education. *2019 Open Doors: Report on International Educational Exchange.* New York: IIE and U.S. Department of State, Bureau of Educational and Cultural Affairs, 2019.

Institute of Military History (ROK). *Hanminjong chŏnjaengt'ongsa* (Chronology of Wars of the Korean People). Seoul: IMH, 1996.

Jameson, Sam. "Economic Superpowers at Odds." *Los Angeles Times,* May 8, 1995. https://www.latimes.com/archives/la-xpm-1995-05-08-fi-63836-story.html.

Jervis, Robert. "Roundtable: T. V. Paul. Restraining Great Powers: Soft Balancing from Empires to the Global Era." *ISSF Roundtable.* 2019. https://issforum.org/ISSF/PDF/ISSF-Roundtable-10-29.pdf.

Jiang, Weidong 姜维东. *高句丽历史编年* (The Chronicle of Koguryŏ History). Beijing: 科学出版社 (Science Press), 2016.

Johnson, Chalmers. *MITI and the Japanese Miracle: The Growth of Industrial Policy, 1925–1975*. Stanford, CA: Stanford University Press, 1982.

Kanagawa, Nadia. "East Asia's First World War, 643–68 CE." In Haggard and Kang, *East Asia in the World*, 67–80.

Kang, David C. *East Asia Before the West: Five Centuries of Trade and Tribute*. New York: Columbia University Press, 2010.

——. "International Order in Historical East Asia: Tribute and Hierarchy beyond Sinocentrism and Eurocentrism." *International Organization* 74, no. 1 (2020): 65–93.

——. "International Relations Theory and East Asian History: An Overview," *Journal of East Asian Studies* 13, no. 2 (2013): 181–205.

Kang, David C., Ronan Tse-min Fu, and Meredith Shaw. "Measuring War in Early Modern East Asia: Introducing Chinese and Korean Language Sources." *International Studies Quarterly* 60, no. 4 (December 2016): 766–77.

Kang, David C., and Alex Yu-Ting Lin. "U.S. Bias in the Study of Asian Security: Using Europe to Study Asia." *Journal of Global Security Studies* 4, no. 3 (July 2019): 393–401.

Kang, David C., Dat Nguyen, Meredith Shaw, and Ronan Tse-min Fu, "War, Rebellion, and Intervention Under Hierarchy: Vietnam-China Relations, 1365–1841." *Journal of Conflict Resolution* 63, no. 4 (2019): 896–922.

Kang, David C., and 夺赴音. "Response: Theory and Empirics in the Study of Historical East Asian International Relations." *Harvard Journal of Asiatic Studies* 77, no. 1 (2017): 111–22.

Kelley, Liam. *Beyond the Bronze Pillars: Envoy Poetry and the Sino-Vietnamese Relationship*. Honolulu: University of Hawai'i Press, 2005.

——. "Convergence and Conflict: Dai Viet in the Sinic Order." In *Sacred Mandates: Asian International Relations since Chinggis Khan*, ed. Timothy Brook, Michael van Walt van Praag, and Miek Boltjes, 81–84. Chicago: University of Chicago Press, 2018.

Kim, Seonmin. "Ginseng and Border Trespassing Between Qing China and Chosŏn Korea." Paper presented at the annual meetings of the Association for Asian Studies, San Diego, CA, April 6–9, 2006.

——. *Ginseng and Borderland: Territorial Boundaries and Political Relations Between Qing China and Choson Korea, 1636–1912.* Berkeley: University of California Press, 2017.

Kim, Woosang. "Alliance Transitions and Great Power War." *American Journal of Political Science* 35, no. 4 (1991): 833–50.

——. "Power, Alliance, and Major Wars, 1816–1975." *Journal of Conflict Resolution* 33, no. 2 (1989): 255–73.

——. "Power Parity, Alliance, Dissatisfaction, and Wars in East Asia, 1860–1993." *Journal of Conflict Resolution* 46, no. 5 (2002): 654–71.

——. "Power Transitions and Great Power War from Westphalia to Waterloo." *World Politics* 45, no. 1 (1992): 153–72.

Kim, Woosang, and James Morrow. "When Do Power Shifts Lead to War?" *American Journal of Political Science* 36, no. 4 (1992): 896–922.

Kim, Youngjin. *Imjin waeranr 2nyŏn chŏnjaeng 12nyŏn nonjaeng* (Imjin War: Two-Year War, Twelve-Year Contest). Seoul: Sŏnggyun'gwandaehakky och'ulp'anbu (Sungkyunkwan University Press), 2021.

"Kishida Wants to Boost Defense Spending, but How to Fund It Remains a Question." *Japan Times*, May 26, 2022.

Ko, Chiu Yu, Mark Koyama, and Tuan-Hwee Sng. "Unified China and Divided Europe." *International Economic Review* 59, no. 1 (February 2018): 285–327.

Kugler, Jacek, and Douglas Lemke, eds. *Parity and War: Evaluations and Extensions of The War Ledger.* Ann Arbor: University of Michigan Press, 1996.

Kye, Seung B. "Huddling Under the Imperial Umbrella: A Korean Approach to Ming China in the Early 1500s." *Journal of Korean Studies* 15, no. 1 (2010): 41–66.

Kyŏngin Publishing Editorial Department. *Koryŏsa, vol. 3, Uwang 14nyŏn (1388) mujinnyŏn* (History of Koryŏ: The 14th Year of King U (1388), the Year of Mujin). Seoul: Kyŏnginmunhwasa (Kyŏngin Publishing), 2006.

Lai, Christina. "Realism Revisited: China's Status-Driven Wars Against Koguryŏ in the Sui and Tang Dynasties." *Asian Security* 17, no. 2 (2021): 139–57.

Lawder, David. "U.S.–China Trade War Has Cost up to 245,000 U.S. Jobs: Business Group Study." *Reuters*, January 14, 2021.

Le, Tom. "A Japanese Security Sea Change? Let's See Change First." *Critical Asian Studies* 54, no. 4 (January 4, 2023). criticalasianstudies.org Commentary Board, January 4, 2023. https://criticalasianstudies.org/commentary/2023/1/3/commentary-tom-le-a-japanese-security-sea-change-lets-see-change-first.

Lebow, Richard Ned, and Benjamin Valentino. "Lost in Transition: A Critical Analysis of Power Transition Theory." *International Relations* 23, no. 3 (2009): 389–410.

Ledyard, Gari. "Cartography in Korea." In *Cartography in the Traditional East and Southeast Asian Societies*, ed. J. B. Harley and David Woodward, 234-342. Chicago: University of Chicago Press, 1994.

——. "Confucianism and War: The Korean Security Crisis of 1598." *Journal of Korean Studies* 6 (1989): 81–119.

——. "Yin and Yang in the China–Manchuria–Korea Triangle." In Rossabi, *China Among Equals*, 313-354.

Lee, Jeong-ho. "US Using Trade War to Stop China Overtaking It: Ex-Singapore Diplomat Kishore Mahbubani." *South China Morning Post*, September 4, 2019.

Lee, Ji-Young. *China's Hegemony: Four Hundred Years of East Asian Domination*. New York: Columbia University Press, 2016.

Lee, John. "Trade and Economy in Preindustrial East Asia, c. 1500–1800." *Journal of Asian Studies* 58, no. 1 (February 1999): 2–26.

Lee, Jungshin. "Koreans Perception of the Liaodong Region During the Chosŏn Dynasty." *International Journal of Korean History* 21, no. 1 (2016): 47–84.

Lee, Kenneth. *Korea and East Asia*. Westport, CT: Greenwood, 1997.

Lee, Ki-baek. *A New History of Korea*. Cambridge, MA: Harvard University Press, 1984.

Lee, Peter, and Theodore de Bary. *Sources of Korean Tradition*, vol. 1, *From Early Times Through the Sixteenth Century*. New York: Columbia University Press, 1997.

Lemke, Douglas. "Power Politics and Wars Without States." *American Journal of Political Science* 52, no. 4 (2008): 774–86.

Lemke, Douglas, and William Reed. "Regime Types and Status Quo Evaluations: Power Transition Theory and the Democratic Peace." *International Interactions* 22, no. 2 (1996): 143–64.

Lemke, Douglas, and Suzanne Werner. "Power Parity, Commitment to Change, and War." *International Studies Quarterly* 40, no. 2 (1996): 235–60.

Lewis, James B. "Introduction." In *The East Asian War, 1592–1598: International Relations, Violence and Memory*, ed. James B. Lewis, 1-8. London: Routledge, 2014.

Li, Tao 李燾. 續資治通鑑長編 (Extended Continuation to the Comprehensive Mirror in Aid of Governance), Juan 19. Beijing: 中华书局 (Zhonghua Book Company), 1995.

Lieberman, Victor. *Strange Parallels: Southeast Asia in Global Context, c.800–1830*. Cambridge: Cambridge University Press, 2003.

Liff, Adam P. "Whither the Balancers? The Case for a Methodological Reset." *Security Studies* 25, no. 3 (2016): 420–59.

Lijphart, Arend. "The Comparable-Cases Strategy in Comparative Research." *Comparative Political Studies* 8, no. 2 (1975): 158–77.

Lim, Darren J., and Zack Cooper. "Reassessing Hedging: The Logic of Alignment in East Asia." *Security Studies* 24, no. 4 (2015): 697–727.

Lin, Alex Yu-Ting, and Saori Katada. "Striving for Greatness: Status Aspirations, Rhetorical Entrapment, and Domestic Reforms." *Review of International Political Economy* 29, no. 1 (2022): 175–201.

Lin, Hu. "A Tale of Five Capitals: Contests for Legitimacy Between the Liao and Its Rivals." *Journal of Asian History* 44, no. 2 (2010): 99–127.

Liu, Jinghua 刘菁华, Xu Qingyu 许清玉, and Hu Xianhui 胡显慧. 明实录朝鲜资料辑录 (A Compilation of Korea Materials from the Veritable Records of the Ming Dynasty). Chengdu: 巴蜀书社 (Bashu Publishing House), 2005.

Liu, Pujiang 刘浦江. "德运之争与辽金王朝的正统性问题" (Debates on the Cycle of the Five Virtuous Elements and Legitimacy of the Liao and Jurchen Jin Dynasties). 中國社會科學 (Social Sciences in China) 2 (2004): 191–92.

Lo, Jung-Pang. *China as a Sea Power, 1127–368: A Preliminary Survey of the Maritime Expansion and Naval Exploits of the Chinese People During the Southern Song and Yuan Periods*. Singapore: National University of Singapore Press, 2012.

Lorge, Peter. "Military Institutions as a Defining Feature of the Song Dynasty." *Journal of Chinese History* 1, no. 2 (2017): 269–95.

——. *The Reunification of China: Peace Through War Under the Song Dynasty*. Cambridge: Cambridge University Press, 2015.

——. *War, Politics, and Society in Early Modern China, 900–1795*. London: Routledge, 2005.

Luo, Lixin 羅麗馨. "豐臣秀吉侵略朝鮮" (Toyotomi Hideyoshi's Invasion of Korea). 國立政治大學歷史學報 (Journal of History of National Chengchi University) 35 (2011): 33–74.

Ma, Xinru, and David Kang. "Why Vietnam is not Balancing China: Vietnamese Security Priorities and the Dynamics in Sino-Vietnam Relations," *Journal of East Asian Studies* 23, no. 3 (2023): 363–86.

MacKay, Joseph. "The Nomadic Other: Ontological Security and the Inner Asian Steppe in Historical East Asian International Politics." *Review of International Studies* 42, no. 3 (July 2016): 471–91.

Macrotrends. "Nikkei 225 Index—67 Year Historical Chart." https://www.macrotrends.net/2593/nikkei-225-index-historical-chart-data.

Magaziner, Ira C., and Robert B. Reich. *Minding America's Business: The Decline and Rise of the American Economy*. New York: Harcourt Brace Jovanovich, 1982.

Mahmud, Aqil Haziq. "US Should 'Stay Very Far Away' from Physically Confronting China Over Taiwan: Ng Eng Hen." *Channel News Asia*, November 4, 2021. https://www.channelnewsasia.com/singapore/taiwan-china-us-tension-ng-eng-hen-2290256.

Mair, Victor. "Sky High Horse Fat." *Language Log*, May 2, 2012. https://languagelog.ldc.upenn.edu/nll/?p=3931.

Mearsheimer, John. "Better to Be Godzilla Than Bambi." *Foreign Policy* 146 (January–February 2005): 47–48.

——. *The Tragedy of Great Power Politics*. New York: W. W. Norton, 2001.

Mearsheimer, John, and Stephen Walt. "The Case for Offshore Balancing: A Superior U.S. Grand Strategy." *Foreign Affairs* 95, no. 4 (July–August 2016): 70–83.

Miller, Harry. *State versus Gentry in Late Ming Dynasty China*. New York: Palgrave, 2008.

Millward, James. "Qing and Twentieth-Century Chinese Diversity Regimes." In *Culture and Order in World Politics*, ed. Andrew Phillips and Christian Reus-Smit, 71-92. New York: Cambridge University Press, 2020.

Mote, Frederick W. *Imperial China 900–1800*. Cambridge, MA: Harvard University Press, 2003.

Moul, William. "Power Parity, Preponderance, and War Between Great Powers, 1816–1989." *Journal of Conflict Resolution* 47, no. 4 (2003): 468–89.

Murphy, R. Taggart. *The Weight of the Yen: How Denial Imperils America's Future and Ruins an Alliance.* New York: W. W. Norton, 1997.

Noland, Marcus. "North Korea and the Right to Food." Testimony Before the United Nations Commission of Inquiry on Human Rights in the Democratic People's Republic of Korea Public Hearings, October 30, 2013.

Norihito, Mizuno. "China in Tokugawa Foreign Relations: The Tokugawa Bakufu's Perception of and Attitudes Toward Ming–Qing China." *Sino-Japanese Studies Journal* 15 (2003): 108–44.

O Chongnok. *Chosŏnch'ogi yanggyeŭi kunsajedowa kukpang* (Military Institutions and Dynastic Defense in Northern and Eastern Borders in Early Chosŏn). Seoul: (Kukhak Charyowŏn), 2014.

Organski, A. F. K. *World Politics.* New York: Knopf, 1958.

Organski, A. F. K., and Jacek Kugler. *The War Ledger.* Chicago: University of Chicago Press, 1980.

Pak, Wŏnho. "Myŏng-gwaŭi kwan'gye" (Relations with the Ming). *Han'guksa* (History of Korea) 22 (1995): 279–93.

Palais, James. *Confucian Statecraft and Korean Institutions.* Seattle: University of Washington Press, 1996.

Park, Eugene. "War and Peace in Premodern Korea: Institutional and Ideological Dimensions." In *The Military and South Korean Society,* ed. Young-Key Kim-Renaud, Richard Grinker, and Kirk W. Larsen, 1–13. Washington, DC: George Washington University, 2006.

Park, Kyuri. "Goldilocks' Signal for Cooperation in East Asia: China's Rise, Hedging, and Joint Military Exercises." Manuscript, Stanford University, 2022.

Park, Saeyoung. "The Death of Eastphalia, 1874." In Haggard and Kang, *East Asia in the World,* 239–62.

Park, Seo-Hyun. *Sovereignty and Status in East Asian International Relations.* Cambridge: Cambridge University Press, 2017.

Pei, Minxin. *China's Trapped Transition: The Limits of Developmental Autocracy.* Cambridge, MA: Harvard University Press, 2008.

Pempel, T. J. "Back to the Future? Japan's Search for a Meaningful New Role in the Emerging Regional Order." *Asian Perspective* 39, no. 3 (July 2015): 361–80.

Perdue, Peter. *China Marches West: The Qing Conquest of Central Eurasia.* Cambridge, MA: Harvard University Press, 2005.

——. "Strange Parallels Across Eurasia." *Social Science* 32, no. 2 (2008): 263–79.

Perry, Elizabeth. "Chinese Conceptions of 'Rights': From Mencius to Mao—and Now." *Perspectives on Politics* 6, no. 1 (March 2008): 37–50.

Peterson, Charles. "Old Illusions and New Realities: Sung Foreign Policy, 1217–1234." In Rossabi, *China Among Equals*, 204-242.

Phan, Thanh Giản, ed. 欽定越史通鑑綱目 (The Imperially Ordered Annotated Text Completely Reflecting the History of Viet). Taipei: National Library, 1969.

Pickens, T. Boone, Pat Choate, and Christopher Burke. *The Second Pearl Harbor: Say No to Japan.* Washington, DC: National Press Books, 1992.

Pines, Yuri. *The Everlasting Empire: The Political Culture of Ancient China and Its Imperial Legacy.* Princeton, NJ: Princeton University Press, 2012.

——. "The Limits of All-Under-Heaven: Ideology and Praxis of 'Great Unity' in Early Chinese Empire." In Pines, Biran, and Rüpke, *The Limits of Universal Rule,* 79-110.

Pines, Yuri, Michael Biran, and Jörg Rüpke, eds. *The Limits of Universal Rule:: Eurasian Empires Compared.* Cambridge: Cambridge University Press, 2021.

Powell, Robert. "Bargaining Theory and International Conflict." *American Review of Political Science* 5, no. 1 (2002): 1–30.

Pye, Lucian W. "China: Erratic State, Frustrated Society." *Foreign Affairs* 69, no. 4 (1990): 56–74.

Rawski, Evelyn. *Early Modern China and Northeast Asia: Cross-Border Perspectives.* Cambridge: Cambridge University Press, 2015.

Robinson, David M. *Korea and the Fall of the Mongol Empire Alliance, Upheaval, and the Rise of a New East Asian Order.* Cambridge: Cambridge University Press, 2023.

Roland, Alex. "*Firearms: A Global History to 1700* by Kenneth Chase." *Journal of Interdisciplinary History* 35, no. 4 (2005): 617–19.

Rosenthal, Jean-Laurent, and R. Bin Wong. *Before and Beyond Divergence: The Politics of Economic Change in China and Europe.* Cambridge, MA: Harvard University Press, 2011.

Ross, Robert, and Zhu Feng, eds. *China's Ascent: Power, Security and the Future of International Politics*. Ithaca, NY: Cornell University Press, 2008.

Rossabi, Morris. "The Reign of Khubilai Khan." In Franke and Twitchett, *Alien Regimes and Border States, 907–1368*, 414–89.

Rossabi, Morris, ed. *China Among Equals: The Middle Kingdom and Its Neighbors, 10th–14th Centuries*. Berkeley: University of California Press, 1983.

Sakai, Naoki. "'You Asians': On the Historical Role of the West and Asia Binary." *South Atlantic Quarterly* 99, no. 4 (2000): 789–817.

Sartori, Giovanni. "Comparing and Miscomparing." *Journal of Theoretical Politics* 3, no. 3 (1991): 243–57.

Scheidel, Walter. "Roman Population Size: The Logic of the Debate." Working paper, Princeton/Stanford Working Papers in Classics Paper no. 070706, July 2007.

Schmitz, Rob. "Who's Lifting Chinese People out of Poverty?" National Public Radio, January 17, 2017.

Schultz, Kenneth A., and Henk E. Goemans. "Aims, Claims, and the Bargaining Model of War." *International Theory* 11, no. 3 (2019): 344–74.

Scobell, Andrew. "China and Grand Strategy: Does the Empire Have a Plan? A Review Essay." *Political Science Quarterly* 137 (2022): 155–60.

Seawright, Jason, and John Gerring. "Case Selection Techniques in Case Study Research: A Menu of Qualitative and Quantitative Options." *Political Research Quarterly* 61, no. 2 (2008): 294–308.

Sechser, Todd S. "Goliath's Curse: Coercive Threats and Asymmetric Power." *International Organization* 64, no. 4 (2010): 627–60.

Segal, Gerald. "Does China Matter?" *Foreign Affairs* 78, no. 5 (September–October 1999): 24–36.

Sejong Sillok (Veritable Records of King Sejong). Seoul: Sejong Taewang Kinyŏm Saŏphoe, 1991.

Seonjo Sogyeong Daewang Sujeong Sillok (Revised Veritable Records of King Seonjo). Year 24 March 1. https://sillok.history.go.kr/id/knb_12403001_004.

Servan-Schreiber, J. J. *The World Challenge*. New York: Simon & Schuster, 1980.

Seth, Michael J. *A Concise History of Korea*, 2nd ed. Lanham, MD.: Rowman & Littlefield, 2016.

Shambaugh, David. "The Coming Chinese Crackup." *Wall Street Journal*, March 6, 2015.

Sharman, J. C. *Empires of the Weak: The Real Story of European Expansion and the Creation of the New World Order*. Princeton, NJ: Princeton University Press, 2019.

Shi, Zhan 施展. 枢纽: 3000 年的中国 (The Hub: 3000 Years of China). Guilin: 广西师范大学出版社 (Guangxi Normal University Press), 2018.

Shirk, Susan L. *China: Fragile Superpower*. New York: Oxford University Press, 2007.

Stockholm International Peace Research Institute (SIPRI). "Trends in World Military Expenditure, 2022." https://www.sipri.org/publications /2023/sipri-fact-sheets/trends-world-military-expenditure-2022.

Simmons, Beth A., Frank Dobbin, and Geoffrey Garrett. "Introduction: The International Diffusion of Liberalism." *International Organization* 60, no. 4 (2006): 781–810.

Song, Nianshen 宋念申. 发现东亚 (Finding Asia). Beijing: 新星出版社 (New Star Press), 2018.

St. Onge, Peter. "How Paper Money Led to the Mongol Conquest: Money and the Collapse of Song China." *Independent Review* 22, no. 2 (Fall 2017): 223–43.

Steele, Abbey, Christopher Paik, and Seiki Tanaka. "Constraining the Samurai: Rebellion and Taxation in Early Modern Japan." *International Studies Quarterly* 61, no. 2 (June 2017): 352–70.

Strangio, Sebastian. "Indonesia and Malaysia Reiterate Concerns About AUKUS Pact." *Diplomat*, October 19, 2021. https://thediplomat.com /2021/10/indonesia-and-malaysia-reiterate-concerns-about-aukus-pact.

Sugiyama, Masaaki 杉山正明. 忽必烈的挑战: 蒙古帝国与世界历史的大转向 (The Challenge of Kublai: The Mongol Empire and the Great Turn of World History). Trans. Junyu Zhou 周俊宇. Beijing: 社会科学文献出版社 (Social Sciences Academic Press), 2017.

Sun, Weiguo 孫衛國. 大明旗號與小中華意識——朝鮮王朝尊周思明問題研究 *(1637–1800)* ("Great Ming" and "Little China"—Studies of the Chosŏn Period Trend of Revering the Zhou and Longing for the Ming, 1637– 1800). Beijing: 商务印书馆有限公司 (Commercial Press), 2007.

Swope, Kenneth. "Crouching Tigers, Secret Weapons: Military Technology Employed During the Sino-Japanese-Korean War, 1592–1598." *Journal of Military History* 69, no. 1 (2005): 11–41.

——. "Deceit, Disguise, and Dependence: China, Japan, and the Future of the Tributary System, 1592–1596." *International History Review* 24, no. 4 (2002): 757–82.

——. *A Dragon's Head and Serpent's Tail.* Norman: University of Oklahoma Press, 2009.

——. *The Military Collapse of China's Ming Dynasty, 1618–44.* London: Routledge, 2014.

——. "Ming Grand Strategy During the Great East Asian War, 1592–1598." In Haggard and Kang, *East Asia in the World*, 108–28.

——. "Perspectives on the Imjin War." *Journal of Korean Studies* 12, no. 1 (Fall 2007): 154–61.

Tackett, Nicolas. *The Origins of the Chinese Nation: Song China and the Forging of an East Asian World Order.* Cambridge: Cambridge University Press, 2017.

T'aejo Sillok. (Veritable Records of King Taejo). Seoul: National Institute of Korean History.

Taizong Wen Huangdi shilu 54 (太宗文皇帝實錄卷之五十四). 1986. In *Qing shilu* (清實錄), 722:2–723:1. Beijing: Zhonghua shuju. Scripta Sinica Database 漢籍全文資料.

Tammen, Ronald L., Jacek Kugler, Douglas Lemke, Allan C. Stam III, Carole Alsharabati, Mark A. Abdollahian, Brian Efird, and A. F. K. Organski. *Power Transitions: Strategies for the 21st Century.* New York: Chatham House, 2000.

Tanner, Harold M. *China: A History.* Indianapolis: Hackett, 2009.

Taylor, Keith. *A History of the Vietnamese.* Cambridge: Cambridge University Press, 2013.

Thucydides. *History of the Peloponnesian War*, translated by Richard Crawley. Dover Edition, 2017.

Vogel, Ezra F. *Japan As Number One: Lessons for America.* Cambridge, MA: Harvard University Press, 1978.

von Glahn, Richard. *An Economic History of China: From Antiquity to the Nineteenth Century.* Cambridge: Cambridge University Press, 2016.

——. "Myth and Reality of China's Seventeenth Century Monetary Crisis." *Journal of Economic History* 56, no. 2 (1996): 429–54.

Vortherms, Samantha, and Jiakun Jack Zhang. "Political Risk and Firm Exit: Evidence from the US–China Trade War." Research paper,

University of California San Diego, 21st Century China Center, Research Paper no. 2021–09, September 1, 2021.

Walker, Brett L. *A Concise History of Japan.* Cambridge: Cambridge University Press, 2015.

Waltz, Kenneth. "The Emerging Structure of International Politics." *International Security* 18, no. 2 (Fall 1993): 44–79.

Wang, Gaoxin 汪高鑫. 二十四史的民族史撰述研究 (The Studies on the Ethno-Historical Recounts in Twenty-Four Histories). Hefei Shi: 黄山书社 (Huang Shan Book Club), 2016.

Wang, Jiahua 王家骅. "略论丰臣秀吉侵朝战争的原因" (A Brief Discussion on the Reasons for Toyotomi Hideyoshi Invading Korea). 日本研究 (Japanese Studies) 3 (1985): 35–38.

Wang, Laite 王来特. "朝贡贸易体系的脱出与日本型区域秩序的构建" (The Disengagement of the Tribute Trade System and the Construction of a Japanese-Type Regional Order). 日本学刊 (Journal of Japanese Studies) 6 (2012): 136–60.

Wang, Sixiang. *Boundless Winds of Empire: Rhetoric and Ritual in Early Chosŏn Diplomacy with Ming China.* New York: Columbia University Press, 2023.

Wang, Yuan-kang. "Roundtable on Steve Chan, *Thucydides Trap?*" *ISSF Roundtable* XII-2, November 9, 2020.

Wang Zhen 王臻. "朝鲜壬辰战争诸问题再探讨" (On the Issues of the Imjin War). 求索 (Seek) 2 (2016): 26–30.

Wang, Zhenping. *Tang China in Multi-Polar Asia.* Honolulu: University of Hawai'i Press, 2013.

Werner, Suzanne, and Jacek Kugler. "Power Transitions and Military Buildups: Resolving the Relationship Between Arms Buildups and War." In Kugler and Lemke, *Parity and War*, 187–207.

White House. "Statement on Indo-Pacific Economic Framework for Prosperity." May 23, 2023. https://www.whitehouse.gov/briefing-room/statements-releases/2022/05/23/statement-on-indo-pacific-economic-framework-for-prosperity/.

Wohlforth, William C. "Unipolarity, Status Competition, and Great Power War." *World Politics* 61, no. 1 (2009): 28–57.

Womack, Brantly. *China Among Unequals: Asymmetric Foreign Relations in Asia.* Singapore: World Scientific, 2010.

Wright, David C. "The Northern Frontier." In *A Military History of China*, ed. David Graf and Robin Higham, 57–79. Lexington: University of Kentucky Press, 2012.

Wu, Han 吴晗. 朝鲜李朝實錄中的中國史料, *1354–1438* (China Materials in the Veritable Records of Korea's Yi Dynasty, 1354–1438), vol. 1. Beijing: 中華書局 (Zhonghua Book Company), 1980.

Xiong, Victor Cunrui, and Kenneth James Hammond, eds. *Routledge Handbook of Imperial Chinese History*. London: Routledge, 2019.

Yao, Dali 姚大力. 追寻"我们"的根源:中国历史上的民族与国家意识 (Tracing the Roots of "Us": Ethnic and National Consciousness in Chinese History). Beijing: 生活读书新知三联书店 (SDX Joint Publishing Company), 2018.

Yao, Guangxiao 姚廣孝 et al., eds. 明太祖實錄 (Veritable Records of the Ming Emperor Taizu). 1418.

Yasunori, Arano. "The Formation of a Japanocentric World Order." *International Journal of Asian Studies* 2, no. 2 (2005): 185–216.

Ye, Longli 叶隆礼. 契丹国志 (Records of the Khitan State). Shanghai:上海古籍出版社 (Shanghai Ancient Books Publishing Company), 1985.

Yin, Weiwen. "Climate Shocks, Political Institutions, and Nomadic Invasions in Early Modern East Asia." *Journal of Conflict Resolution* 64, no. 6 (2020): 1043–69.

Yu, Chaech'un. "15 segi Myŏng-ŭi Tongp'alch'am chiyŏk chŏmgŏ-wa Chosŏn-ŭi taeŭng" (Ming's Occupation of the Tongp'alch'am Region in the 15th Century and Chosŏn's Reaction). *Chosŏn sidaesa hakbo* (Journal of Chosŏn Dynasty History) 18 (2001): 7.

Yuan, Jingdong. "Averting US–China Conflict in the Asia–Pacific." *International Affairs* 92, no. 4 (2016): 977–86.

Zarakol, Ayşe. *Before the West: The Rise and Fall of Eastern World Orders*. Cambridge: Cambridge University Press, 2022.

Zhang, Feng. *Chinese Hegemony: Grand Strategy and International Institutions in East Asian History*. Stanford, CA: Stanford University Press, 2015.

Zhang, Peiheng 章培恒, and Yu Suisheng 喻遂生. 二十四史全译:明史 (Full Translation of the Twenty-Four Histories: The History of the Ming Dynasty). Shanghai: 汉语大词典出版社 (Hanyu Da Cidian Publishing Company), 2004.

Zhao, Gang 赵刚. "德川幕府对外关系史料考" (Historical Examination of Tokugawa Shogunate's Foreign Relations). 日本学刊 (Journal of Japanese Studies) 1 (2006): 136–60.

Zhou, Xin. "Is China Rich or Poor? Nation's Wealth Debate Muddied by Conflicting Government Data." *South China Morning Post*, May 29, 2020.

Zong, Huiyu 宗惠玉, and Jin Rongguo 金荣国. "也论丰臣秀吉侵朝战争的原因" (Discussion of Toyotomi Hideyoshi's Invasion of Korea). 东疆学刊哲学社会科学版 (Dongjiang Journal of Philosophy and Social Sciences) 4 (1993): 53–57.

"'6亿人月入1000元'是最有效的清醒剂" ("600 Million People Earn $1,000 a Month" Is the Most Effective Sobering Agent). 第一财经 (China Business Network), June 3, 2020.

INDEX

Brotherhood Treaty, 151–52
bureaucracy, 84–85, 136–37
Bureau of Military Affairs, 84–85
Burma, 89, *89*
Buzan, Barry, 196–977

CCP. *See* Chinese Communist
  Party
Central Asian steppe: banner
  system from, 125; China and, 54,
  117; history of, 87–88; peoples of,
  44–45, 47. *See also* Mongols
Chan, Steve, 23, 29–30, 83
Chen Shangsheng, 129
Chiang Kai-shek, 115, 130
China: access to, 95–96; Belt and
  Road Initiative to, 190–91;
  borders of, 69, 87, 98–99,
  143–45, 199–200; bureaucracy in,
  136–37; Bureau of Military
  Affairs in, 84–85; CCP in,
  191–92, 194, 197–99; Central
  Asian steppe and, 54, 117;
  communism to, 130; culture of,
  140–41; diplomacy with, 20,
  59–60, 189–90; dynasties in, *51*;
  East Asia and, 30–31, 61–62, 97,
  108–9, 126–27, 201–2; in East
  Asian history, 112–14, 131–32,
  189; Europe and, 7–8, 53–54,
  197; foreign policy of, 132;
  hegemony of, 11–12, 15, 44–48,
  53; higher education to, 167–68;
  history of, 65–66, 73–74, 235n9;
  Humiliation of Jingkang in,
  76–77; Japan and, 14, 25,

100–101, 104–5, *106*, 107–12, 115,
  136, 166–70, *169*, 181–82; Korea
  and, 35, 55–56, 129–30, 141–48,
  188; to Kublai Khan, 65; Mair
  on, 225; Manchus in, 115,
  129–30; Mandate of Heaven in,
  68, 72–73, 92, 127, 129; in
  maritime trade, 78; military of,
  111–12; in modernity, 15, 29,
  170–74, *171–73*, 196; Mongols
  and, *89*, 147–48; National
  People's Congress in, 192;
  philosophy of, 200–201; South
  Korea and, 177; Taiwan and,
  121–22, 183, 191, 197, 199; Turkey
  and, 63; United States and, 3–4,
  16–18, 159–60, 174–81, *179*, 190,
  196–97; Vietnam and, 4, 44–45,
  49–50, 55, 58–60; violence in, 57;
  wealth of, 85, 87. *See also specific*
  topics
China Population History
  (Ge Jianxiong), 202–3
Chindŏk (queen), 138
Chinese Business Network,
  192–93
Chinese Communist Party (CCP),
  191–92, 194, 197–99
Chinggis Khan: Allsen on, 85;
  ancestors of, 64; history of,
  87–88, 93; legacy of, 13, 66, 79
Chiu Yu Ko, 53
Chong, Ian, 31
Chŏngjong (king), 146
Chŏng Tuhŭi, 103
Chongzen (emperor), 118

GPSR Authorized Representative: Easy Access System Europe, Mustamäe tee 50, 10621 Tallinn, Estonia, gpsr.requests@easproject.com